"Stunningly original. *Swoon* reads like a novel, a pop culture history and a feminist manifesto rolled into one.
Like Greil Marcus – but sexier."
GRAHAM COXON, BLUR GUITARIST AND AUTHOR OF *VERSE, CHORUS, MONSTER!*

"A groundbreaking study of female love – and lust – from Byron to the Beatles. Right from the first page, Bea Martinez-Gatell hooks you in with sensational stories of scandal but then unfolds a serious message. The policing of women's desire, *Swoon* argues, says so much more about us, the society we live in and our fears of feminine sexuality than it does about the individuals involved. What a pleasure it is to read something that takes women's pleasure seriously!"
DR KIRSTY SEDGMAN, CULTURAL STUDIES EXPERT AND AUTHOR OF *ON BEING UNREASONABLE*

"With wit, precision and empathy, Bea Martinez-Gatell fever-charts the evolution of passionate female fandom – the swoon – and playfully (but wisely!) breaches the facades of the objects of desire who provoked and stoked it."
JAMES KAPLAN, AUTHOR OF *FRANK: THE VOICE* AND *SINATRA: THE CHAIRMAN*

"*Swoon* won't just sweep you off your feet – it will make you think and laugh, too. Finally, a book that takes fangirls as seriously as we deserve!"
ZAN ROMANOFF, AUTHOR OF *BIG FAN*

"Though the fangirl has been derided and dismissed by the male press and mainstream culture for 200 years, her passion and persistence created the brightest stars in the celebrity galaxy. Bea Martinez-Gatell's *Swoon* is a fascinating cultural history of fangirls and their enormous yet overlooked impact on pop culture and beyond."

Dr Candy Leonard, author of *Beatleness: How the Beatles and Their Fans Remade the World*

"An enthralling and revisionist history of modern celebrity, shifting our attention from the usual cast of culture heroes to their female fans. Bold in its transatlantic and transhistorical reach and written with real passion and authority, *Swoon* shows how these frequently disparaged women and girls have challenged expectations around gender and art and pushed for social change. From Byromania to Lisztomania to Beatlemania, these are voices and stories that continue to resonate."

Dr James Grande, literary scholar and editor of *The Keats-Shelley Review*

"Tender, hilarious and profoundly moving, *Swoon* reveals the fascinating and often complex relationship between artists and audiences through the ages. This is a page-turning history of love, lust, fandom and cultural change that reminds us of what it means to be human."

Cristina Cordero, Cuarteto Casals violist

SWOON

FANGIRLS, THEIR IDOLS AND THE COUNTERCULTURE OF FEMALE LUST – FROM BYRON TO THE BEATLES

BEA MARTINEZ-GATELL

Biteback Publishing

ISBN 978-1-78590-882-8

10 9 8 7 6 5 4 3 2 1

A CIP catalogue record for this book is available from the British Library.

Set in Adobe Caslon Pro and Brother 1816

Printed and bound in Great Britain by
CPI Group (UK) Ltd, Croydon CR0 4YY

She gazed in wonder, 'Can he calmly sleep,
While other eyes his fall or ravage weep?
And mine in restlessness are wandering here –
What sudden spell hath made this man so dear?'
– LORD BYRON, *THE CORSAIR*

CONTENTS

Preface   ix

Prologue: The Heroine   xv

1.   IMAGINATION, LONDON, 1812   I
     Bad Romance

2.   ECSTASY, BERLIN, 1842   41
     In Love With a Feeling

3.   DESIRE, HOLLYWOOD, 1926   89
     The Lure of the Flesh

4.   ROMANCE, NEW YORK CITY, 1944   141
     It's Always You

5.   SEX, MEMPHIS, 1954   191
     Sacred and Profane

6.   REVOLUTION, LIVERPOOL, 1963   241
     From Me to You

Afterword: Thank You Girl   295

Acknowledgements   307

Bibliography   313

Notes   327

Index   341

PREFACE

Ridiculed, derided and brushed into the margins of history, the fangirl has had many names. Today, she might be a Swiftie, an Arianator or just plain Stan. At the turn of the twentieth century, she was the Matinee Girl, shamelessly swooning and weeping in the stalls of the Edwardian theatre. Her hero was the Matinee Idol – the dashing star of romantic melodramas and musicals. 'Usually she is in bunches,' wrote one critic, 'two or three in a crowd, and invariably she is noisy. All through the play one hears snatches of conversation such as: "Isn't he just darling!", "I think he's the most handsome man I ever saw."'[1]

Theatre critics were not impressed. Forcing audiences to consume increasing amounts of 'dramatic saccharine written to appeal chiefly to the limited intelligence of immature girlhood' was having a damaging effect on the theatre, they said.[2] And as I sit writing the final pages of this book two days before Christmas 2024 and thousands of TikToks scattered with pink glitter and heart emojis transform Ivy League valedictorian turned alleged CEO killer Luigi Mangione into a thirst trap, inappropriate adoration is still making headlines: 'Why is the world swooning over an alleged killer?' The historical hotties in this book are not murderers, but nearly all of them provoked a fusion of bafflement and concern when the girls started swooning in their days. The Matinee Girl may well have been labelled the most harmful influence on the American theatre of 1907, but there was no denying the power of her pocketbook or the potential influence of her daydreams.

I've been studying fangirl history since I arrived at university as an excitable, newly feminist film and literature student still recovering from an acute case of Leomania in the early 2000s. I was surprised to be informed, in my first 'film, gender and identity' class, that the gaze was male. If the gaze was male, then what were all those *Titanic* posters for? Two DiCaprio dissertations (filled with important photos required for academic purposes) later, I graduated and the *Romeo + Juliet* posters came down. The Jean-Luc Godard ones went up, eventually to be replaced by pretentious abstract art prints in proper frames. As my interests and obsessions changed, so did the fangirl. She had a name now. And a verb: people were fangirling about everything from Donald Trump to ice cream. The internet had pushed her so far into the mainstream that I'd almost forgotten about looking back – until Baz Luhrmann released his 2022 *Elvis* biopic. How could the man who had given the wonder and beauty of Leo and Claire Danes falling in love through a fishtank to the fangirls of the '90s have done this to the Elvis girls of the past!?

Luhrmann's *Elvis* is a story we know well: handsome male genius unleashes his sexual magnetism on the world and women lose their minds. In Elvis's first concert scene in Luhrmann's film, girls begin involuntarily releasing monstrous otherworldly screams as he shakes those famous hips for the first time. They look both ecstatic and terrified, as if they don't understand what it is they're feeling, let alone doing. Soon they're up and out of their seats like zombies rising from the dead, grabbing at our hero as he backs away from them in terror. 'Are you trying to kill my son!?' screams his mama. In line with countless male star mythologies, the fangirl in this film is either a sexually aggressive monster or a vapid, clueless idiot. It's Elvis's divine genius that makes him a star, not the power (and pocket money) of his largely female early fanbase. By the time I walked out of the cinema, I had decided it was time to write this book.

From Frank Sinatra in the 1940s to Robert Pattinson or Harry Styles more recently, many of the biggest male stars in pop culture past and present built their early careers on their romantic appeal to young women. The dreamy swooning teenager gazing at pictures of her idol in magazines or screaming in hordes at a pop concert is a stock character in the textbooks of fame. And yet no history book has, until now, told her story from the start. Is it because she's too trivial? Someone in publishing once advised me it might be better off as a blog post ('Are you sure there's enough material to fill a whole book?'). Too repetitive perhaps? Apart from the outfits, and the guy signing autographs, is there really a difference between one hysterical crowd of screaming, crying, grabbing girls in 1844 and another in 1944? Or is it because we're still bound by centuries-old assumptions about which audiences – and which feelings – deserve to be taken seriously?

When I sat down to begin researching this book, I was looking forward to a joyfully lovestruck exploration of early movie, music and book culture. The plan was to look at the six moments in pop culture history when fangirl 'manias' erupted most fervently around a particular star – I'm sure you can guess a few. These were super-ficially heterosexual fandoms in which the male stars' success was thought to be founded on their romantic appeal to young women – a phenomenon that was seen as both troubling and ridiculous. Very often, these men – like Elvis, Frank Sinatra and of course the

Beatles – went on to shed their dreaded initial 'teen idol' status and be reborn as some of the most iconic artists of all time. The fangirl has always been a footnote in their stories; a stepping stone on her idol's road to later, more 'serious' stardom. I wanted to use this book to take the 'not serious' phase seriously. What was it about these stars, in their early days, that elicited such passionate, all-consuming devotion from their fans and how did these swoonish beginnings shape the 'more serious' artistry to come?

What I discovered was that these stories had both everything and nothing to do with the men at the centre of them. These were six moments in history when gender and society themselves were going through seismic moments of change. Who we choose to swoon about is as much, if not more, about us and the times we live in as them. Behind every swoon and every squeal, the seeds of a revolution were stirring.

Fans are everywhere these days, and their cultural and economic power is undeniable (just ask Taylor Swift), but in the earliest days of celebrity and pop culture, polite society was at first confused and then concerned – especially when female fans and male stars were involved. Fandom became a moral and cultural battleground. What was at stake was women's right to want things they weren't supposed to want, feel things they weren't supposed to feel and express all these things loudly, shamelessly and in public. By the time we come to the '60s, where this book ends, the history of the fangirl is subtly but inextricably linked to the birth of the women's liberation movement itself. And it doesn't end there. In much the same way that they turned their heroes into icons, those silly, screaming, swooning girls were giving birth to pop culture as we know it today.

It's impossible to write an authentic history of the fangirl without engaging emotionally – I learned that after a few false starts

– so this is not an objective history. It's a map of the human heart in all its messy, beautiful, fascinating weirdness. From daydreaming about saving Lord Byron's soul to swooning with my friends over pictures of John, Paul, George and Ringo in old copies of *Beatles Monthly* magazine, I've fallen in love with every star in this book, but I've fallen in love with their fans even more. These were girls and women who, in big and small ways, broke all the stifling, repressive rules about how they were supposed to think, feel and behave in eras when passionate self-expression often came at a real cost. I hope that as you step into these six very different moments in time with me, you will fall in love with them too.

Bea Martinez-Gatell
Barcelona
December 2024

PROLOGUE

THE HEROINE

In November 1813, two portraits sat next to each other on display at Thomas Phillips's art studio in Central London. The first, a man, was easily recognisable. With his dark wavy hair, flowing open collar and deathly pale, eerily marble-like complexion, Lord Byron could have stepped straight off the pages of a Gothic romance novel. Fresh from the publication of *The Bride of Abydos*, his latest 'heroic poem', Byron was the literary sensation of the moment. Long before the Hollywood star factory of the 1920s and '30s perfected the recipe for celebrity, Byron was inventing it for himself.

For the past year, Europe had been in the grips of Byromania. His books were wildly popular, each one selling more copies than the last, but it was gossip about his life that was just as important to his success. Equally thrilling and scandalous, the public devoured every new tale of Byron's misdemeanours and affairs with the same fervour as they did the romances from his pen. For the first time in history, the brooding, soulful heroes on the page and their handsome, enigmatic creator were intoxicatingly interchangeable.

Byron enjoyed walking the fine line between infamy and celebrity: his poems were filled with mysterious allusions to dark rumours about his own life. But just how autobiographical were they, *really*? The latest rumour – an incestuous affair between Byron and his half-sister Augusta – might finally have been a step too far, even for him. In Phillips's studio however, unphased, he looked serenely out of his portrait and across the room towards the second painting: a young woman dressed in a pageboy uniform, blonde hair cropped short, seductively offering up a tray of fruit to someone just beyond the frame.

Lady Caroline Lamb had not been pleased about the portrait display or everything that the positioning of that particular portrait of her next to Byron's implied. The previous year, after receiving an advanced copy of *Childe Harold's Pilgrimage*, the book that would make Byron's name, she had sent him a fan letter. It was uncommon, at the time, for people to write letters like this to authors they'd never met, but there was something about Byron's writing that drew people in. He wrote with an openness and intensity that made readers feel as if they knew him. His poetry seemed to cry out for participation.

'I have read your Book & can not refrain from telling you what I think,' wrote Caroline. 'I think it is beautiful. You deserve to be and you shall be happy. Do not throw away such talents as you possess in gloom & regrets for the past.'¹ She went on to explain that, as a lady, it wouldn't have been appropriate for her to include her name, but it should be easy enough for him to find out who she was, if he so wished. She asked him to burn the letter – she knew how inappropriate it was to be writing to him like this – but closed with a flirtation: her greatest wish was to one day meet him and to know him.

Over the coming years, Byron would receive hundreds of letters like this one. The anonymous authors, nearly always women, would express being compelled, as if by some supernatural force, to write to him. His poetry, they said, made them feel all kinds of new sensations: intense, physical emotions – feelings they couldn't quite explain but didn't have a name for either. Often, like Caroline, they wrote to console him. He seemed so melancholic and despairing in his poems. They hoped their letters would, in some way, be of help. Other times, sensing in Byron a kindred spirit, they sent copies of their own poems or wrote to share tragic or sometimes even mundane anecdotes from their own lives.

At first, he'd been perplexed. He couldn't understand why these strangers were writing to him on such intimate terms. It was so unusual, in fact, that the first time he received a fan letter, he presumed it was from a relative. But as this collection of strange love letters grew, so too did his understanding that a new type of relationship was forming. The power he had over these readers was intense, but the relationship seemed to go two ways. He now belonged to his readers as much as he belonged to himself.

Byron had resolved early on that he would never answer these letters, but there was something about Caroline's that was different. A poem she'd included was rather good, and he was intrigued by the idea that she might be of noble birth like him. After making enquiries, he discovered that she was the eccentric wife of the Hon. William Lamb, MP and future British Prime Minister. At twenty-six, Caroline was just a few years older than him and known not just for her wit and intelligence but also for her headstrong and passionate nature. Rumour had it she'd been illiterate until her teens, married for love (unusual for the time) and had just come out of a shockingly indiscreet affair with a soldier. The world of the Regency aristocracy was rife with infidelity, but Caroline sounded either nonchalant or actively contemptuous of the unwritten rules of secrecy and silence that safeguarded reputations. Byron had a taste for 'wild women'. He was now just as intrigued as she was.

Byron and Caroline moved in similar social circles, so it was inevitable that they would meet. When they finally did, they were intensely drawn to each other. They shared an irreverent attitude to life, a mutual curiosity for the world and a deep love of the arts. Caroline, who saw herself as a romantic free spirit, admired Byron's poetry, as well as his refusal to live by the rules and expectations of society. Byron, in turn, was impressed by Caroline's intelligence and sharp sense of humour. He was also intrigued by *her* rebelliousness and emotional intensity. He described her as 'the cleverest, most agreeable, absurd, amiable, perplexing, dangerous, fascinating little being that lives now or ought to have lived 2,000 years ago'.[2] Their relationship began as a true intellectual friendship, but soon neither could deny the intense physical chemistry they shared as well. 'When you first told me in the carriage to kiss your mouth and I durst not,' Caroline later wrote to him, 'and after thinking it such a crime it was more than I could prevent from that moment – you drew me to you like a magnet and I could not indeed have kept away.'[3]

The melodrama that followed quickly became one of the set-pieces of the Byron myth. It seemed to both confirm the extreme, unholy power of his celebrity and be the perfect metaphor for everything that Regency society feared about his potentially dangerous effect on women and fans.

Through the early summer of 1812, the couple shamelessly appeared together in public. Caroline's husband was forced to look the other way, but the scandal seriously threatened to put an end to his burgeoning political aspirations. They were so 'torturously in love' that they began making plans to elope, but Caroline's behaviour became increasingly obsessive. 'She absolutely besieged him,' recalled the poet Samuel Rogers, a mutual friend. 'After a great party at Devonshire House, to which Caroline had not been invited, I saw her – yes I saw her – talking to Byron, with half her body thrust into the carriage which he had just entered.'[4] Other times, knowing how he liked her to dress as a boy, she would disguise herself as a pageboy to visit him unseen. Frequently, these visits were welcomed and planned, but when she arrived unannounced, bitter arguments would be followed by passionate, apologetic reconciliations.

Byron had strong feelings for Caroline, but he was selfish, easily bored and – ironic for a celebrity known for flouting the rules and expectations of society – concerned for both of their reputations. When he finally broke off the relationship after a few short months, Caroline refused to go quietly. She bombarded him with letters pleading with him to press on with the elopement. One letter, signed 'your wild antelope', contained a rose gold locket with a lock of her pubic hair inside. 'I asked you not to send blood,' she wrote, 'yet do – because if it means love I like to have it – I cut the hair too close & bled much more than you need – do not you the same … sooner take it from the arm or wrist.'[5]

No blood was returned. Byron was hiding from Caroline in Scotland at this point, but Caroline – heartbroken, desperate and increasingly distressed – threw herself into winning her lover back at any cost, including any fragments of her reputation that remained intact.

She resurrected her pageboy act to break into his house in Piccadilly. The plan had been to get him alone to talk to him about their future together, but finding him absent, she was overcome with rage. When Byron returned home later that night, he found the words 'REMEMBER ME' scrawled in the flyleaf of his copy of the Gothic novel *Vathek* – a twisted fairy tale of sin, sex, fallen angels, ghosts and a hero's slow, debaucherous descent into hell due to his own insatiable desires and ungodly life choices. The incident would inspire a suitably Gothic response; one of Byron's bitterest and cruellest Caroline poems:

> Remember thee! Remember thee! …
> Remorse and shame shall cling to thee
> And haunt thee like a feverish dream! …
> Thy husband too shall think of thee …
> Thou false to him, thou fiend to me!

Still undeterred, Caroline's rampage continued. The rumour mill was aghast at reports that she had smashed a glass and threatened to stab herself after a tense exchange with Byron at a ball. She didn't stab herself, but there was a scratch deep enough to draw blood. Or was it that she actually *had* stabbed herself with a pair of scissors? Accounts were conflicting. Some people said she'd fainted multiple times, others that she'd been carried home by her mother-in-law, dress soaked in blood.

It wasn't until December that Caroline finally conceded defeat. Just before Christmas, she held a Byron burning ceremony. Caroline led an army of girls, dressed in white, around a bonfire in the village of Welwyn, near her country estate of Brocket. Her servants wore livery with shiny new buttons. She'd had them engraved with the words '*Ne crede Byron*' ('Don't believe Byron'), an inversion of the Byron family motto. As her homemade effigy went up in flames, she threw relics and mementos of their relationship onto the pyre and recited a poem she'd written especially for the occasion:

> Burn, fire, burn, while wondering boys exclaim,
> And gold and trinkets glitter in the flame.

Ah, look not thus on me, so grave, so sad,
Shake not your heads, nor say the lady's mad.
Judge not of others, for there is but one
To whom the heart and feelings can be known.
Upon my youthful faults few censures cast,
Look to my future and forgive the past.

Caroline would never be forgiven in the eyes of polite society. By the end of the year, Byron had cemented his reputation as 'mad, bad and dangerous to know' (a phrase coined by Caroline herself shortly after meeting him). But Caroline was just mad. Obsessed with her idol and living in a fantasy world, she was the most famous and tragic victim of Byromania. As Byron himself wrote to a friend, her imagination had been 'heated by novel reading which made her fancy herself as a heroine of romance and led her to all kinds of eccentricities'.[6] When she published *Glenarvon*, a fictionalised account of the affair a few years later, she cemented her fate. For the rest of her life, Caroline would be defined by her Byron obsession – her refusal to let go, her desire to *be him* as well as be with him and the shameful public spectacle she had made of the whole thing.

Caroline was a complicated person. Recent historians have argued that she most likely suffered from bipolar disorder, but her vilification, regardless of diagnosis, reflected an intense double standard. While Byron's larger-than-life reputation as a scandalous figure only added to his mystique, the narrative of Caroline's social downfall reduced her to passivity. She was an erotomaniac. A sex addict. A disturbed victim of lust for a man that had completely escaped from her control. If Byron was the world's first celebrity, then Caroline was the world's first celebrity stalker fan. Her literary efforts were dismissed as a kiss and tell or, as Byron put it, a 'fuck and publish'.[7] Her influence on his work was forgotten. Her depiction as a deranged groupie, even today, in many modern accounts of the affair, casts Byron as the victim of rabid female desire that will stop at nothing to consume him as well as his literary works.

Caroline's story was unique, but this nightmarish depiction of Byron's female fans was not. Contemporary reviews were filled with references to the 'insatiable' appetites of hysterical readers said to be far more interested in Byron's body than his body of work.[8] 'The feelings, the earthly desires, the animal passions, are alone and always the object' of Byron's appeal, contended one review in the *London Magazine*.[9] And it wasn't just reviews. Byron's own writings were rife with allusions to female readers as soul-sucking vampires feeding on his books to satisfy their lust for him. 'I've been more ravished myself than anybody since the Trojan War,' he once famously wrote.[10]

As Byron's 'most famous fan', the story of Caroline's Byromania was more than a melodramatic tale of unrequited love and celebrity obsession or even a tragic story of undiagnosed mental illness. It reflected deep cultural anxieties about the changing role of women in society and a nervousness about women's relationship with popular culture and visible expressions of female desire that would continue well into the twentieth century. Like Bertha Mason, 'the madwoman in the attic', the Byronic Mr Rochester's first wife in *Jane Eyre*, Caroline's crime was not her 'madness' – it was her visibility. She was a physical embodiment of the 'strange, wild and disturbed friendship' that Byron seemed to have formed, through his writing, with his fans.[11] Bertha, after all, is most terrifying because her passion, sexuality and capacity for rage are a part of every woman, including Charlotte Brontë's pious heroine Jane. Bertha, sent mad by that passion, hidden away from the world by her husband, is a warning. A reminder, to Jane, of what happens to nineteenth-century women who allow themselves to be ruled by feeling, emotionality and lust.

There's a large box in the Murray Archive at the National Library of Scotland. It was once tied with pink ribbons. It is stuffed full of letters from women – from courtesans to schoolgirls – of every walk of life and social class. Many are gushing, adoring and flirtatious; they talk of 'enthusiastic fire', 'melting hearts' and 'animated souls'. Many are also bold, self-reflective and self-aware.

Byron, and the majority of his biographers, may have dismissed these 'foolish', 'lovesick girls' as neurotics, reading the letters as symbols of his power over women, trophies that he hoarded until his death. But in putting pen to paper and expressing their romantic fantasies and often complicated feelings and emotions to a man who was not only a stranger but a lord – far above them in social class – these women were actually doing something quite radical.

In a world that required women to sit down and shut up; a world where Caroline Lamb's legacy would be as a madwoman and not, as Dickens would later describe her, as 'a really clever woman – a heroine, in a way'; a world where female desire existed almost completely in relation to needs, rules or expectations of men, in their small way, as we shall see, every fan letter was an insurrection.[12]

Forbidden Fruit, Auguste Toulmouche (1865)

© Glasshouse Images / Alamy Stock Photo

1

IMAGINATION, LONDON, 1812
BAD ROMANCE

The line raced through the girl's fingers. Her imagination had rushed away. It had sought the pools, the depths, the dark places ... And then there was a smash. There was an explosion. There was foam and confusion. The imagination had dashed itself against something hard. The girl was roused from her dream. She was indeed in a state of the most acute and difficult distress. To speak without figure she had thought of something, something about the body, about the passions which it was unfitting for her as a woman to say.
– Virginia Woolf, 'Professions for Women' (1931)

Isabella Harvey was seventeen when she first wrote to Lord Byron. She knew it wasn't a good idea, but she couldn't stop thinking about him. He was on her mind constantly. In her thoughts, her prayers, her daydreams. It was odd to feel this way about a person she'd never met, she knew that. But at the same time, it felt completely normal – like he was a part of her in some way. Whatever their souls were made of, it was the same thing. What was stranger than her feelings was the violent, irrepressible urge to write.

If she was going to do this, she decided it was best to do it under a pseudonym. She settled on the name 'Zorina' after an Italian school friend. It had a continental glamour that seemed to fit with the heroines of his poems: Medora, Gulnare, Zorina. He would like that. But more importantly, she would have any replies sent to Mr Weston's Post Office on Fitzroy Street – no one in her family could know about this. Aristocratic ladies like Caroline Lamb might be established enough to break the rules and damn the consequences, but for middle-class girls like Isabella, virtue and reputation were everything. Byron was not the type of man a young lady should be corresponding with. Especially not a letter like this. 'Zorina' was the perfect solution.

There's something special that happens when a person writes anonymously: it frees them. 'Man is least himself when he talks in his own person,' said Oscar Wilde (himself a massive Byron fan). 'Give a man a mask and he will tell you the truth.' For women in the late eighteenth and early nineteenth centuries, this was even more resonant and potentially explains the Regency obsession with masquerade balls. There were very few places that a girl or woman could experiment with who she was or express herself at all.

According to ladies' conduct books with stern titles like *An Enquiry into the Duties of the Female Sex* or *Strictures on the Modern System of Female Education* (recommended reading for ladies at the time and nearly always written by men), the ideal woman of the 'long' eighteenth century was passive and passionless by nature. Her key words to live by were modesty, chastity and restraint. This extended to every part of a woman's life – from ideally not eating in public to making sure no one ever found out that you were too funny or clever. Even reading too much or reading the 'wrong things' in the 'wrong way' were thought to be bad for a woman's health as well as her reputation.

And then there were the rules on chastity. Since passion and desire were seen as unnatural in women, the concept of chastity covered all impure 'irregular thoughts' or imaginings that a woman might have, as well as anything she might do about them. Female desire was about repression, denial and inhibition of self. This was arduous and isolating, but girls were taught that it was about self-protection. Men were said to be so sexually rapacious and predatory that potential seduction (leading to pregnancy and therefore ruin) was everywhere. Just so much as looking at a man in the wrong way could 'inflame his desire', putting a lady at risk.

Corresponding, amorously, with a man you weren't married or engaged to was something to be approached with extreme caution. As the author of *The Complete Art of Writing Love Letters; or, the Lover's Best Instructor* advised women in 1795:

> Either the man conceals his basest designs under the cover of the most virtuous and honourable pretences; or the Lady encourages those addresses which she is resolved to disappoint ... It behoves our youth to walk with the utmost wariness in this dangerous path, which though strewed with roses and lilies ... they too frequently tread on serpents that lurk beneath the beauteous and fragrant flowers.[1]

HOT-PRESS DARLING

Byron wasn't the type of guy who even bothered to conceal his 'basest designs'. At the peak of Byromania in 1812, as his fanmail from women began to pile up, he wrote to his publisher John Murray to complain about the fact that his admirers were anonymous. 'If I can discover them & they be young as they say they are, I could perhaps convince them of my devotion.'[2]

On the surface, Byron was exactly the type of rakish seducer that ladies' conduct books had been warning young women about for years. He was said to 'fall on chambermaids like thunderbolts', drink his wine out of a cup made from a human skull he'd found in his garden and on his wedding night, he (literally not metaphorically) apparently set fire to his bed while screaming, 'Good God, I am surely in hell!'[3] Wherever he went, he left a trail of broken hearts and fallen women in his wake.

These rumours were true. What was also true – though he would never have liked to admit it – was that Byron knew a lot about isolation, secret hidden desire and victimisation himself. Born in 1788, a year before the French Revolution, George Gordon Byron was the only son of fortune-hunting sea captain 'Mad' Jack Byron and Catherine Gordon, an impoverished Scottish heiress (she had not been impoverished when she first married Jack). He was born with a deformity to his right foot, then known as a 'clubbed foot', that would cause him shame, insecurity and a limp for the rest of his life. He believed it was a sign that he was cursed by the devil. He was emotionally and physically abused by his mother, sexually abused by his nanny and bullied by nearly everyone at school. When he was fifteen, in an incident that would mark him for the rest of his life, he overheard his cousin Mary Ann, who he was secretly and madly in love with, cruelly deride him: 'Do you think I could care anything for that lame boy?'[4]

Resolved not to be defined by his disability, Byron worked hard to become a great athlete. His sport was swimming. By the time he left school, he had grown into a handsome, charming, popular young lord. He liked to read, party and buy clothes. 'That Boy will be the death of me and drive me mad – I fear he is already ruined. At eighteen!!!' wrote his mother.[5] But beneath the jokes, the reckless spending and perpetual debauchery, something deeper felt wrong.

Throughout his life, Byron would be in love with the idea of being in love but – perhaps due to this childhood of trauma and abuse – never fully able to grab hold of it in reality. This was compounded by the fact that he was bisexual, often finding it easier to form closer attachments with men. In England, homosexuality was a criminal offence. Like his female readers, Byron was forced to hide and sublimate a secret, desiring part of himself. And just like Zorina and his other anonymous fans, he often found it easier to write behind a mask.

The first flush of Byromania came in the weeks and months after the publication of *Childe Harold's Pilgrimage*, a fictionalised account of Byron's travels through Europe during his 'grand tour' the previous few years. Freed from the stuffy, repressive confines of Regency society, the trip had been a revelation.

Harold, his literary alter ego, is a young knight with a dark, mysterious past. Tired of his decadent partyboy lifestyle back in England – 'with pleasure drugge'd, he almost longed for woe', he says – he decides it's time for a 'change of scene'. A precursor to countless spirit-of-the-age travelogues from the restless, tortured brotherhood of self-mythologising man-genius (think Hemingway, Kerouac and Dylan) who set off for foreign lands, or hit the road in the quest for authenticity and freedom, there's no direction to Harold's wanderings. His search is for himself.

Like Byron, the poem was a bundle of tantalising contradictions – inspired by the classics but startlingly modern in its politics and sentiment. It felt epic but also, seemingly, deeply personal. As Harold mopes and glowers his way across Europe, his world-weary disillusionment is tempered by a deep and genuine longing for something more. This spoke to a whole generation of readers, struggling themselves from jadedness and '*Weltschmerz*' (world grief) in the fallout from the French Revolution and subsequent Napoleonic Wars. They connected with Harold, felt his pain and saw themselves in his words. But they were also curious about the mysterious, broken-hearted young lord who had written the book. This confessional-style writing was completely new. Was it fact or fiction? Rumour had it, Lord Byron was just as tortured and romantic as his protagonist. Also that he was gorgeous. And single. That old adage 'a reformed rake makes the best husband' suddenly felt true again.

In his preface to the poem, Byron had flirted with readers. 'It has been suggested to me by friends, on whose opinions I set a high value, that in this fictitious character, "Childe Harold", I may incur the suspicion of having intended some real personage,' he wrote. 'This I beg leave, once for all, to disclaim – Harold is the child of imagination.' Readers were having none of it. There were far too many similarities between Byron and Harold for them to believe that. It would have been impossible, they thought, for anyone to have written so beautifully and so truthfully about love, melancholy and *Weltschmerz* without having experienced those feelings first-hand. They became convinced that Byron *was* Harold, and he was only too happy to let them run with it.

Until then, as a charming but eccentric debt-ridden minor lord who believed he was cursed by the devil, Byron had existed on the periphery of the British aristocracy. Now, he was the darling of London. His fame seemed to 'spring up, like the palace of a fairytale, in one night', recalled his friend and fellow poet Thomas Moore.[6] The whole thing had been 'electric'. There was so much hype around the book that the first print run of *Childe Harold* sold out in three days, carriages jostled outside his apartment with invitations to dinners and balls, anyone who knew anyone who knew him (even vaguely) implored them for an introduction and the letters from admirers streamed in. 'This poem is on every table, and he himself courted, visited, flattered, and praised,' wrote the Duchess of Devonshire. 'He really is the only topic of almost every conversation – the men jealous of him, the women of each other.'[7]

It seemed that the whole of London had gone 'stark mad about *Childe Harold* and Byron'. But when Caroline Lamb's 22-year-old cousin, the high-minded Annabella Milbanke, coined the term Byromania, it was the women she took aim at. In her poem, 'The Byromania', Annabella depicted Byron as a dangerous cult leader, bringing women under a poisonous spell. That rake reform fantasy that seemed to beckon, so irresistibly, from the stormy depths of that wounded, feeling heart was a trap:

> Woman! How truly called a 'harmless thing!'
> So meekly smarting with the venom'd sting
> Forgiving saints! – ye bow before the rod,
> And kiss the ground on which your censor trod …
> Reforming Byron with his magic sway
> Compels all hearts to love him and obey

This was the summer of the Caroline–Byron affair, but Caroline was not the only woman Byron was involved with. Nor was she the only woman who seemed to have completely lost her mind at the shrine of *Childe Harold*.

Lady Falkland, for example, the widow of Byron's friend Lord Falkland (killed the previous year in a duel), had become convinced that Byron was secretly in love with her. She had apparently discovered this while reading *Childe Harold*, which she interpreted to be addressed to her. 'It is not a loveless heart I offer you,' she wrote to him, 'but a heart where every throb beats responsive to your own.'[8]

This type of romantic melodrama was typical of Byron's fan letters from this period, which were arriving with increasing frequency: 'You must excuse this madness', 'I can resist no longer', 'instantly destroy what was intended *for your eyes only*', 'an impulse grateful as irresistible impels me to acknowledge your pen has called forth the most exquisite feelings I have ever experienced', 'should curiosity prompt you, and should you not be afraid of gratifying it, by trusting yourself *alone* in the Green Park at seven o'clock this evening you will see *Echo*'.[9]

Annabella was devoutly religious and therefore horrified at the undignified, unwomanly spectacle of Byromania. She reserved her most barbed couplets for Caroline and the other women who increasingly seemed to be attempting to channel their hero themselves:

> See Caro smiling, sighing, o'er his face
> In hopes to imitate each strange grimace
> And mar the silliness which looks so fair
> By bringing signs of wilder Passion there
> Is human nature to be cast anew,
> And modelled on your Idol's Image true?
> Then grant me, Jove, to wear some other shape,
> And be an anything – except an Ape!!

These lines would be strangely prophetic. By the time Annabella wrote them, Byron (apparently boyishly playful and good-humoured in private around friends) had fully embraced the theatrical anguish of his Childe Harold persona in public. His fans couldn't get enough of it, and big feelings (preferably wild, melancholic and/or devoured by passion and remorse) had become the hot new thing.

Within a few years, as his celebrity continued to grow beyond anything the world had seen before, Byron and 'being Byronic' would become symbols of youthful rebellion and sex appeal as our hero trailed 'the pageant of his bleeding heart' across Europe.[10] Admirers learned his poetry word for word and were said to 'practise before the glass in the hope of catching the curl of the upper lip and scowling brow in imitation of their great leader'.[11] And if Byron was what women wanted, then Byron was what they were going to get. Young men 'caught the fashion for deranging their hair, or of leaving their shirt-collar unbuttoned' – 'open shirt collars, melancholy features, and a certain dash of remorse were ... indispensable', according to Edmund Reade in 1829.[12] But who exactly was imitating who?

Between 1812 and 1816, a period he would later refer to as his 'reign', Byron put out a flurry of new works, known collectively as the 'Turkish Tales'. Today, he's better known for his more 'serious', 'mature' works like *Manfred* and *Don Juan*, but these romantic swashbucklers would be the making of him. Like a Hollywood franchise that found a winning formula, *The Giaour*, *The Bride of Abydos*, *The Corsair*, *Lara* and *The Siege of Corinth* all featured the most crowd-pleasing elements of *Childe Harold*:

- A sexy, brooding anti-hero
- An exotic foreign location
- Idealised tragic love
- Scandalous adventures
- Reportedly drawn from real life.

With every new tormented hero – the pirate captain of *The Corsair*, the vampiric infidel of *The Giaour* or the incestuous lover of *The Bride of Abydos* – standing in for the poet himself, readers had unique access to Byron and his world. The heady mixture of scandal and the beauty and honesty with which Byron apparently laid his tortured soul bare were irresistible. Although, as the literary historian Andrew Elfenbein has pointed out, Byron's most scandalous escapades (the dramas that are, today, most closely associated with his legend) actually began after his *Childe Harold* success. 'His scandalous aura arose almost as if to justify the qualities of his poetry,' he says.[13]

Was it that fame had finally given Byron the freedom to admit and indulge his darkest, most immoral impulses? Or was he just method acting – giving his adoring audience the infamous Lord Byron of their nightmarish daydreams? Either way, there was (and still is) something incredibly sexy about an outlaw. Byron had known this for a long time. His literary ancestors were the great anti-heroes of the past, most notably Milton's smouldering fallen archangel, Satan, from *Paradise Lost*. Cast down from heaven for daring to challenge the tyranny of God, Satan was – until Byron – the ultimate poster-boy for the tormented pursuit of moral individualism.

What Byron added to the mix (in addition to his beautiful, terrible, most confounding self) was romance. This was the hero-villain as lover. The great-grandfather of a long line of moody, brooding sex symbols from Mr Darcy through Heathcliff to Edward Cullen and Christian Grey, Byron taught the world that 'girlish innocence can triumph over manly experience through the redemptive power of love'.[14] Both hero and victim, the Byronic Hero's cynical, remote exterior is really just an act of self-protection – a product of the ravages of the world that have forced him to harden his heart. What lies beneath is the most feeling and sensitive man. As Byron himself wrote in *The Corsair*:

> His heart was form'd for softness, warp't to wrong
> Betrayed too early, beguiled too long.

These lines were the most quoted across all of Byron's fan letters. And it *is* an achingly compelling fantasy. Lone, wild and strange the Byronic Hero may be, his darkness and misanthropy only serve to intensify his connection with his beloved – the one woman in the world with the power to see the real him. It makes her goodness and her love even more radiant. She is the purest good. The only truth. The one thing in the world that can give meaning to his otherwise hellish existence.

There's no God in Byron's world. *She* is his only possibility for redemption, which is strangely empowering – in a way. Imagine being the one person in the world with the power to calm *that* storm. 'Without one hope on earth beyond thy love / And scarce a glimpse of mercy from above,' he writes:

> Yes – it was love – if thoughts of tenderness
> Tried by temptation, strengthened by distress
> Unmoved by absence, firm in every clime
> And yet – oh more than all! – untired by time;
> Which nor defeated hope, nor baffled wile,
> Could render sullen were she to smile

The infinite depths of his torment are really just a promise of his profound capacity to love the right woman passionately.

It's no surprise that Byron's earliest fans, women who felt they had gotten to know the 'real Lord Byron' through his writing, were attempting to save him. This was the model of love he had given them, and he seemed to be *desperately* in need of it.

'You are unhappy – a being feared and mistrusted,' wrote one anonymous admirer. 'The interest I feel – the eager wish for power to contribute (tho' but a mite) to your happiness arises from sympathy adding strength to compassion.' She included a copy of the

Bible with her letter, urging him to embrace Christianity as an antidote to his pain. Another woman, similarly anonymous, explained
that it was his writing itself that had proved his goodness to her:
'I am told my Lord Byron is an infidel but no, it cannot be, I have
fought your cause and said, he who can so feelingly describe the
purest of sentiments, must acknowledge a God of love.'[15]

Even Annabella Milbanke – the woman who had initially
mocked the idea of 'reforming Byron' – came over to the dark side
in the end. After finally meeting him at a party, she caught the
Byromania herself. She remembered the exact moment her feelings
changed. They'd been standing together in the middle of the room:

> I felt that he was the most attractive person; but I was not *bound* to
> him by any strong feelings of sympathy till he uttered these words,
> not to me but to my hearing – 'I have not a friend in the world!' ...
> I vowed in secret to be a devoted friend to this lone being.[16]

Annabella became convinced that she *was* the one woman in the
world who actually could save that beautiful, tortured soul. And for a
brief enchanted moment – fuelled in part by the fact that Byron had
mounting debts and Annabella was a wealthy heiress and in part by
his need to distract the public from escalating rumours that he was
sleeping with his sister – he wondered if it might actually be true.

'I am thankful that the wildness of my imagination has not prevent-
ed me from recovering the path of peace,' he wrote to her. 'My plans
– my hopes – my affection into love – I could almost say – devotion to
you – forgive my weaknesses – love what you can of me ... and I will
be – I am whatever you please to make me.'[17] Reader, she married him.

I know it may be painful to imagine now, but rake reform (aka taming fuckboys) was advertised as a manifestation of girl power in the eighteenth century.

Young women, like Annabella and Byron's anonymous saviours, were raised to believe that female power lay in virtuous domesticity. If a man like Byron could be reformed and therefore 'tamed', through marriage to a good woman, into renouncing his rakish vices and philandering ways, that was a win for the fairer sex – an expression of female power and a vindication of domestic life. The sharing of feelings, especially of sympathy as mentioned by many of Byron's anonymous reformers, were thought to be an important part of the 'conversion process'.

The belief that rakes could be reformed, and that it was the mission of virtuous women to help them, was propagated by sentimental novels like Samuel Richardson's *Pamela*: England's first bestseller and the first novel to spark a wave of popular enthusiasm that we would recognise as fandom today. It's the story of a fifteen-year-old servant girl, Pamela, who finds herself in a morally questionable situation when her new employer, the rakish Mr B, begins making unwanted sexual advances. Through the novel, which is told as a series of letters, Mr B's attempts at seduction become increasingly dark, manipulative and scheming, but Pamela remains steadfast in her virtue. By the end of the novel, Mr B has been converted to goodness.

In the novel's pivotal scene, Mr B reads the letters that Pamela had been writing to her friends and family, which describe her experience of his abuse. Seeing the world through her eyes is the turning point in his path to redemption. Pamela and her virtue make him want to be a better man. They fall in love, get married and are finally able to consummate their love with Pamela's saintly virtue still intact. This good girl/bad boy redemption story would become a staple plotline in novels of the second half of the eighteenth century and – from *Bridgerton* to *Beauty and the Beast* – is still with us today.

Feminist literary critics like Tania Modleski who have studied the enduring popularity of these stories have theorised that part of women's enjoyment of good girl/bad boy narratives, which most often culminate in marriage, is the power struggle. When the bad boy gets down on one knee to propose, he literally *is* on his knees: the woman has dominated him. Modleski calls this a 'revenge fantasy', but the revenge is over the patriarchy more than the bad boy himself.[18] In forcing him to connect with his feelings, it's a victory of emotion – something that both eighteenth-century men and women were, on the whole for different reasons, required to repress.

Byron was a perfect candidate for reform because his inner softness and ability to feel were already so visible in his poems. It wasn't just that he needed to be saved; he wanted to be saved! His fanmail is filled with heartfelt confessions of female feeling and often suffering too. 'I have known what it is to have my youth blighted by unkindness, to be feared, hated, neglected,' said the lady who sent him the Bible. Another, who called herself 'Rosalie', was bolder: 'Has he a mind that possesses the power of friendship? And that feels the ingratitude, and malice of an unfeeling, prejudiced and misjudging world? … Does he seek a virtuous, innocent and faithful friend?' She explained that she couldn't share her identity, but he could reply by posting a message in the *Sunday Observer* 'bearing the name Antonio'.[19]

This was more than sympathy or even romance. Byron's confessional writing – in all its messy, tortured, feeling humanness – connected with people in a way that poetry never had before. As yet another woman who said she 'could not affix her name' explained:

I must be allowed to observe that your Lordship is not addressed by one of those frivolous beings, who conclude that it is very sentimental and captivating to sigh away an hour over Lord Byron's poetry, merely because it is what is deemed the fashionable reading of the day, but it is one, whose deeply wounded spirit was occasioned in early youth, for several years past to shun all society as an intolerable annoyance.

His fans were writing to him because they identified with the feelings and emotions he described – and because his impassioned, confessional writing had given them a model and language that they could use to express these thoughts and feelings in themselves. That so much of his fanmail came in the form of poetry is testament to this fact. As modern readers, we might look at these letters and see only cringeworthy torrents of hyperbole and melodrama, but in 1812, that was the point. In sitting down to write to Lord Byron, these women had found a safe place to feel and express – to experiment with being Byronic themselves.

For many women, this emotional connection was born out of the magic of reading itself. They often described reading Byron in almost supernatural, mystically eroticised terms, as if, through the alchemy of his words, Byron had become a physical presence in their lives. 'Often have I wandered in these gardens with your poem for my companion & with thee conversing have forgot all time,' wrote Anna from Kensington Palace. 'I have hung in rapt attention over every line of *Childe Harold*. I am not a critic but an inexperienced young woman, but the language of genius & of nature must be felt.'[20]

Sometimes they struggled to make sense of these feelings, even when writing to Byron himself: 'This empire you obtained over me by means of your writing,' wrote Zorina. 'How intimately I connected with the author and his works. This was natural, but how happens that the author is now more to me than his writings, that he is the food of my thoughts, the impulse of my life ... the bright dream of my existence.'[21] The infamous courtesan Harriette Wilson was less confused. She wrote to tell Byron that she'd taken her copy of *Don Juan* to bed with her and that it had kept her up all night.

Byron was notoriously ambivalent about his female readers. In public, he scoffed at the idea of catering to female tastes: 'I have not written for their pleasure; if they find theirs in the perusal of my works, it is because they wish it ... I have no intention of writing books for women.'[22] But in private, particularly in the early days, he understood the importance of the women's market, monitored which books sold best with women and enjoyed his status as a Romantic heart-throb. 'Who does not write to please women?' he asked his friend Thomas Medwin, admitting that he was most pleased with the success of *The Corsair* than any other book 'because it did shine, and in *boudoirs*'.[23]

By the time his year-long marriage to Annabella fell apart in a storm of revelations so shocking (and potentially criminal) that he was forced to leave England never to return, Byron wasn't just a celebrity. He was an otherworldly multimedia event. A fictional character in real life. Holed up in Villa Diodati, a beautiful mansion on the shores of Lake Geneva, brooding on past regrets and unspeakable sins, the incarnation was complete. 'He had Childe Harolded himself,' wrote his friend Sir Walter Scott, 'outlawed himself into too great a resemblance with the pictures of his imagination.'[24] But let's not forget that it was his fans' fantasies, as much as his own, that had given birth to all this.

Byromania was born in a whirlwind of curiosity about one, very real, man. But, as we know too well these days, the power of celebrities is not who they are. It's what they mean. For Byron's female fans, this was often deeper and more complex than the 'reforming Byron' fantasy of Annabella's poem. Byron and his celebrity had created new ways for people to enjoy and engage with books. And as his fan letters were beginning to prove – consciously or not – he was inviting women to become active participants in the story. His idealised soulmate may have been virtuous, pure and true, but she was also a lot like him. In his narcissistic fantasies of love as connection with a perfect other self, Byron (one of the most misogynist writers of the Romantic era) was inadvertently creating a radical vision of equality:

> She was like me in lineaments – her eyes
> Her hair, her features, all, to the very tone
> Even of her voice, they said were like mine …
> She had the same lone thoughts and wanderings
> The quest of hidden knowledge, and a mind
> To comprehend the universe.[25]

BAD READERS

By the time he went into exile in 1816, the word 'Byron' was hot property. It wasn't just his books that were big business. Anything associated with Byron that could be marketed and sold was marketed and sold, and even things that couldn't be marketed or sold gained special currency if they were even slightly connected with him.

Zorina, in one of her letters to Byron, described how she had danced with a young man at a ball only because he was said to be a distant relation of his. She did admit a quick realisation that he was no substitute for the original, but whether it was dancing with a supposed relative, buying a printed portrait or copying favourite lines from a poem into a commonplace book (a type of scrapbook that was popular at the time), Byron's most ardent readers wanted a physical piece of him, to have and to hold. Many fan letters contained requests for portraits, signed poems and locks of hair. In typical Byron style, the poet is said to have bought a dog to help him keep up with the demand for hair. This was definitely a very Byron thing to do, but it also tells us something about how his most enthusiastic female readers were viewed.

From the very earliest days of his celebrity, women were said to have been vital to Byron's popular success. This was partly because women were the largest demographic of readers in England at the time and partly also because Byron's most popular early poems, the 'Turkish Tales', combined two genres that were considered to be 'female'. They had all the drama and romance of a novel and the real-life intrigue of a memoir or 'secret history'.

Men read and enjoyed them too (in equal numbers) and, as we've seen, no one was immune to Byron's extra-textural mystique. But in newspapers and magazines, there quickly emerged a story of two very different types of Byron reader. There were the 'good' highbrow readers of Byron's work, generally male and upper class – a select minority. They appreciated the quality of his writing. And then there were the 'bad' readers: the ladies who had turned him into a 'popular idol'. These women were said to be dangerously gullible, borderline hysterical and far more interested in Byron's body and character than in his books.

Seduced by gossip and under the spell of the poet's good looks, the typical female reader of Byron, according to critics, devoured his poetry (if she even read his poetry at all) in pursuit of the same cheap thrills she found in the Gothic romances of Ann Radcliffe and Horace Walpole. At best, these misguided fantasies were a phase to be outgrown. At worst, as the story of Lady Caroline Lamb illustrated, the Byronic appeal to sensation and sentimentality could lead to bad behaviour, mental instability and downfall. And the most concerning part of all of this was: you didn't even have to be reading Byron's books to fall under that corrupting yet irresistible influence.

From 1812 onwards, Byron's devastatingly handsome face was everywhere. Those blue eyes. That curled lip. That steamy open collar that showed just enough of his neck for a lady to imagine all kinds of terrible things and, of course, that trademark brooding 'underlook'. Women who met him in person reported breathlessness and heart palpitations. Others fainted. 'That beautiful, pale face is my fate,' wrote Caroline Lamb in her diary on the night of that first, fateful meeting. One Lady Lovell, on a trip to Rome, is said to have averted her daughter's eyes when they came across Byron in St Peter's Square. 'Don't look at him,' she said, 'he's dangerous to look at.'[26]

Since so much of Byron's stardom itself radiated from the secrets supposedly hidden within his person, the act of looking itself took on new depths, meanings and dimensions. For Byron's first female readers, women of the British aristocracy, glancing curiously or gazing longingly across ballrooms and dinner tables, the invitation to look was very real. Byron may have been a stranger, but through his writing, they had already seen his soul. This was a dangerous illusion – a fascination with the body of a man that could lead to very real seduction and seemed to be igniting the most dangerous of all passions: lust.

This was bad enough when it was afflicting women in his social circle, but as this 'enchantment' extended to women who didn't know him and would never meet him, it became even more concerning. From the perspective of his critics, that beautiful face, a supposed well of secret hidden truths and unutterable depths, was about as deep as a dirty puddle. And the same could be said of his writing. That moody, brooding character supposedly protecting a sweet and savable soul, was just a cynical act he was putting on for calculated and nefarious objectives: mind control. As John Gibson Lockhart wrote in his satirical *A Letter to the Right Hon. Lord Byron by John Bull*:

> You are a great poet, but even with your poetry you mix too much of that at present very saleable article against which I am now bestirring myself. The whole of your misanthropy, for example, is humbug … But you thought it would be a fine interesting thing for a handsome young Lord to depict himself as a dark-souled, melancholy, morbid being and you have done so … Every boarding-school in the empire still contains many devout believers in the amazing misery of the black-haired, high-browed, blue-eyed, bare-throated Lord Byron. How melancholy you look in your prints![27]

In the eyes of many critics and fellow writers, Byron was a sell-out, manipulatively using his handsome face and affected emotions to sell books to clueless young women who didn't understand the true meaning of his work – a classic case of catering to the lowest common denominator. This wasn't a reformable rake. This was a fame-hungry narcissist who took pleasure in illusion, sensation and chaos. As one reviewer summarised, even after his death: 'Byron is a poet of passion – indeed, of all others, *the* poet of passion. Love is with him selfish, an unrestrainable idolatry – wild and mighty, but fickle and forgetful. It is, while it lasts, a tempest, a hurricane, and it scratches where it alights.'

In his *Letter*, Lockhart included a scene in which women from Jane Austen novels gather together to gossip about the Byrons' separation trial while fawning over a portrait of him:

Now, tell me, Mrs Goddard, now tell me, Miss Price, now tell me, dear Harriet Smith, and dear, dear Mrs Elton, do tell me, is not this just the very look, that one would have fancied for Childe Harold? Oh! What eyes and eyebrows! Oh! What a chin! – well, after all, who knows what may have happened. One can never know the truth of such stories. Perhaps her Ladyship was in the wrong after all – I am sure if I had married such a man, I would have borne with all his little eccentricities – a man so evidently unhappy – Poor Lord Byron! ... I am sure any woman of real sense would have done so ... poor Lord Byron! – well, say what they will, I shall always pity him.

If these women believed that Byron *was* the heroes of his poems and that his bad behaviour should be ignored or forgiven on account of his melancholy, they would follow and believe anything, including the 'delusions and illusions' and 'filthiness' of his 'disgusting and horrid' poems.[28] They were a danger to themselves. And to everyone else.

For conservative and religious critics, this sympathy for Byron was part of a much bigger problem: an appetite in poetry readers, and in Byron readers in particular, for wild and passionate emotions. The age of sentiment had taken hold and readers were obsessed with emotional intensity. They wanted to feel deeply rather than think clearly; to lose themselves in sensation; to experience the sublime rush of anguish and ecstasy that can only come from the darkest and most secret corners of a poet's naked heart. And so, reviewers accused Byron of feeding this lust for vulgar stimulation by 'seizing upon all of his most hidden thoughts ... and flinging them out into the open air' – shamelessly airing his dirty feelings in public.[29]

And if his heroes were bad, many of his heroines were worse. These were women who took the sexual initiative – expressed desire in words 'which would be indecent even in the mouth of their lovers'. They made 'strong love to a man', which was 'not very decorous, nor very natural'.[30] And if gossip was true, this Byronic degeneracy was making its way into the real world. These *were* the thoughts, feelings and behaviours that Byron was igniting in fans. 'How long, indeed, an abused public, and our fair country women in particular, will suffer themselves to be held in the silken chains of a poetic enchantment … is more than we can tell,' cried the *Christian Observer*.[31]

Newspapers and magazines pleaded with him to do the right thing:

> He is a lord and a poet, he will always be read by women. I entreat him, then, not to lose the glorious opportunity afforded him, of strengthening those minds, which it were a foul shame to weaken; let him awaken their capabilities, by exciting their moral ambition, instead (of doing what every boy can do) melting their hearts.[32]

Did Byron listen? Of course he didn't. His poems got darker, sexier and more blasphemous. The women who loved him were bad readers – of Byron, his books and potentially of life itself.

The idea of 'good readers' and 'bad readers' had already been around for a while. Most closely associated first with romance novels, then sentimental and Gothic literature, it had been picking up speed through the second half of the eighteenth century as literacy rates soared and publishers began catering to new, more popular, tastes. By the time Byron was writing, popular meant female.

Books were expensive to produce, historically making them luxury items. But in 1779, publishers realised they could make more money renting books out than they could selling them. This led to the birth of the first lending libraries, the infamous circulating libraries. For a small subscription fee, anyone could borrow a book for a few days, and since it was middle- and upper-class ladies who had the most spare time to read, by 1800, they had overtaken men as the primary market for books in England.

Women's reading had always been a contentious issue. Everyone acknowledged that it was, in theory, a good thing: the reading woman was a sign of modernity and civilisation. But reading meant thinking and feeling. These were two very dangerous things for a woman to be doing. As the increasing number of female readers gave rise to an increasing number of female writers and books targeted specifically at women, religious and conservative critics began to worry.

Reading could educate, inform and entertain, but it could also be a dangerously seductive activity. Too much reading could lead to laziness and the neglect of womanly duties in the home, while reading the wrong things or reading in the wrong way could fill a woman's mind with radical ideas, prime her for real-life seduction or worse. 'The increase of novels', said a 1792 pamphlet entitled *The Evils of Prostitution and Adultery*, 'will help to account for the increase of prostitution and for the numerous adulteries and elopements that we hear of in the different parts of the kingdom.'[33]

Unlike male reading, which spoke to the intellect, female reading was thought to connect directly with the body. Female readers were said to 'crave', 'devour' and 'consume' books.[34] Their reading was often described in physical terms: lolling on sofas or luxuriating in bed. Writers, cultural commentators and even artists depicted reading as an increasingly dangerous form of sensuality – a bodily pleasure that was not only subtly associated with sexual desire but conflated with it – and not in a heteronormative or healthy way. Reading was a private activity: something a lady could indulge in alone, behind closed doors and, most troublingly, without a man.

The epic popularity of Gothic romances around this time seemed to confirm the carnal effect that books had upon women. Ladies' transgressive, physical enjoyment of the fear and sensation elicited by these delightfully 'horrid' books was interpreted as sexual.[35] In Charles Williams's satirical cartoon, *Luxury, or the Comforts of a Rum-p-ford*, a young woman toasts her naked bottom by a roaring open stove. She has a copy of Matthew Lewis's filthy, blasphemous Gothic classic *The Monk* in one hand and the other inside her petticoat. (Is she doing what we think she's doing!?)

'In vain youth is secluded from the corruption of the living world', wrote the brilliantly named cleric Vicesimus Knox in *On Novel Reading*. 'Books are commonly allowed them with little restriction, as innocent amusements; yet these often pollute the heart, inflame the passions … and teach all the malignity of vice in solitude.'[36]

As the circulating libraries gave rise to popular literature (fun, disposable romance and horror stories you might want to borrow and read but not necessarily own), concerns about the dangers of women's literacy and the power of fiction, in particular, to debauch female minds soon converged around the figure that Ian Watt, in his seminal *The Rise of the Novel*, called the Novel-Reading Girl.[37] Young, dumb and dangerously gullible, she became one of the most prevalent figures in both fiction and cultural criticism of her day. Addicted to books and left to her own devices at the library, she was not picking out the type of literature that was good for her in any way.

Conduct books and literary magazines teemed with articles and letters deploring her pernicious, low-brow taste for romance and Gothic literature. These 'pathetic tales of love and madness' were designed to inflame the imagination, they said. They 'dressed out vice in pleasing colours', poisoning vulnerable young women with dangerous fantasies:

> The dissipated rake, who glories in his debaucheries, is painted often as humane, generous, and benevolent; whilst the heedless female, for the sake of these accomplishments, forgets his want of principles, his diseased body, and his rotten heart ... Many young girls, from morning to night, hang over this pestiferous reading, to the neglect of industry, health, proper exercise, and to the ruin both of body and soul.[38]

Many writers of the day took the imperilled, deluded Novel-Reading Girl as their theme. In *The Female Quixote*, *The Heroine* and *Northanger Abbey*, a young woman imagines she is the heroine of a novel. Too much reading has given her false expectations about life, which she believes will be as exciting, dramatic and romantic as in books. Sometimes, like in Jane Austen's *Northanger Abbey* – at its heart, a coming-of-age story – the series of misunderstandings that follow are used for comedy. But other times, this overly enthusiastic 'misreading' of both books and life took a novel-reading heroine to infinitely darker places.

Most famously, writing much later in the nineteenth century, Gustave Flaubert would immortalise the wayward female reader in *Madame Bovary*. His heroine, Emma Bovary, is the bored wife of a provincial doctor. Her obsession with romance novels and belief that a more exciting, fiction-like life is out there somewhere lead her into a sordid world of affairs, shopping addiction and ultimately debts, destitution and suicide. Convulsing on her deathbed after drinking a bottle of arsenic, she violently coughs up buckets of ink-black blood. The message was clear. Books – especially the romantic ones – could be dangerous.

Books may have been potentially harmful to women on a personal level, but there was a second, much more epic fear nestled in all this talk of 'bad readers' and 'degrading thirst for outrageous stimulation'. It was the spectre of the French Revolution. The dramatic scenes reported out of Paris in 1789 – angry mobs rising up to overthrow the monarchy, rivers of blood in the streets and baskets full of dismembered heads mouldering at the foot of the guillotine – could have come straight from the pages of Radcliffe or Lewis. These novels – or so it seemed – were appealing to exactly the same thirst for violence and disorder as the revolutionaries themselves.

'But, alas!' wrote a concerned citizen in an article entitled 'The Terrorist System of Novel Writing', 'so prone are we to imitation, that we have exactly and faithfully copied the SYSTEM OF TERROR, if not in our streets, and in our fields, at least in our circulating libraries and our closets'. The Gothic romance had 'made terror the order of the day'.[39] The Molotov cocktail of these 'terrorist novels' and their delusional, sensation-seeking female fans were now a threat to national security, especially since the revolution itself had been caused, in part, by the printing press.

It was, after all, passionately written political pamphlets, newspapers and books – the type of writing that appealed to the heart not the head – in the hands of the newly literate but uneducated masses that had helped spread the revolutionary ideas in the first place. To many people, this was a cautionary tale of what could happen when you used literature to rile up people's emotions and then put them behind a charismatic leader. And in France, women had been just as active as men in overthrowing the *Ancien Régime* and the bloodthirsty Terror that followed. In fact, it was a mob of hysterical women who had started the whole thing.

The inciting incident of the revolution, the Women's March on Versailles, during which 6,000 pike-wielding ladies stormed the Palace of Versailles demanding a fairer price for bread and the head of Marie Antoinette, was seared in the popular imagination as a nightmarish spectacle of women out of control. As Edmund Burke described in *Reflections on the Revolution in France*: 'The horrid yells, the shrilling screams, and frantic dances … all the unutterable abominations of the *furies of hell* [burst forth] in the abused shape of [these] vilest of women.'[40]

For conservative Brits like Burke, living in constant fear that a revolution in England was just around the corner, the idea that books containing radical ideas might fall into the hands of 'bad readers' like women or working-class people was a very real concern. Byron, the Gothic hero of the public imagination, may not have directly been calling for revolution, but he was definitely stirring up passions and his liberal politics were widely known. You didn't have to dig too deep to imagine how his hysterical appeal to the bodies of women could – in one dramatic flash of that infamous underlook – become a catalyst for revolution, terror and disorder.

Like a vampire, infecting the minds and imaginations of impressionable young women, spreading through the printing press, clouding their minds with feeling and emotion while presenting a radically liberal outlook to life, Byron's bestselling poems like *The Corsair* might have seemed, superficially, like romantic adventure stories, but who knew where all this romantic emotionality might lead. Didn't *The Corsair* end with a hareem girl turning violent and killing her master because of her love for a Byronic Hero? This was not going to end well.

The historian Jon Mee has called this phenomenon 'dangerous enthusiasm'.[41] Visible expressions of emotion in the eighteenth and nineteenth centuries, he says, were seen as dangerous because of their associations with civil unrest. In England, this can be traced all the way back to religious 'fanaticism' during the English Civil War. Since women were understood to be less rational and more sensitive to physical arousal than men, they were seen as more susceptible to enthusiasm – a relation of both hysteria and lust.

'Enthusiasts' and 'fanatics' were thought to be people with no stable identity of their own – like women themselves – empty voids waiting to be filled up with other people's ideas. Eventually, this same philosophy would lead to the birth of the word 'fan' itself, along with notions (that are arguably still with us) about the moral weakness and unseemly or dangerous excesses of the fan.

These ideas came together so powerfully in Byromania because Byromaniacs *were* women and because their enthusiasm was thought to be sexual in nature. Add to this the fact that Byron seemed to be inspiring not only thoughts but action in his admirers, and his fanmail takes a more serious turn. As Byron scholar Ghislaine McDayter explains: 'To flaunt the social order so flagrantly and to express desire so openly might be alarming on an individual basis, but it was profoundly worrying when it was done en masse.'[42]

England believed that its ability to protect its nation from revolution and terror lay in its women, that national security depended upon 'the character and order of British households'.[43] If Byron and his writing could inspire ladies into these shamefully public expressions of lustful enthusiasm, then what type of revolutionary awfulness could, or would, this poet of passion inspire them to next?

LITTLE VOLCANOES

There's a scene in Emily Brontë's *Wuthering Heights* in which Heathcliff, Byron's most famous literary descendent, pours scorn on his young wife Isabella.

Recently married, she has exchanged the 'elegancies and comforts' of her former life with family and friends for the isolated wilderness of her marriage to him. 'She abandoned them under a delusion,' he says, 'picturing in me a hero of romance … I can hardly regard her in the light of a rational creature, so obstinately has she persisted in forming a fabulous notion of my character and acting on the false impressions she cherished.'

For better or worse, Byron, like Heathcliff, *did* capture the female imagination. His fans *did* cherish their romantic notions of him and often *did* obstinately persist in doing so. Fandom is an active process. And as we've seen so far, these imaginings had just as much – if not more – to do with Byron's fans themselves than they did with him. Reading Byron, writing to him and, as time went on, increasingly, writing *about* him became ways for women to explore and express the secret hidden depths, desires and Byronic power in themselves.

The first person to do this was Caroline Lamb. *Glenarvon*, her semi-autobiographical account of their affair, has all the sexy, tortured, bad-but-good melodrama you want, need and expect from a Gothic romance starring Byron as an evil lord who seduces women for sport, is planning a political rebellion and also happens, secretly, to be a vampire. It's a campy, underappreciated Gothic classic. It's also an important exploration of active female desire and of fandom itself. Halfway through the novel, when their relationship ends, Calantha (Lamb's fictional alter ego), who's been seduced by the Byronic Lord Glenarvon, turns the tables. In the second half of the book, she's the one who becomes Byronic to chase him.

Glenarvon may have been the final nail in the coffin of Lamb's reputation, but it was a bestseller. It sold out immediately and went through multiple editions. It also played an important role in cementing Byron's reputation as the dangerously seductive vampire that lived on in the popular imagination. It was reviewed not in the book section but in the gossip columns.

During their relationship, Byron had praised Caroline's passionate imagination: 'Then your heart – my poor Caro,' he wrote to her. 'What a little volcano! That pours lava though your veins & yet I cannot wish it a bit colder.'[44] Volcanoes were Byron's favourite phallic metaphor for creativity: he famously described writing itself as 'the lava of imagination'.[45] But now, as writers like Lamb began to steal his identity – copy his Gothic style to create Byronic Heroes and Heroines of their own – he was beginning to feel ravished and abused by what he perceived to be the vampiric female imagination.

Like many male celebrities who would come after him, Byron believed that his status as a 'popular idol' (fodder for a thousand girlish daydreams) was undermining his ability to be a serious artist. During his early days of fame, in the 'Turkish Tales', he'd given readers what they wanted. But now, as his writing became more experimental, his popularity was beginning to wane. Book sales were down and reviewers who associated him with his earlier Gothic style now accused him of writing 'inauthentic' Byronic works. He blamed women. 'I have been their martyr,' he said. 'My whole life has been sacrificed to them and by them.'[46]

Behind these exasperated diatribes about the insatiable demands of his female readers were anxieties about the 'feminisation' of the literary world. Byron felt threatened by both female readers and the increasing number of female writers like Lamb. If the trashy, low-brow Gothic and romantic tastes of women were setting the agenda for what the market wanted, then what hope was there for true (male) artists like him? His feelings on the subject culminated in his mock epic *Don Juan*. In his re-writing of the story of this infamous womaniser, the gender and power dynamics are reversed. Juan is an innocent man accosted, victimised and seduced by a long line of lusty women intent on ravishing him. The predator had become the prey.

By the time he published *Don Juan*, Byron's fanmail was infrequent. The scandalous revelations of his separation trial had split the public. Many women now sided with Annabella, who they saw as a role model for leaving him. They could no longer justify reading Byron's increasingly blasphemous work. But there was still a hardcore set of fans who (to his surprise) remained devoted to him. 'I have … a love letter from *Pimlico* from a lady whom I never saw in my life – but who hath fallen in love with me for having written *Don Juan*!' he wrote to his sister. 'I suppose she is either mad or naughty.'[47]

Byron had always been both fascinated and mystified by his fanmail. He pretended not to care or notice but apparently returned to the letters frequently, 'with complacency', and boasted to friends about how many there were.[48] I'm pretty sure he missed them when they dried up, and if he wanted to understand them, he got his chance in 1824.

When Isabella Harvey (alias Zorina) first wrote to Lord Byron, she was just as obsessed as any of the women in *Don Juan*. Her first letter contains all the trademark hyperbole and melodrama of a classic Byromaniac:

My Lord –

I tremble in addressing you, yet I cannot remain silent ... I know not how to execute the extraordinary step I am taking. You will scarcely understand because you could never have felt the powerful influence that great minds obtain over weak ones.

But it soon evolves into a touching, strangely self-reflective meditation on her experience of being a Byron fan, in a world in which fandom is so new that there isn't even a word for it yet:

My imagination has perhaps dressed you in attributes that do not exactly belong to you, but such as I can imagine you, you are the bright dream of my existence ... I cannot define my feelings – I have vainly sought to analyse my heart. I know that it is full of you, and surely I need not blush to own it, for I have never seen you; thank heaven then it cannot be love ... To you I am indebted for almost all the happy hours I have spent, my day-dreams have been so full of you – how romantic you would think me, did I tell you of all the projects I have formed of which you were the hero ... I feel awe of you ... Sometimes I fear your anger, at others a strange hope fills my bosom that the devotion of a young heart cannot be unacceptable to you – that you will accept the offering and deign to write to me.

What is both wonderful and fascinating about this letter is the fact that Isabella is fully aware of the role that her own imagination is playing in the enjoyment she gets from Byron. He's a fantasy. And yet she's decided to write and tell him about it. Real-Life Byron and Fantasy Byron are not mutually exclusive in her world.

To her surprise, Bryon did respond to her letter. The two engaged in a back-and-forth correspondence for a few months in 1824 – the final months of his life. Fed up with women who imagined him to be something he wasn't, Byron initially wrote to tell Isabella to go find someone else to fantasise about. She (as you can imagine) was having none of it:

> You tell me I am deluded by my imagination with regard the sentiments I bear you. No matter if it be illusion, how much more delightful it is than reality. I abjure reality forever. You wish for me to find worthier objects on whom to waste my feelings (it would indeed be wasting them), and you say that I am unconscious of their transient duration. Oh no! I am not, and I should little care if their bright reign is *brief* ... But do not bid me turn my thoughts from you, you would be disobeyed, and I would deceive myself with the hope that you would not wish it.[49]

As the correspondence continued, it became clear that Isabella saw Byron less as a dream lover but more as an imaginary friend. A father figure, in fact. While she did flirtatiously send him a portrait of herself – 'a mere coloured sketch of a young lady in a scarlet frock' – she also began addressing him as 'my dear papa'. He (softening in his old age?) addressed her as 'my child'.[50]

Byron was prematurely grey with loosening teeth at this point, living in exile in Genoa and feeling very old for thirty-six. He'd written to his sister the previous year to reminisce about his admirers from earlier, happier, more popular times:

> Do you remember Constantina and Echo ... and all my other inamorate – when I was 'gentle and juvenile – curly and gay' – and was myself in love with a certain silly person. But I am grown

very good now – and think all such things vanities which is very proper at thirty-four.

He arranged to send Isabella a copy of the very best portrait of himself from 1815. I guess there was still a little bit of that vanity left, and I'm sure it was good to imagine himself as the picture in *her* mind. To be the 27-year-old in the portrait again.

Zorina may have been the only person to say it directly, but the desire to enjoy Byron as an object of fantasy and to keep him there, in the blissful world of perpetual longing and imagination, was (to his dismay) common. Fans who met him in real life most often spurned his attempts to seduce them. 'Another wild embrace, and with a desperate effort I tore myself forever from the truly noble Lord Byron,' wrote Eliza, a young poet from London (not sure where she got 'noble' from in this story).[51] Many of his most fervent admirers, including the courtesan Harriette Wilson, asserted that what they wanted from Byron was 'intellectual and spiritual love' or for him to see them as a sister.[52] Obviously, the word sister, in Byron's world, was a bit of a loaded term, but the sentiment was clear. This was about equality of spirit – brain more than body.

Harriette's story is particularly compelling. Given her job as a celebrity sex worker (her clients were a who's who of Regency England – everyone from the Duke of Wellington to the Prince Regent himself), you would have imagined her to be fairly relaxed about the idea of getting intimate with her idol. But it seems that Byron meant more to her than that. Her letters are deeply romantic and flirtatious, but from the very first (a request to meet) she was clear about what she did and didn't want from him: 'If you think it is to make anything like *love* to you', she wrote, 'don't come.'

They never did meet. But in her memoirs, Harriette included

a scene in which they did. In her fantasy (presented as truth), she describes meeting Byron at a masquerade ball. He is 'unmasked' – so beautiful, she says, that she would have been 'afraid to have loved him'.[53] In a candid 'one author to another' type of conversation, they discuss the nature of love, truth and *Glenarvon*. In Harriette's story, Byron is nothing like the vampiric seducer of the popular imagination; he's a philosopher of fame. She used their imagined meeting in her book as evidence that she was an intellectual herself.

Harriette, Caroline and Zorina weren't the only fans to rewrite or borrow Byron for their own purposes. He died in 1824, but as a whole generation of women who had been avid readers of his life and work as girls reached adulthood, the Byronic Hero became a recurring character in the work of female authors. 'Not only did the Romantic movement as a whole unleash the creative energies and larger ambitions of Victorian female novelists', says literary historian Caroline Franklin, 'but the public voice of Byron in particular engaged them in transnational issues of political, racial and sexual freedom.'

In 1827, poet Letitia Landon gazed up at a portrait of her hero. In 'Stanzas Written Beneath the Portrait of Lord Byron Painted by Mr West', he is an object of both love and inspiration. Byron was especially meaningful to Landon because she was marketed as 'The Female Byron'. Her work was often mistaken for his, and she learned a lot about how to manipulate and handle fame from his example. But, as ever with Byron, the 'strange feelings' she describes in this poem are complicated. She feels his presence, she says. But puzzling over his face, searching for those secret hidden truths behind the brushstrokes, she can't work out if his 'magic of mind' is there or really just a portrait-inspired figment of her own imagination.

Dreams of being Byronic or falling in passionate, rebellious love with a Byronic Hero were alluring fantasies. But as writers like Landon, the Brontë sisters and Harriet Beecher Stowe among others began incorporating Byron into their work, the question became: 'What would loving a Byronic Hero, or being a Byronic Heroine, mean for a woman in real life?'

For some, like Stowe, this was about exorcising their own adolescent hero worship. As a girl, she had fantasised about saving Byron's soul. When she was fourteen, she even wrote a play, in verse, called *Cleon*, about him being converted. The Byronic struggle between good and evil was a huge influence on her bestselling anti-slavery classic *Uncle Tom's Cabin*. But after meeting Lady Byron (Annabella, now an old woman) in 1853 and learning the truth about Byron's abusive behaviour during their marriage, Stowe wrote 'The True Story of Lady Byron's Life', an exposé of 'the real Lord Byron' and impassioned defence of Annabella for leaving him.

The article got so much hate mail that it nearly brought down *The Atlantic*. In one of many satirical cartoons, Stowe is depicted as a witch, wielding a quill instead of a wand. There's a snake labelled 'scandal' at her feet. She's conjuring Byron – half man, half devil – from beyond the grave. 'Woman!' he says. 'Why do you call me up before the world in this monstrous and distorted shape?'

The scandal that blew up around the article was just as intense and hysterical as the one that had surrounded Byron during the separation trial itself. 'The True Story of Lady Byron's Life' and Stowe's subsequent book *Lady Byron Vindicated* may have pitted Byron's aristocratic libertinism against the virtuous 'cult of true womanhood', but there was still a little something of him in her determination and commitment to her cause. Like Byron, Stowe 'wrote as a crusader bravely challenging her own society', says

Caroline Franklin. 'She believed that it was her mission to speak for those ... who could not or dared not speak for themselves ... She claimed the right of a woman to speak openly about sexuality in public.'[54] *Lady Byron Vindicated* was an exposé of an abusive marriage but also a feminist treatise on the injustices and inequalities faced by Victorian women as a whole.

One of the most annoyingly attractive things about Byron was his ability to be so many different things at the same time: hero, villain, lover, victim, masculine, feminine, broken, strong. It is both beautiful and fitting that, of all the writers and artists who took inspiration from the many things he was or could be, his truest heir was a woman.

As children, the Brontë sisters were fascinated by Byron's life and works. Sitting around their kitchen table at the parsonage in Haworth, his tales of amoral heroes and intense but destructive, impossible love spoke to their imaginations. Byronic Heroes of their own invention, like the Duke of Zamorna, featured heavily in their juvenilia and fantasy worlds of Angria and Gondal. Their first novels, published under pseudonyms, each in their own way, explored the fantasy and reality of the Byronic Hero. For Anne, like Stowe, this was about rejection. For Charlotte, ambivalence. But in the 'untamed ferocity' of *Wuthering Heights*, Emily Brontë not only channelled that Byronic spirit but added to it. Her story of human nature, family secrets and tragic, all-consuming love has outlived anything Byron ever produced himself.

Wuthering Heights is a woman's answer to Byron's incest tragedy *Manfred*. Heathcliff, like Manfred, is a man haunted to the point of madness by the memory of a lost love and his own inner demons. 'I loved her, and I destroyed her!' says Manfred of his dead sister Astarte. But in *Wuthering Heights* – even in death – Heathcliff's

Cathy will not allow herself to be destroyed. As his true and perfect soulmate, she is just as wild, restless and ungovernable as him. Her final words become a statement of desirous intent: 'They may bury me twelve feet deep, and throw the church down over me, but I won't rest till you are with me.'

Heathcliff is a classic Byronic Hero – strangely alluring in his brooding, forsaken brokenness. But it's Cathy and the other women in the novel who control the narrative. These are female characters who speak their desires and act on them. Cathy, in her wildness, is the epitome of this. But even the innocent, novel-reading Isabella, who pictures Heathcliff as a 'hero of romance', is the one who pursues him. 'I have a right to kiss her, if she chooses,' he says. And towards the end of the book, like Annabella, she chooses to leave him. That was a brave and unconventional thing for a woman to do in 1847.

Halfway through the novel, Cathy tries to put her feelings for Heathcliff into words. The language is pure Byron:

My great miseries in this world have been Heathcliff's miseries, and I watched and felt each from the beginning; my great thought in living is himself. If all else perished, and *he* remained, *I* should still continue to be; and if all else remained and he were annihilated, the universe would turn to a mighty stranger; I should not seem a part of it ... My love for Heathcliff resembles the eternal rocks ... a source of little visible delight but necessary ... I am Heathcliff! He's always, always on my mind: not as a pleasure, any more than I am always a pleasure to myself, but as my own being.

'I am Heathcliff!' would become one of the most iconic and

romantic lines in English literature. Today, it represents an idealised type of romantic love that poets like Byron were, in part, responsible for inventing. But in 1847, when Brontë published her book, the idea that a woman could be just as wild, strong, passionate, tormented and desirous as a man was revolutionary and challenging. 'I am Heathcliff!' was a statement of sameness and equality that defied the oppressive gender divisions and constraints of the early nineteenth century. That vision of sameness had its literary roots in Byron.

Like Heathcliff for Cathy, Byron was an object of both desire and identification for his female fans. A passionate twin spirit as much as a hero of romance. Through him and the universal humanness of his poetry, they found new ways to understand and express their own identities, tell their own stories and harness the power and joy of the 'lava of imagination' for themselves.

The Awakening Conscience, William Holman Hunt (1853)

2

ECSTASY, BERLIN, 1842
IN LOVE WITH A FEELING

But the beginning of things, of a world especially, is necessarily vague,
tangled, chaotic, and exceedingly disturbing. How few of us ever
emerge from such beginning! How many souls perish in its tumult!
The voice of the sea is seductive; never ceasing, whispering, clamoring,
murmuring, inviting the soul to wander for a spell in abysses of
solitude; to lose itself in mazes of inward contemplation. The voice
of the sea speaks to the soul. The touch of the sea is sensuous,
enfolding the body in its soft, close embrace.
– KATE CHOPIN, *THE AWAKENING* (1899)

The King's Theatre was stifling, but as the audience fell silent and turned their eyes to the stage that July evening in 1831, Mary Shelley felt the exquisite crackle of fear run down her spine. It had been thirteen years since she shocked and terrified Europe with her first novel, *Frankenstein*, but her monster had been a projection – a creature summoned from the depths of her nightmares and imagination. Tonight, she was going to meet a real one.

When it was announced that the Italian violinist Niccolò Paganini was coming to London, the whole city had erupted in a flurry of whispers and shivers of the type that hadn't been seen since the peak of Byromania. Paganini was known as 'the devil's violinist', and looking at his portrait (if you were brave enough), you could believe it. Where Byron had been strikingly beautiful, Paganini was wiry and cadaverous. People who'd seen him play said he wielded his violin with a force that transcended human skill, as if he'd made a pact with the devil himself. In fact, those who'd known him back in the old country said he had.

Everyone wanted tickets to the Paganini concert, and he knew it. He'd already made himself obscenely wealthy touring Europe, so his demands for the King's Theatre were unheard of: two-thirds of all ticket sales, with prices so exorbitant that newspapers even began calling for a boycott. The papers raged. The theatre manager squirmed. Paganini didn't care! He knew the chance to see a man who'd sold his soul to the devil was priceless.

When he took to the stage, the whole audience gave a collective gasp. He was even more horrific than they'd imagined – all angles and lines – it was glorious! And then there was the sound: whining and wailing, soaring and plunging, keening and climbing. The bow cracked like a whip. His fingers raced up and down the fingerboard as if he, or it, was possessed. One lady screamed. Others fainted. Countless more clutched at their companions for support. Men stiffened in their seats, trying to resist the pull of this black magic, but what none of them could do was look away.

'Heard Paganini today,' wrote Mary in her diary. 'He is divine – he had the effect of giving me hysterics – yet I could pass my life listening to him – Nothing was ever so sublime.'[1] She would later describe his power as 'enchantment'.[2] Women adored Paganini. He was old, ugly and spellbinding – the type of hot that filled even the most devout women with sinful agitation. It made the idea of soul saving irrelevant. Those skeletal fingers and sunken eye sockets promised something even darker than Byron's poetry: a night with the devil himself. But it was a young man who would become his most devoted admirer.

A year later, as cholera swept through Paris, killing hundreds of people a day, a young pianist sat in the shadows of the Opera House watching Paganini hold his audience in collective ecstasy. Franz Liszt was barely twenty-one, still in search of his artistic identity, but the moment Paganini ripped into those first dizzying arpeggios of his twenty-fourth caprice – a piece so fiendishly complex that other violinists considered it unplayable – he understood. This was power that transcended technical brilliance. It was performance as sorcery. Music as spiritual possession. But what truly mesmerised him wasn't just the demonic virtuosity: it was the way Paganini held the audience in the palm of his hand.

In that moment, Liszt had a vision of his future. He would take this dark art and remake it as something holy. The next morning, hands bleeding from practice, he wrote feverishly about his revelation to a friend: 'What a man, what a violin, what an artist! Heavens! What suffering, what misery, what tortures in those four strings!'[3] If Paganini was the Mephistopheles of music, Liszt would become its missionary. He would channel that same ecstatic power not for self-glorification but for the uplift of the human spirit. *Génie oblige*, he would later declare: genius comes with obligation. The ladies of Europe were about to discover that holiness can be just as seductive as hell.

A STAR IS BORN

People who knew Franz Liszt when he came to Paris in 1823 recall a 'pale and haggard' young man with 'unspeakably attractive features'.[4] He was twelve years old, with big blue eyes, silky fair hair and the ethereal aura of a fairy-tale prince. His piano playing was just as mesmerising: part solace, part storm, pure drama.

'He was able to reproduce all the passions at the keyboard,' said Madame Boissier, whose daughter Valérie would eventually become one of his piano students (and love interests), 'terror, fright, horror, despair, love'.⁵ His first few years in Paris were a whirlwind of salon performances and growing acclaim. When he was thirteen, he premiered his first opera at the Paris Opera House then set off on a European tour where he was compared to a young Mozart.

Society ladies, in particular, were completely taken with him. They would shower him with kisses and burned almonds, offering him sweets with one hand while stroking his hair with the other. But when his father died, suddenly, he was thrown into an existential crisis. He was sixteen by now, but he'd already been playing piano for nearly a decade. He was beginning to feel like 'a performing dog'.⁶

Liszt was one of many boy prodigies who were all the rage in nineteenth-century Europe. Born in 1811 in rural Hungary, he'd been destined for greatness from the moment a comet blazed across the sky on the night of his birth. His whole life so far had unfolded like a storybook, and maybe that was the problem.

When he was eight, his father, a lowly accountant and amateur musician, had recognised his musical talent, sold his gold watch to buy him his first piano and begged local noblemen to fund his musical training. His first piano teacher was both thrilled and horrified by what he saw: 'He was a pale, sickly-looking child who swayed on the piano stool as if drunk ... throwing his fingers arbitrarily all over the keyboard.' But even without any formal training or knowledge of harmony, there was unmistakable genius in his natural instincts – it was as if 'nature herself had formed a pianist'.⁷

Like Elvis a century later, Liszt had an uncanny ability to absorb and transform everything he heard. The Romani music that drift-ed through his cottage window at night became an obsession that fused with his classical training to create a sound that was haunt-ingly original. Years later, he recalled one particular Romani violin-ist who 'used to play for hours on end … his musical cascades fell in rainbow profusion, or glided along in a soft murmur'. This experi-ence, he wrote, 'must have distilled into my soul the essence of some generous and exhilarating wine' like 'one of those mysterious elixirs concocted in the secret laboratories of alchemists'.[8]

By his late teens, all that early promise had blossomed into un-deniable pedigree. Trained by Antonio Salieri – the music director of the Austrian imperial court (most famously misremembered by history as the mortal enemy of Mozart) – and reportedly blessed by a kiss on the forehead from an ageing Beethoven himself, Liszt had already dazzled audiences from Vienna to London. But Paris was the capital of the musical world. This was the place to be for virtuoso pianists looking to prove themselves.

The old aristocracy and their uptight conservative tastes were fading. In the wake of the French Revolution and Napoleonic Wars, they were being replaced by a new breed of cultural power player with money to burn and reputations to build: industrialists, bankers and entrepreneurs. Once upon a time, classical music had been an exclu-sive luxury for kings, queens and aristocrats. Now, it was a spectacle for the rising middle class. They loved seeing and being seen at lavish soirées, throwing their money about at the opera and holding court at concert halls. And it was virtuoso concerts they loved most. These were self-made musicians who, like them, had made their names (and their money) through raw talent, ambition and hard work. Every ri-diculously flashy arpeggio and excessive, dramatic flourish felt like a champagne toast to their shared ascendance.

As the virtuosos flourished, the whole city became a commercial entertainment machine. 'Concert-goers watched with relish as one pianist attempted to outplay another – gladiators of the keyboard locked in combat, fighting it out in the open arena of the concert hall,' says biographer Alan Walker. These 'steel-fingered, chromium-plated virtuosos' filled their calendars with challenges and piano duels, while the venues themselves were locked in rivalries of their own.[9] Even the piano makers Erard and Pleyel joined in, racing to showcase their latest models – and to sign up virtuosos to endorse them. Every piano was bigger and better, and every show was wilder and grander – a spectacle of music, marketing and flash.

Liszt could have dominated this new musical battleground in an instant, but instead, he vanished. While his rivals battled for fame in Paris's concert halls, he set off for the continent. For the next few years, he would busy himself having passionate affairs with countesses (often simultaneously), reading philosophy (moody and German) and wandering around Europe being tortured (his hero, and spirit animal, was Byron). He lived exactly as a Romantic should – wallowing in love, literature and spiritual truth – a long way from the commercial spectacle of the stage. He got so good at the whole mysterious-absent-genius thing that one newspaper actually declared him dead.

But during these years of wandering, Liszt was processing what he'd learned from his heroes. From Byron, he absorbed the power of being the perfectly tormented outsider. From Paganini, the sorcery of showmanship. And from Beethoven, he learned how music could be both intimate and infinite. When he finally returned to the concert stage in 1838 and '39 for a series of performances in Paris, Hans Christian Andersen was there to witness the result:

'An electric shock passed through the salon,' he wrote. The whole audience was transfixed by Liszt's magnetic aura, but it was the women who truly fell under his spell. 'Most of the ladies rose' when he walked in, Andersen said. 'It was as if a ray of sunshine passed over every face, as if all eyes received a dear, beloved friend.'[10]

As he sat down at his piano, Liszt looked sick, in that gorgeously melancholic my-piano-is-my-only-salvation Romantic genius kind of way. He shook his mane of hair, stretched his arms, clicked his knuckles and then placed his fingers on the keys and waited... and waited... and waited... Only then, finally, did he begin.

The moment his fingers pressed down on the keys, Schubert's 'Erlkönig' burst to life. On paper this was a dramatic story anyway – a father pursued by a demon-king galloping through a storm-lashed forest, cradling his dying child in his arms. But as Liszt's fingers raced across the keys, he summoned real hoofbeats, real wind-howls, real terror. It was as if he had opened up a secret door into a world where music and the physical world became one. All the mysteries of the universe were momentarily visible – or you could feel them at least.

Liszt's body shook. His hair flew all over the place. The piano convulsed. In the audience, women and men seemed to be shaking too – some cried out, others had tears in their eyes. 'He was a demon nailed fast to the instrument whence the tones streamed forth,' wrote Andersen.

They came from his blood, from his thoughts ... But as he played, the demon vanished. I saw that pale face assume a nobler and brighter expression: the divine soul shone from his eyes, from every feature; he became as beauteous as only spirit and enthusiasm can make their worshippers.

When he finished, you got the feeling that you'd just been ravished. From the wreckage, flowers began to shower the stage. 'Beautiful young girls, and old ladies who had once been young and beautiful, cast each her bouquet. He had cast a thousand bouquets of tones into their hearts and heads.'[11]

This was the beginning of a period Liszt scholars call his 'years of transcendental execution', but Keith Richards would probably have called it the greatest rock tour of all time: eight years of piano smashing and existential rapture, baby. Finally ready to conquer the world (but only on his own terms), Liszt spent 2,000 francs on a carriage and hired a man called Gaetano Belloni as his personal secretary (or the world's first ever tour manager) and barnstormed Europe.

During this period, Liszt would play over 1,000 shows, single-handedly invent the solo music recital and turn the piano sideways. Before him, pianists had always played with their backs to the audience, but Liszt wanted everyone to see his hands. And his face. 'He gives his proud head a toss,' wrote American pianist Amy Fay,

> throws an electric look out of his eagle eye, and seats himself with
> an air as much as to say, 'Now I am going to do just what I please
> with you'... You feel at once that he is a great genius, and that you
> are nothing but his puppet, and somehow you take a base delight
> in the humiliation![12]

'He must be heard', wrote fellow composer Robert Schumann, 'and also seen – for if Liszt played behind the scenes, a great deal of the poetry of his playing would be lost.'[13] Everywhere he went, he was met with huge crowds desperate to see, hear and ideally to meet with him. 'There have been nothing but dinners and suppers, music and champagne, counts and beautiful women,' wrote Schumann's pianist fiancée, Clara Wieck: 'He has turned all our lives upside down. We are all wildly in love with him, and yesterday he again played like a god at his concert.'[14] Rumours of ladies' overwhelming enthusiasm for Liszt soon took on a life of their own. They were reported to be throwing themselves at his feet and wearing his portrait in lockets. Crowds of them would descend upon his hotels in the hope of catching his eye (some even dressed as men to get past security).

If the rumours were true, this was the biggest mass outpouring of female fan love since Byron, but female music fans had already been avid swooners over musicians, in general, for some time. In fact, their devotion was becoming a secret barometer for musical greatness. The cult of Paganini had a 'flying squadron of infatuated women' who followed him wherever he went.[15] Beethoven's admirers had knitted him stockings and baked him puddings that he 'devoured with huge gusto'.[16] Many opera singers even had fan clubs.

Back in the eighteenth century, Italian castrati singers like Farinelli and Marchesi had sent women wild with love in opera houses up and down Europe. Fan club members wore ribbons with the initials of their favourites around their waists. In Vienna, they even wore medallions of Marchesi's face, sometimes five at a time ('one for each arm, one on the neck and two for the buckles of their shoes').[17] In London, writer Fanny Burney recalled a male acquaintance's outrage about the effect the castrati had on women: '"Why now, there was one of these fellows at Bath last season," he said, "I vow I longed to cane him every day! All the *fair females* sighing for him! Enough to make a man sick!"'[18]

The castrati were men who had been castrated before puberty to preserve their ethereally high voices, and they inspired almost religious devotion. Ladies collected wax dolls of their favourites and noblewomen battled it out to take them as lovers. They were the ultimate fantasy: passionate, cultured and 100 per cent risk-free (no pregnancy = no scandal). Farinelli, the greatest of them all, caused such a sensation when he came to England that women's cries of 'One God! One Farinelli!' were denounced as blasphemy, but cheers of 'Long live the knife!' followed him wherever he went.

'Farinelli employs everybody's thoughts & time & our Ladys are stark mad in ye country to hear from him,' wrote a Norfolk man in a letter to his sister.[19] But this madness was nothing compared to the 'veritable insanity' that would become Lisztomania.[20] 'Women always seem intoxicated when Liszt plays,' wrote writer and occasional music critic Heinrich Heine, who captured the visceral, sexually charged atmosphere of a Liszt concert in his novel *Florentine Nights*: 'Pallid faces in the hall, heaving bosoms, panting breaths during the pauses and at last tumultuous applause.'[21] At the end of concerts, ladies would flock around him and 'assail him with questions', many of them inappropriate and shockingly personal (someone once asked him the age of his celebrity friend George Sand and to describe her appearance – can you believe it!?).[22]

Reports of increasingly unbridled displays of female enthusiasm reached their peak when he arrived in Berlin at the beginning of 1842. The most famous caricature of this visit shows Liszt at his piano, waving grandly at his crowd of mainly women as they applaud in ecstasy and gaze at him through binoculars. Flowers and kisses rain down. Some are so excited they've jumped up out of their seats.

The few men who are there look confused and overwhelmed: they're catching swooning women as they collapse. Others battle to hold their most hysterical companions back. Just one man is interested. Very interested, actually. He's peering intently through binoculars with a laurel wreath tucked into his hat – I guess he's hoping to meet and honour his hero after the show. But something about his posture, or maybe his intensity, gives the impression that his foppish devotion is being lumped into the same deviant bucket as the ladies. At the centre of it all, a woman, pressed right up to the very front of the stage, holds her wine cup high as if she's trying to drink in the music straight from the piano. Her face is a wild, dishevelled mix of drunken joy and erotic delirium.

'It is true that Berlin did go mad,' wrote German physician Adalbert Cohnfeld. 'Liszt was feted, serenades were performed in his honour, a woman knelt before him and begged to kiss his fingertips, while another embraced him in public at one of his recitals ... Many were robbed of their senses by him.'[23]

A few centuries later, Liszt's most well-respected modern biographer Alan Walker was equally repulsed. 'It was at Berlin that "Lisztomania" swept in,' he wrote.

> The symptoms, which are odious to the modern reader, bear every resemblance to an infectious disease, and merely to call them mass hysteria hardly does justice to what actually took place ... Swooning lady admirers attempted to take cuttings of his hair, and they surged forward whenever he broke a piano string in order to make it into a bracelet. Some of these insane female 'fans' even carried glass phials about their persons into which they poured his coffee dregs. Others collected his cigar butts, which they hid in their cleavages.[24]

Liszt was apparently disturbed – so disturbed he decided to extend his stay in Berlin by several weeks. During those ten weeks, he played twenty-one concerts and performed eighty works. The Prussian royal family attended nearly all of his performances. King Wilhelm IV awarded him the *Ordre Pour le Mérite* in recognition of his extraordinary achievements. He was elected to the Prussian Academy of Fine Arts, serenaded by huge crowds of all-male university students and even larger crowds lined up to see him wherever he went.

On the day he left the city, an eyewitness described how

> a carriage drawn by six white horses pulled up outside his hotel, and to the cheering of the crowd Liszt was almost carried down the steps and lifted into the carriage … Thirty smaller carriages, each of them drawn by four horses and filled with students, accompanied him, as did a number of individual riders dressed in academic regalia. Countless other carriages followed, and a crowd of several thousand seethed all around the departing travellers.[25]

The carnival followed him all the way to the Brandenburg Gate, where they were finally forced to say goodbye. 'It was as if a reigning monarch were taking leave of his people,' says Walker. He was leaving 'not like a king, but as a king'.[26] Collecting cigar butts might have been odious, but I guess turning a pianist into a king was just Berlin being Berlin.

MAD ABOUT THE BOY

A few days after Liszt left Berlin, the city that had thrown him a thirty-carriage parade suddenly developed a collective case of 'I wouldn't be caught dead at his concerts'. In the cold light of day, it was mortified it had so shamelessly thrown itself at a pianist under the influence of a bit of piano smashing and a few well-timed hair tosses. What a relief to remember it was only the women who had gotten silly and embarrassed themselves.

'Praise God! Mr Liszt has left,' exclaimed a music magazine.

The paroxysms of his adorers has reached the limit of madness. At the moment it is raining caricatures to mock the fanaticism of some sectors. A lady was recently arrested in the street, calling Mr Liszt by the most intimate names at the top of her voice. She was visited by doctors and led like a madwoman to the Charité hospital to be treated there.[27]

This story, like many of the more hyperbolic accounts of female fan hysteria circulating, was obviously a fabrication. In this case, it was most likely inspired by a cartoon of a woman being carted off to the madhouse published shortly after Liszt's visit. As the historian and musicologist James Deaville has pointed out: many of the most famous tales of Lisztomania that were blithely repeated as fact were (and still are) inspired by second- or even third-hand accounts. Lazy journalism is one thing, but lazy scholarship hints at the idea that there are some 'facts' so entrenched in cultural bias that even respected historians don't see the need to investigate or question them.

The story of Lisztomania is just as much the story of how and why rumours and satirical cartoons become facts as it is about the early history of female fandom. And yet Lisztomania would be seared in the popular imagination as the first true case of female fan hysteria – one continually dusted off and rolled out every time a new moral panic over female fans and male stars came along. This tells us something about how history has chosen to tell (and gender) the story of the birth of pop culture. If we want to understand how and why this happened, we need to take a look at what was really happening in those hot, sweaty, candlelit concert halls.

At first, critics had described Liszt's power over audiences as 'bad enthusiasm' and it applied to everyone.[28] They were shocked to see people of every social class falling over themselves to bend the knee to a pianist. Not many years earlier, musicians like Liszt had been little more than servants, paid to entertain royalty and aristocrats on demand. Now, here was Mr Nobody From Nowhere strutting about in honours and medals from every king and queen in Europe. The aristocracy seemed to have accepted him as one of their own. This was a sign of a changing social order – one where talent, charisma and popularity were beginning to challenge noble birth and military might as foundations of power.

'These Parisians who have seen Napoleon,' wrote Heine, 'the great Napoleon, who had to engage in battle after battle to keep them focused on him and to get their approval, these same Parisians shower our Franz Liszt with acclamations!'[29] Both Liszt and Napoleon were charismatic, self-made men who had conquered Europe, but while Napoleon did it with cannons and cavalry, Liszt did it by turning the humble piano into a weapon of mass seduction. By the time he arrived in Berlin, Clara Wieck's assertion that he was the great 'smasher of pianos' was right: he'd categorically perfected the art of musical performance as full-body assault.[30]

How could a lady (or gentleman or entire city for that matter) not find herself completely undone as she watched this beautiful man stride up to the piano, tear off his gloves and fling them to the floor before running his fingers through his tumbling mane of dark hair and then unleashing himself all over the instrument? He would attack the keys with such force that strings would snap as the piano shook violently beneath him. When technicians rushed in to try to replace them, he'd push them away. Once, he got so into it, he actually fainted at the keyboard.

Critics may have described him as 'the Napoleon of the Piano', 'the greatest key-chopper, the most enraged piano-shatterer and string-breaker of our century', but they also seemed to get awfully carried away describing how this 'kindly monster' treated 'his beloved, the piano, now sweetly, now tyrannically, decorates her with kisses, tears her to pieces with sensual bites, embraces her, plays with her, pouts, scolds her, strikes, grabs her by the hair, then hugs her all the more sweetly, more intimately'.[31] No one – not even the most hardened of male music critics – was immune to his charms.

When Heinrich Heine coined the term Lisztomania in 1844, it was this ability to conquer anyone and everyone that he was trying to make sense of. 'He is here,' he wrote, 'the bad, beautiful, ugly, mysterious, fateful, and sometimes very childish child of our times … Franz Liszt, whose magic power compels us … But what is the reason?'[32] He admitted that, in a music world where there always seemed to be some star of the moment or other, he hadn't paid much attention when people began raving about Liszt. He'd been waiting for his star to pass. But it hadn't. In fact, he'd just become more and more godlike as time went on.

After attending a concert in Paris, Heine said he'd been shocked to see sophisticated Parisians – 'busy and blase people' – shower Liszt with such riotous applause that it felt like it lasted for days. This, he believed, had more to do with illness than art. These people were suffering from 'the spiritualistic sickness' of their age: 'the electric effect of a demonic nature on a crowd that is all pressed together, the infectious power of ecstasy, and perhaps the magnetism of music itself'.[33]

If Heine's words sound a bit fantastical, it's because the ones he needed didn't exist yet. Liszt was a megastar. He was smashing out hit after hit. And he had gone viral. In a Europe still haunted by waves of cholera and tuberculosis, the idea of Lisztomania as a disease was particularly resonant. Like a pathogen, Liszt's influence infected indiscriminately across class, gender and place. His carriage meant he could travel more widely than any train-bound virtuoso before him and he was so famous he didn't even need papers to cross borders.

By the time he rolled into a new city, the press (his carrier) had always whipped it into a frenzy of anticipation. And like the true disease it was, the effect was physical. It brought to mind the infamous Methodist preachers of eighteenth-century England like George Whitefield, who would weep, shout and gesture dramatically from his pulpit as his body became a vessel of divine passion, whipping his congregations into religious frenzy – hardly what you'd expect to see in a concert hall. And just like in those Methodist services, the more Liszt thrashed about at the keyboard, the more excited the audience seemed to get. It was as if his passion itself was contagious.

While both men and women were prone to a little excitement now and then (especially in the Romantic era), this type of physical loss of control in the face of art, music and literature was seen as inherently female. For centuries, doctors had theorised that women, with their 'delicate constitutions' and supposed tendency toward sympathy, were more vulnerable to the physical power of art – it's part of what had made reading Byron so dangerous. As historian and musicologist Dana Gooley explains: women's 'fine, sensitive nerves were thought to make them highly excitable'.[34] Their responses to music and poetry were thought to come directly through the body, without the intellectual or aesthetic understanding expected of men.

These ideas were so deeply tied to the female body that when Heine set out to make sense of Liszt's spellbinding effect on his audience, he turned – whether mockingly or earnestly – to a specialist in 'women's ailments'. The doctor's response, complete with a knowing smile and rambling discourse on 'magnetism, galvanism, electricity, contagion … hysterical epilepsy, and the phenomenon of titillation', was more sexual innuendo than medical diagnosis.[35] With references to aphrodisiacs and ancient women's fertility rites, the doctor was basically saying what everyone already knew but couldn't quite say out loud: Liszt was sexy as hell, and everyone was feeling it.

The mid-nineteenth century was the golden age of pseudoscience, when theories about everything from phrenology to mesmerism promised to unlock the mysteries of human behaviour. Celebrity was still so new that people were scrambling to explain it – desperate to break it down in ways they could analyse, categorise and explain. In 1838, a German reviewer had described Liszt as 'a physiological-psychological-artistic triad'.[36] Others thought his power came from 'animal magnetism' – the fact that 'communication was in fact a kind of transfer of vital fluids between bodies and that people's minds touched each other in mysterious ways'.[37] They couldn't quite put their finger on what it was that Liszt was radiating, but whatever it was, it was electric.

By consulting a women's doctor about why everyone was acting 'hysterical', Heine was playing into – and subtly mocking – the fact that it was the whole of Europe that was fangirling, as they say. But the joke backfired. The press latched onto the idea of Lisztomania as a female malady. It was a useful distraction from the truth, and it made sense. Only women could fall in love with a pianist and get carried away by their emotions, no? Even Berlin went back and embellished the story of what had happened. Many of the reports and caricatures of the Berlin incident were actually created years after the fact. The irony was that in the very same article where he'd consulted his 'women's doctor', Heine admitted that there might be a much simpler explanation: 'Sometimes it seems to me that this whole ensorcellment can be explained by the fact that no one in the entire world knows better than our Franz Liszt how to organise his successes, or rather, their *mise en scène*.'[38]

Like his hero Byron before him, Franz Liszt was an extremely handsome and talented man who understood the power of theatre. From his earliest days as a child prodigy, he'd been honing the art of both performance and publicity. Women had been some of his most enthusiastic supporters in his youth, and he would never forget it. As his celebrity grew, he made sure they were both physically and symbolically centre stage.

People attending a Liszt concert for the first time were startled to find themselves at something that felt more like an intimate soirée than a formal concert. Liszt would arrive early so he could work the room like a perfect host, greeting guests, making introductions and squeezing through the crowd to walk ladies to their seats. He even installed a 'circle of ladies' – carefully selected aristocratic VIPs – on stage with him during performances. He would chat with them between pieces, delighting them with what the Leipzig press described as 'a mix of innocence and ingratiating charm learned in the Parisian salons'.[39]

The women on stage were the perfect symbols of his meteoric rise, as well as a model of the right way to receive his genius. Here was a man who had risen from nowhere to the very top, now laughing and flirting with the aristocracy's richest and most beautiful tastemakers. In the concert hall, he would drink black coffee and behave as if he were at home. His casualness thrilled his fans and enraged his critics. Everything about him, from his notoriously long and unruly hair (actually quite neat in real life, apparently) to the gossip about his unconventional personal life (he was living in sin, and had three children, with a married countess who wrote novels), was a study in the allure of contradictions: scandalous and revered, showman and artist, earthly and otherworldly. By the time he ignored the steps and jumped up onto the stage for the show to begin, the whole audience had been reduced to a quivering mass of love and anticipation.

Curiously, however, music critics in many cities were disappointed to find that the scenes of mass hysteria they'd heard so much about failed to manifest in the performances they attended. 'All the strange events and historic world phenomena that Liszt's playing provoked in other places were absent!' wrote a reviewer in Mainz.

There were no fainting individuals being carried out of the hall; rather, it would have been more likely to carry listeners into it. The women indeed stretched their dove-like necks to absorb something of Liszt's playing, but they did not contort themselves as in other German cities, where they would twist their heads all the way around as he threw his long locks from one side to the other in jubilation-induced delirium.[40]

The reality was that women were enjoying themselves *a lot*, but they weren't throwing themselves at the stage – well, only sometimes, briefly (when there was a broken string going). Mostly, they were watching, listening and losing themselves in the music, just like everyone else. The true ravishment was of the soul. Subtle physical reactions that might seem tame to us now – swooning, trembling, sighing, even crying – were powerful displays of feeling in those days. So was the riotous applause that was one of the most defining features of Lisztomania.

Centuries later, writer Sheila Rowbotham would describe rock 'n' roll as music that 'went straight to your cunt and hit the bottom of your spine'.[41] Well, this is where it started. But if rock 'n' roll was hot, dirty, visceral abandon, this was true, deep, soul-to-soul transcendence – the type of music where you see God.

Liszt believed that music and spirituality were deeply connected. As a young man, he'd nearly joined the priesthood but eventually decided the piano could be an even more powerful pulpit. Music, he believed, could 'lead the crowd' and 'fill them with adoration and divine love' more directly than any sermon.[42] In his essay 'On the Situation of Artists and Their Condition in Society', he described his dream of creating a music through which 'all classes of people [would] be joined together in a common, religious, grand, and sublime feeling'. He imagined this ecstatic music of togetherness and revelation 'bursting from the fields, the hamlets, the villages, the workshops and the cities'.[43] Lofty? Absolutely. Our boy was ambitious. And talented. But you know what? This is exactly what people saw and heard when they came to see him.

After returning home from a concert in Paris, 26-year-old Malwida von Meysenbug described the 'river of enchantment' that flooded her soul: 'I could have wept from the happiness of knowing that man can conquer matter in this way,' she wrote, 'that terrestrial forces submit to him, enabling him to fill life with a foretaste of perfect beauty … The harmonies of this evening are still resounding within me like a persistent echo, and the happiness with which they have filled my soul will not quickly fade.'[44]

Spectators and journalists alike, struggling to articulate the intensity of what they were seeing and feeling, went to metaphors of the body to try to explain it. 'Liszt appeared to us like a tragic God. Through his harmonies, [he] made the finest nerves of the breast tremble,' wrote one admirer. 'He seemed like the highly charged conductor of an electric machine. When he is moved, electrical waves radiate outward. We feel electrified along with him.'[45]

For Liszt, connecting with the crowd in this way was part of his mission. Like a steampunk televangelist, he was the first performer to truly engage in the social and emotional back-and-forth with his audiences in a way that we take for granted in live performances today. He would read the room, gauge the energy and adjust his programme mid-concert based on the audience's reactions. Sometimes he would even take requests from the crowd. As one admirer put it: 'No artist in the world understands better than Liszt how to survey at a glance the character and the most hidden recesses in the hearts of his audience.'[46] And despite the media's obsession with madwomen, it wasn't just women's hearts he was reading.

Through his European tours, Liszt had men as well as women of all ages and demographics – from princes to peasants – swept into states of ecstatic delirium. 'We had never in our lives heard anything like this,' wrote music critic Vladimir Stasov, who saw him in St Petersburg. 'We had never been in the presence of such a brilliant, passionate, demonic temperament ... Liszt's playing was absolutely overwhelming.'[47]

After the concert, Stasov described how he and his friend 'were like madmen', rushing home to immortalise their feelings in writing. 'Then and there, we took a vow that thenceforth and forever, that day, 8 April 1842, would be sacred to us, and we would never forget a single second of it till our dying day.' Critic and composer Yuri Arnold, similarly, found himself devastated after seeing Liszt for the first time. He described being 'completely undone by the sense of the supernatural, the mysterious, the incredible'. Like Stasov, he hurried home to process what he'd seen. 'As soon as I reached home,' he wrote, 'I pulled off my coat, flung myself on the sofa, and wept the bitterest, sweetest tears.'[48]

AND I AM A MATERIAL GIRL

Seeing Franz Liszt work his magic on the keyboard was clearly a physical and emotional experience for nearly everyone who saw him, but the press continued to paint two very different pictures of how audiences were receiving him. When women swooned, it was a physical response to his sexual magnetism. When men did the same thing, it was a testament to his virtuosic genius. As we've seen, this gendering of audience response was coloured by assumptions about how men and women experienced the arts differently. It also served to reinforce Liszt's carefully cultivated image as the ultimate Romantic genius.

During the Romantic era, when the concept of genius as we know it today – that it is something we are born with, not something that can be learned or acquired – was gaining popularity, it became inextricably linked to the idea of male sexual potency. The ideal Romantic genius was supposed to embody a fusion of masculine power and feminine sensitivity (he was a studly alpha male who brooded, suffered and then gave birth to art). Women gave birth to babies, so they couldn't be geniuses.

With his long flowing hair, violent piano attacks and magical ability to open up an ecstatic window into the transcendental beyond, Liszt was the perfect androgynous genius – nearly too perfect. By placing his very pretty body so visibly centre stage, he was beginning to push the rules of the feminine man a bit too far. Like Elvis in the '50s, his critics saw him as a 'circus freak' who was feminising himself by putting his body on display for audience pleasure and, more embarrassingly, for money. Even in the face of spiralling debts, Byron, the prototypical Romantic genius, would never have accepted payment for his work.

In the context of this precarious feminised state of being, tales of the hysterical swooning ladies of Lisztomania and even Liszt's off-stage image as a 'ladies' man' were a useful way to restore the proper order of his genius. It's a myth that's persisted with such force that these days people are more likely to know Liszt through Ken Russell's insane 1975 rock opera *Lisztomania* than anything that actually happened in real life. Russell's Liszt is played by Roger Daltrey of the Who in a film that features a giant piano penis that transforms into a spaceship, hundreds of naked groupies with perms and Ringo Starr as the Pope. By the end of the film, he becomes a messianic rock hero battling vampire-Nazi Richard Wagner in space with a laser-shooting piano.

For Ken Russell, Liszt's piano may have been a penis, but in the nineteenth century, this was an instrument that was leading a fascinating, and secretly subversive, double life – one that connected Liszt and his female fans in much more interesting and meaningful ways. In public, it was a swaggering symbol of male virtuosic genius, but in the private world of thousands of middle-class homes, the piano belonged to women. As the nineteenth century progressed, just as the cult of the virtuoso was coming into its own, the piano had become a domestic status symbol. Families bought pianos to announce their social aspirations and cement their place in society: young ladies were taught to play as a sign of attractiveness and refinement. As Maria Edgeworth reminded readers of *Practical*

Education in 1798: musical skill improved 'a young lady's chance of a prize in the matrimonial lottery'.[49]

Anyone who's ever seen a nineteenth-century costume drama knows the scene: young woman sits at the piano pretending she doesn't know or care how intently her favourite suitor is watching her. Even if her skills aren't great, like Jane Austen's Emma, who plays only 'tolerably well', she understands what this performance means. Look how quickly her mind jumps to scandal when her rival Jane Fairfax receives a mysterious pianoforte as a gift from an anonymous admirer. A piano, in the nineteenth century, is never just a piano.

Anthony Burgess once described the 'aura of gamy eroticism' that surrounded virtuoso pianists like Liszt and Chopin who used the piano as 'a monstrous aphrodisiac'.[50] Men with musical instruments are undeniably irresistible (a recent study found that women were more likely to give their phone number to a man in the street if he was carrying a guitar), and Liszt had countless love affairs, but was his brand of sexy really just about seduction? Or was watching this beautiful long-haired, fine-featured fairy-tale prince of a man pour his soul out through the keys just as much about recognition?

Lifelong Liszt fan George Eliot (who got to meet him once) gave us a much richer look at what watching a man play piano might have meant to women in the nineteenth century in her novel *Daniel Deronda*. Herr Klesmer is a talented young pianist whose magical fingers have the power to send storms through the piano. Klesmer is in love with his music student Catherine, but his humble social position means he can't tell her. Playing the piano becomes a way for him to express all the things he cannot say with words, and in one particularly romantic scene, it becomes a prelude to their actual love confession. It isn't so much that the piano is an object of seduction; it's more that it makes visible feelings and emotions that are already there. For women, as for Klesmer, music was often a way to express things that they would not have been allowed to say out loud.

Women who saw Liszt play often wrote, in letters and diaries, about his aesthetic perfection, but most often they focused in on the emotionality of his performances.[51] 'In Liszt I can at last say that my ideal in something has been realized,' wrote Amy Fay. 'His personal magnetism is immense, and I can scarcely bear it when he plays. He can make me cry all he chooses.'[52] His 'feminine' side made him both otherworldly and relatable. Even frenemy pianist Clara Wieck couldn't help noting, in her diary, that he was 'a very attractive person' while watching him throw himself into musical abandon with a mixture of wonder and critique. 'His passion knows no bounds, not infrequently he jars on one's sense of beauty by tearing melodies to pieces.'[53]

For Clara, like all female pianists be they amateur or professional, this kind of unrestrained piano smashing was off limits. She'd been drilled by her father, since childhood, to play with ladylike grace, propriety and restraint. This made Liszt's aggressive style and dramatic gestures both mesmerising and transgressive. The wonder, for women, of watching him lose himself in the music was, in part, the illicit thrill of watching a transcendentally androgynous man who spoke the same language of musical passion as them. Here, in the flickering, candlelit glow of the concert hall, was a brief, liberatory moment where they could imagine, and vicariously experience, being just as wild, expressive and unrestrained themselves.

In the spring of 1844, 21-year-old Marie Duplessis, one of the most famous courtesans of her day (later immortalised by her lover Alexandre Dumas Jr as *The Lady of the Camellias*), attended a Liszt concert in Paris. She was so moved by his performance that she rented a piano and began teaching herself to play. Marie didn't need piano skills to attract men, and she was certainly never going to become a professional, but she threw herself into practising increasingly difficult pieces. Sometimes she would even stay up all night struggling to get the most difficult passages right. When she finally met Liszt, a few years later at the opera, she told him his playing had 'set her dreaming'.[54]

Marie and Liszt were two of the most beautiful and fabulous people in nineteenth-century Europe, so of course they embarked on a brief yet passionate affair. He would later describe her as 'so graceful, high-spirited, and full of a childlike abandon ... undoubtedly the most perfect incarnation ever of womanhood'.[55] And yet there was no way he would ever have made it official. He'd just been offered a position as the court music director in Weimar. For all the married countesses he romanced and even lived with, rocking up with a former courtesan would have ruined his carefully constructed image.

In many ways, their story is the perfect allegory for Liszt's relationship with his female fans. These are women who were always present in his story in the abstract but have rarely been considered as people in their own right beyond being either symbols of his genius or pawns in the debate over who he did or didn't sleep with. For most of the female audience members who found momentary liberation in his music, the reality of that freedom most often remained out of reach. That's not to say that the impact was not profound. Even as she lay dying of tuberculosis in 1847, Marie's thoughts returned to him. 'Take me, take me anywhere you like,' she wrote to him. 'I shan't bother you. I sleep all day. In the evening you can let me go to the theatre, and at night you can do with me what you will.'[56]

This final plea is a reminder of how deeply women of the nineteenth century were constrained. Even Marie, a woman who had made her own money and was living a uniquely independent and unconventional life, found herself bound to the idea of her body as currency when it came to imagining what true freedom might look and feel like. For most women, even liberation itself had to be accessed – or even imagined – through a man. This tension was made visible by William Holman Hunt in one of the most famous piano paintings of the Victorian era. In *The Awakening Conscience*, a kept woman like Marie sits on her lover's lap in a room filled with gaudy new furniture that advertises her status as a purchased luxury. In an inadvertent yet perfect Liszt reference, the man has flung his gloves to the floor and is playing her instrument. Here is the nineteenth-century piano in all its contradictions: at once a symbol of proper domesticity and unspeakably sensual and bodily pleasure, of upward mobility and subjugation, of possibility and constraint.

At first glance, this is a classic 'fallen woman' painting. The gloves on the floor seem to predict our heroine's fate: that her upper-class lover will discard her once he's done with her. But as he plays, the music seems to have sparked an epiphany. She's rising from his lap, gazing out the window, glimpsing all kinds of possibilities in the world outside her gilded cage.

Art historians tell us the sheet music on the piano is a country tune that reminds her of her childhood – of her pre-fallen innocence – a sign that maybe, through God, she will find redemption. Really, what he's playing doesn't matter as much as what she's thinking and feeling. In this moment, music has conjured a vision of freedom and possibility beyond prescribed and predestined roles and fates. In the expansiveness and wonder in this woman's eyes, we see the same music-induced rapture described by Liszt's female fans. 'A new world opened for me,' wrote Malwida von Meysenbug after seeing him in 1843. 'What is, in comparison, the brief imperfection of our existence, when we can participate in a world of the spirit in which development is limitless?'[57]

The idea that women might be experiencing moments of true imaginative freedom at Liszt's concerts was not something most critics and later even historians were interested in thinking about, let alone spending time attempting to understand. What they saw was unusually high numbers of women (still vastly outnumbered by men) attending his shows and welcome receptions and the fact that these women seemed excited. Given the deep-rooted belief that female enthusiasm was inherently bodily and irrational, critics interpreted this excitement as nothing but sexual excess. Women were abandoning all self-restraint for a false idol, they said. And Liszt – far from elevating them – seemed to be colluding in it: turning himself into an object of spectacle and desire.

It's not that sex wasn't part of it – Liszt was so sexy that even male music critics were writing piano erotica for men by men in their reviews. But in caricature after caricature, we see him depicted as a carnal deity surrounded by ecstatic, swooning female fans. It seems that, when it comes to Lisztomania, the line between sexual and religious ecstasy was very fine. The 'bad enthusiasm' of audiences that could potentially have made him dangerous now just made him ridiculous. It was easier that way. And so the image of the delusional, love-crazed female Lisztomaniac continued to be mythologised into 'fact'.

In 1842, the satirical journal *Berlin as It Is and as It Drinks* dedicated an entire issue to Lisztomania jokes. Meet Baroness von Sinnen – the woman so consumed by her adoration for Liszt that her name literally means 'out of her mind'. Reclining on a divan embroidered with his face, gazing at his portrait, she calls for her servant. 'Bring my special crystal glass,' she cries, 'the one with his portrait engraved on it. While you're at the sideboard, pour some eau de Liszt on my handkerchief.'[58]

This scene contains every Lisztomania cliché in the book: an aristocratic woman abandoning her dignity, her living room transformed into a temple, her devotion expressed through consumption. Even her words of adoration are vacuous: 'O most refined blossom of soulful, divinely wild Romanticism, how I worship you!' she gushes. 'How manly and noble is your entire being – your coat, your waistcoat, your shirt, even your buttons! Everything about you is *physiognomy*! Ah, I am exhausted by such high regard!'[59]

People always said you had to see Liszt to truly experience him, but satires like this implied that, for women, that in-person pleasure was purely of the body. His artistry has been reduced to a series of objects that can be collected and consumed. Like Byron's female readers a generation earlier, the female Liszt fan became the poster girl for much bigger anxieties about celebrity and the rise of consumer and popular culture in general. Critics grumbled that virtuosos like Liszt had turned the sacred art of music into a cult of personality. What these men were selling was themselves – and to such an extent that many of their admirers had never even seen them play. This mass enthusiasm – coded feminine – was evidence of the vulgar, bodily and lower-class instincts corrupting public decency and taste.

Liszt himself puzzled, in his diary, over the fifty people who descended on his hotel room each day while he was in Berlin. 'What do all these people want of me?' he wrote. 'Most of them, money; some of them (especially the young people) just to see me in any way, shape, or form; others to be able to say that they have seen me and that they visit me.'[60] The music was becoming secondary. No mention of hordes of lustful women, though. Perhaps they were all at Le Bon Marché.

Le Bon Marché was the world's first department store. It opened in Paris in 1838 – the same year Liszt returned to the stage – and within a decade, it was offering a new and revolutionary kind of rapture. Émile Zola's description of the magic, in his novel *The Ladies' Paradise*, makes it sound a lot like a Liszt performance: 'The enormous department store made her heart swell, held her in thrall, oblivious to everything,' he wrote. Here was another temple of sensation, where women could lose themselves in endless corridors of wonder and possibility. At the same moment that Liszt was enchanting audiences in the concert halls of Europe, these grand palaces of pleasure were inviting women to look, touch and spend. If Liszt gave them a vision of life beyond duty, modesty and restraint, shopping gave them an excuse to leave the house and actually do something about it. Each, in its own way, made female desire visible. And each seemed to hint that – for those willing to dirty their hands by pandering to women and their silly, irrational and often embarrassingly excessive tastes – marketing and selling pleasure and fantasy to women could be wildly profitable.

Everyone remembers the stories about women tearing each other's hair out over Liszt's gloves and broken piano strings or wearing his coffee dregs in necklaces, but those lucky ladies were a rarity. A newspaper, reporting a glove incident in Luxemburg, pointed out that 'Liszt [had] thrown down his gloves before every piano in Europe. It was at Luxembourg alone that someone had the temerity to pick them up.'[61] Most of his admirers got their souvenirs the normal average way: they bought them. With money.

By 1844, the market was flooded with Liszt merchandise – gloves, handkerchiefs, sheet music, anything that could carry his face or name. Women who bought transcriptions of his most virtuosic pieces became a particular target for mockery – what was the point, people asked, of buying music you couldn't play? Husbands should have counted themselves lucky their wives were buying sheet music and not wax dolls like in the castrati era (rumour had it they were actually dildos). Businesses of all types were learning to cater to female interests and aspirations. And in Liszt's case, this went back much further than the concert hall. Women had been investing in him and his music from the start.

Long before anyone was buying or even conceiving of Lisztomania merch, Liszt had risen to fame in a world where female patronage was essential currency. He was the product of salon culture. Salons were regular gatherings in private homes where Europe's cultural and intellectual elite would come together to hear music, discuss art, politics and literature and forge social connections. By tradition, it was the wife of the household who ran these gatherings, welcoming guests and steering conversation. In Paris alone, there were around 850 salons by 1830. As waves of revolution and industrialisation created a new type of modern woman – one with an increasing amount of free time, money and connections – these spaces became more and more important as centres of social and cultural power.

Here, in the comfort of their own homes, some of the most daring and forward-thinking women of their age became cultural and economic power brokers. They arranged performances, commissioned new works and connected artists with publishers and theatres – they were the original influencers and they had great taste. Throughout his career, salons were essential to Liszt's ability to build his reputation and promote his genius. Two of his most devoted supporters were Countess Louis Plater and Marie von Mouchanoff-Kalergis – Polish noblewomen who had fled forced marriages back home and were now living in exile in Paris. Having redirected their fortunes to supporting the arts, their salons became vital centres of music culture where artists like Liszt and Chopin found both early acclaim and enduring support. If Liszt was known for charming the ladies, it was in part because he needed them.

Women's increasing influence in the arts, especially through their salons, soon began making many guardians of traditional culture uncomfortable. 'Paris has a kind of woman who aspires to become what one would call socially preponderant persons, seeing the world only as their booty, taking part in the movement of society only to amass from it what they can,' wrote the Marquis de Custine.[62] Nineteenth-century Europe had seen a shattering of class boundaries and traditional power structures: both men and women were now suddenly competing with each other for cultural authority in the power vacuum that followed. Many historians have argued that this embryonic struggle for cultural power, which was first visible in music and salon culture, was one of the earliest stirrings of what would become the women's movement of the late nineteenth century.

Women's power was still limited and almost completely informal, but even these marginal gains in the music world were enough to provoke anxiety in many men. In Vienna, where political repression had limited men's public roles, women's dominance of cultural life sparked so much resentment that men began staying away from salons and starting their own clubs. Some were even said to have formed an 'Anti-Women Society' in protest.

Art and culture, especially music, was one of the few places that women of the mid-nineteenth century had to channel their increasingly restless desire for autonomy and self-expression. Perhaps this helps explain both the stereotype of the Lisztian hysteric and why the press fixated with such horror on women's enthusiasm for collecting concert souvenirs. Those broken piano strings and cigar stubs that critics dismissed as worthless rubbish were the perfect symbol of a new social order. In transforming these fragments into treasures, women were not indulging in mindless adoration. They were asserting their right to determine what held value. Just as their salons had transformed private homes into centres of cultural power, their concert souvenirs transformed the ephemera of performance into enduring symbols of artistic worth. These were not symptoms of weakness. They were acts of creative power – the same power that had helped launch Liszt's career in those Parisian salons and was now helping to redefine the role of music in both popular culture and public life.

GIRLS TO THE FRONT

It would be nice to imagine that Liszt fully embraced his role as the world's first proper pop star. He didn't. For all his talk of bringing music to the people, by 1843 he was writing grumpy letters to George Sand about how the crowds were getting on his nerves. They only wanted to hear the hits, he complained, and they were so musically illiterate he could play the same piece twice in the same concert and no one would even notice. He'd created a monster. His face was plastered across everything from wine glasses to satin scarves, and bakers were even making little grand piano-shaped cakes with his name on them. His audiences were literally consuming him.

Critics and competitors were, predictably, happy to pile it on. According to many of his fellow composers, the whole future of music was now under threat. Schumann, who spent his days writing love letters to Clara and his nights arguing with his imaginary friends (they were called Florestan and Eusebius), founded a whole music journal partly to complain about declining standards. Having to listen to virtuoso performances was like being forced to 'gulp down the most hackneyed Italian tunes', he moaned.[63] Soon Berlioz, Europe's most lovesick man (and king of orchestral overkill), weighed in. He described Liszt's audiences as vulgar attention-seekers who threw flowers and clapped on command. These weren't real music lovers, he said; they were more like the Roman mob that had cheered for gladiators at the Colosseum.[64] The real problem was that Liszt was making classical music popular. The virtuoso style was bringing Beethoven and Bach to the masses, with showmanship that made people actually want to listen.

Liszt was devastated by accusations he was destroying music. It seemed so unfair. As his biographer, our old friend Alan Walker, put it: 'Was Liszt to blame for the unrestrained conduct of his audiences? That is rather like asking whether "Niagara Falls is to blame for so many suicides".'[65] He tried to fight back. He wrote in to music magazines, insisting he was an artist, not a showman. But he didn't forget where his piano-shaped bread was buttered. If he was Niagara Falls, it was Niagara Falls with a tour manager, a viral marketing strategy and a 2,000-franc carriage.

Behind the scenes, Liszt was still subtly orchestrating the spectacle of his success. He only agreed to come to concerts if he was certain he would be playing to a full house. If he got the feeling he might not be, he'd cancel or move to a smaller venue. At one point, Heine even accused Liszt's tour manager Gaetano of hiring 'claques' (fake fans) and providing them with the laurels and flowers they needed to shower him with adoration. There is little evidence of this, but there is no question that Liszt leaned into the aftershow theatrics.

At one concert, as thundering applause and an avalanche of flowers rained down on the stage, Liszt bent down, plucked a blood-red camellia from the pile and tucked it into his lapel. Heine compared it to the blood of a fallen war hero (painfully ironic, he pointed out, given the very real veterans sitting in the audience). Or maybe Liszt *was* shedding blood for his art, in his way. In his obsession with bringing music to the people, he had unwittingly written a playbook for fame that would soon be adapted and amplified across the world. In doing so, he also found himself face to face with the question that would plague A-list geniuses for centuries to come: how do you maintain artistic credibility when you've become so popular that people are turning you into cakes?

His answer was to quit touring and devote his life to God. Eventually, he would be semi-ordained by the church, which elevated him from storm-fingered golden boy to storm-fingered sexy priest. His adorers would thenceforth address him as Abbé, but the damage was done. As the century rolled on, the battle between serious art and mass entertainment would continue to rage. And just like Lisztomania, it would very often be female fans who got blamed for ruining everything. One thing that can be said of Liszt, however, is that he never subscribed to that particular panic. He always understood the power of female audiences. 'The women and the aristocrats are with me,' he once said. 'With them I will go far.'[66] This statement would be far more prescient than he knew.

As the nineteenth century progressed and the wheels of social change turned, the line between public and private life continued to blur as women began to enjoy greater freedoms outside the home. From Paris to New York, cities were seeing a revolution in how people were spending their leisure time and their money. The birth of the department store was transforming city centres, and the virtuoso craze had already shown that the growing middle class had cash to spare and a thirst for fun. A 'respectable' lady, who used to need a husband or brother to escort her in town (if she didn't want to be mistaken for a prostitute), could now walk the city streets and browse the grand shopping arcades unchaperoned. New leisure activities like visiting the ice-cream parlour or meeting friends for afternoon tea gave her socially acceptable reasons to be in town for the day, but it was the theatre that would become the place to be.

In London and across the Atlantic, on Broadway, afternoon matinees, set up to allow ladies to safely and respectfully attend the theatre while husbands and fathers were at work, brought shopping and entertainment together to perfection. After a day out perusing and patronising the plush new shops near the theatre district, ladies could stop into a play to show off their department store hauls, catch up with friends (and enemies) and check what everyone else was wearing.

Historically, American theatres had been male spaces (basically taverns with stages attached). The only women who attended regularly were prostitutes, who were given free tickets to the gallery to help attract male customers. On the rare occasions that a 'respectable' woman or two did attend a play, the number of ladies present was sometimes reported in the papers. Not that they were missing out on much: people at the theatre generally drank, argued and only occasionally noticed there was a play happening. When writer Alexis de Tocqueville visited from France, he was shocked to see that the audience 'paid not the slightest attention to the stage, but walked about, drank together, and argued as if nothing else were going on'.[67] When they did pay attention, the actors could expect to be pelted with anything and everything from rotten eggs and vegetables to chairs and (in Cincinnati) half a sheep carcass.

Theatre owners had initially started putting on women-friendly shows in the evenings in the hope of taming the frequent riots and debauchery they were tired of dealing with – men apparently behaved a lot better when the ladies were around. But they soon discovered that targeting women wasn't just a calming influence.

It was a goldmine. After performing in his first matinee show in 1855, an actor in Boston admitted he was astounded by the resounding success: 'At that hour and especially on a Saturday, all the male Americans are riveted to their office desks. So what happened? We played to an audience exclusively composed of women ... Prodigious takings for a Saturday.'[68]

In a few short years, these typically bawdy male spaces – centres of prostitution and vice – were transformed into women-friendly temples of luxury and refinement. Out went the prostitutes and drinking. In came the sweet treats and morality plays and then, dropping the pretence that women truly wanted to spend their leisure time thinking about being virtuous, the eternally crowd-pleasing romances, melodramas and gritty realist 'problem plays'.

Theatre critics, who were forced, for work, to attend these matinees, complained about the sea of increasingly elaborate hats that were perpetually blocking their view of the stage, the shameless sentimentality of the plays themselves, as well as other louche displays of the insatiable female appetite for anything and everything saccharine, excessive and/or secretly sexual, for example the eating of chocolate (treating yourself to a fancy tin of bonbons had become an essential part of the theatre-going experience).

'I am a frequenter at the playhouse, and live, therefore, in the odour of chocolate,' wrote one reviewer.

> I know that without chocolate our womankind could not endure the modern drama; and without womankind the drama would cease to exist ... But to see scores of women simultaneously eating chocolate at the theatre is an uncanny thing. They do it in unison, and they do it with an air of furtive enjoyment, as though it were some secret vice, all the better for being sinful.[69]

The chocolate-hating journalist may have ridiculed the secretly sinful spectacle of women's collective chocolate eating, but he was making a more serious point than he knew. Brought together as a group, enjoying the things that they wanted to enjoy, spending their money on things that pleased them, collectively, female consumers were becoming an increasingly powerful cultural force. Female tastes were now controlling the box office. 'If women do not like a play, it is doomed,' explained a theatre manager. 'But if it appeals to them and they flock to it, its prosperity is assured.'[70]

The most visible manifestation of this new economic and cultural power were the Matinee Girls – young women who were said to attend the theatre not for the plays or the bonbons (though they did rather like those too) but for the actors. The dashing and slightly effeminate – in the best, most 'take him and cut him out in little stars' kind of way – leading men: the Matinee Idols.

The Matinee Girl was the great-grandmother of the fangirl exactly as we know her today. From around 1860 onwards, this effusive and excitable teenager invaded the theatre and revelled in the newfound freedom and community it gave her – shamelessly swooning and weeping in her seat (because the acting was *that good*), restlessly waiting outside her hero's dressing room to ply him with flowers, chocolates and violet-scented 'mash letters' (marriage proposals or love notes) and, in extreme cases, crawling right up onto the stage in the middle of a performance. Her active pursuit of this 'adored creature' threw the traditional active/male and passive/female rules of Victorian courtship and propriety right out the Angel of the House's window.[71] So did his acquiescence.

The most popular actors of previous decades like Edwin Forrest and Edmund Kean had been of the 'muscular school' of acting.[72] They projected manly virtues like brooding and fighting on stage and were said to be just as tough and masculine in real life. Their rowdy, often working-class male fans liked to see them bring all that manliness and vigour to hardcore, serious things like Shakespeare's action-packed history plays, which they were obsessed with. They were so obsessed, in fact, that the most famous theatre riot of the nineteenth century, the Astor Place Riot of 1849, actually began as a dispute between die-hard Edwin Forrest fans, the infamous Bowery B'hoys, and fans of British actor-on-tour William Charles Macready over which actor was better at being Macbeth. By the end of the night, twenty-two people had been killed, 141 injured (including fifty policemen) and the identity of the best Macbeth was still open for debate.

The universe of the Matinee Idol was a little dreamier, but he still caused a fair few fights of his own. These 'male professional beauties' played in romances and melodramas and distinguished themselves by how good they looked in tights, how ardently they loved their leading ladies and how much their admirers adored and applaud-ed them.[73] Harry Montague, the first official Matinee Idol, was so popular that 'dainty ladies shoved, and not so gently shouldered, for position at the ticket counter', tried to sneak in through the fire exit when tickets sold out and were constantly being escorted out of performances by security after trying to climb up onto the stage (Montague was the king of the stage crawlers).[74]

Critics derided these 'leaders in unreal romanticism' as money-hungry and vain, forever trying to stay handsome and relevant enough and embarrassing themselves as they got older by insisting on continuing to squeeze back into those Romeo tights when it was definitely far, far, *far* too late.[75] 'A man never knew when he was too old to play Romeo,' said OG Matinee Idol and grandfather of Drew Barrymore, the legendary John Barrymore ('Girls, in the name of humanity, do stop besetting him!').[76] 'In the old days, in the theatre, an aged Romeo was not infrequent. He may have looked like a corseted bloodhound, but he carried his lifted face proudly.'[77]

Theatre critics may have rolled their eyes, cringed and groaned, but, by the late nineteenth and early twentieth centuries, Matinee Idols like Montague and Barrymore were some of the most bankable stars in the theatre. A whole language and culture had sprung up around them and their fans' all-consuming desire to think, see and know as much as was humanly possible about them. 'Rush seats' were the front-row seats that allowed girls to get as close as was legal to the stage. They would queue for hours and then rush to get them as soon as the doors opened. 'Gush columns' were newspaper articles bursting with gossip and much-needed behind-the-scenes information. 'Hero books' or 'him books' were leather-bound diaries in which girls collected pictures and newspaper clippings, as well as their own thoughts and impressions of performances.

In an eight-page special feature on the Matinee Girl phenomenon, *Munsey's Magazine* gave readers a peek of what it might look like inside:

> The first act is almost invariably indicated by a long series of truly feminine ejaculations, such as 'Too sweet for anything!', 'Just perfect!', 'Simply great!' The second is even more intense: 'Superb!', 'Wonderful!', 'Magnificent!', 'Oh!' But the third act is the climax. Exclamation points alone fill the lines, and the paper has bubbled up here and there, where evidently blinding tears have fallen.[78]

It may not have been Liszt, but the rapture was just as sweet. And just as real. On stage and on film, Barrymore, for example, looked *incredible* in tights. When he played the Renaissance painter

Gianetto in *The Jest*, his wife recalled that his costume 'left no faint fragment of his anatomy to the imagination'.[79] Each night, when he appeared on stage for the first time, this spectacle would be met with audible gasps and sighs of women in the audience. The transgressive pleasure of being able to gaze upon (and be delighted by) 'that famous Barrymore figure' was an ecstatic battle of heaven and hell in its own right.[80]

The same theatre critics who had complained about the hats and bonbons soon turned their attention to the Matinee Girl and her pernicious taste for romance and melodrama, which they singled out as the single biggest threat to the seriousness and legitimacy of the theatre in the whole history of the stage. In a series of histrionic opinion pieces with titles like 'The Brutality of the Matinee Girl' and 'The American Girl's Damning Influence on American Drama', they blamed 'sordid money-grubbing tradesmen' and 'illiterate candy eating women' for bringing shame and destruction to the theatre.[81] Women's low-brow tastes for light-hearted spectacle and entertainment and the cult of celebrity that was now taking precedence over high-quality art were just as damaging as each other – everyone knew that Matinee Idols traded on their faces (and legs) as opposed to their talent. 'Unless people of high standing in America get together to support good, respectable productions,' wrote one critic, 'something terrible may happen.'[82]

Enter that terrible thing in human form. He came from Norway and his name was Ibsen. Yes. Father of Realism, Henrik 'Internationally Acclaimed for Writing Plays That Make Me Want to Scream into the Void' Ibsen. Less corseted bloodhounds; more existential dread and marriages collapsing under the weight of suppressed misery. The Matinee Girls adored him. Theatre critics on London's West End were incensed by the sight of hundreds of young women joyfully munching their bonbons through his nasty foreign plays about suicide and venereal disease. These 'sweet young girls ranging from twelve to sixteen years of age' were 'literally drinking in remarks and conversations to which no young girl in her teens should listen'.[83]

It was 1891 by now, but Ibsen was still shocking enough that his plays were normally confined to one-off performances in small theatres – until the Matinee Girls discovered him. When Elizabeth Robins and Marion Lea put on *Hedda Gabler* at the Vaudeville Theatre, what started as yet another experimental matinee stretched into six unprecedented weeks of packed-out performances.

Hedda is the story of a woman who is bored out of her mind. As a new bride, she's supposed to be happy, but she's restless and suffocating in her gilded cage. Her husband is the type of man whose idea of excitement is footnotes. Lucky her Byronic ex-boyfriend is back in town. Or is it? After orchestrating his downfall (with the help of a fireplace and one of daddy's pistols) and facing blackmail from a creepy judge who turns out to be a sexual predator, she decides to shoot herself in her living room – too sweet for anything!

After two weeks of packed, gushingly adored matinees, the Vaudeville promoted *Hedda* to the evening slot. The difference in the audience reactions was stark. A critic for the *Sunday Sun* noted that the older, mixed evening audience 'did not become at all enthusiastic, nor did they openly hoot or scoff. They simply sat still, stolid and silent.' The performers, 'missing the stimulating applause which had been so liberally showered upon their efforts by matinee audiences mainly composed of the cult's devotees', apparently had to resort to 'over-emphasis' just to get any reaction at all. This repeated itself at other Ibsen plays. At *Little Eyolf*, a reviewer recounted how 'some of the female portion … seemed at times much affected, and sobs and tears occasionally greeted such passages in the drama as were especially lugubrious. The males, I regret to say, were more disposed to chuckle irreverently.'[84]

The critics reached for their medical dictionaries again. After condemning Ibsen's heroines as 'repulsive' and 'infinitely perverse', they turned their attention to the women watching them. The *Sunday Review* helpfully noted that while Nora, who leaves her controlling husband at the end of *A Doll's House*, might be 'restless and hysterical', the real concern was that 'fragments of her personality' could 'be found in the character of almost every woman in the audience'.[85] One particularly alarmed reviewer claimed he'd never seen so many 'deformed faces' even 'at an entertainment for the mentally or physically afflicted … at an asylum concert or hospital treat'. Another described the audience as 'spectacled, green-complexioned, oddly dressed females of unhealthy aspect, their bodies seemingly as diseased as their minds'.[86]

And yet, in a way that was remarkably similar to Lisztomania, the female fan enthusiasm the critics were labelling madness actually felt like an existential epiphany to the women who were experiencing it. Lady Burne-Jones was so transported by *The Master Builder* that she forgot she was in a theatre. When she finally came back to herself, she was 'bewildered to find the theatre empty' and did not know how long she'd been sitting there alone.[87] 'This was either the end of the world or the beginning of a new world for women,' wrote Edith Lees after that first Ibsen performance in London. She and her friends emerged from the theatre 'breathless with excitement … restive and impetuous and almost savage in our arguments'.[88]

Plays like these meant so much because, for the first time, they gave women a naturalistic glimpse of their own frustrations and complexities reflected back at them. Many reported feeling a sense of recognition, solidarity and transformation. As a woman who was 'married, and not noticeably unhappy', put it: 'Hedda is all of us.'[89]

The power of great art – be it the brutal honesty of an Ibsen play, the transcendent ecstasy of a Liszt concert or the beauty and wonder of John Barrymore in tights – is the way it is both a mirror and an escape. It reveals things we didn't know but makes them feel inevitable. For the women of the nineteenth century, these revelations were even more meaningful given where and how they were taking place. 'When women attended a matinee,' says historian Susan Torrey Barstow, 'their experience of the play was in some way shaped by the unwonted thrill of independence they enjoyed for the afternoon, and by their sense of community with the other hat-wearing, chocolate-eating, star-gazing members of the audience … quite self-consciously escaping domesticity for the brief space of an afternoon.'[90]

Girls who attended matinees described the thrill of travelling to get there and back on the omnibus, navigating bustling city streets, being caught up in the crush of people and fighting to get the best position in the pit. These were rare moments for girls and women to experience being part of a crowd. Coming back to the serenity and silence of home afterwards only served to intensify the experience.

The Matinee Girls weren't the first female audience members to discover this particular joy. Decades earlier, Liszt's concerts had created similar moments of excitement and escape from the everyday, and it's easy to imagine that the ecstasy of seeing him live was shaped by similar forces. Even Heinrich Heine's doctor noted the power of the 'sultry hall filled with innumerable wax candles and several hundred perfumed and sweating human beings'.[91] The music itself was enough to lift your soul out of your body, but as anyone who's ever seen their favourite band or performer live knows, the context amplified it. Add to this the fact that, with his pre-show walkabouts and circle of on-stage aristocratic ladies, Liszt seemed to be actively inviting female attention, and it makes perfect sense that women felt emboldened to adore him – unlike many men of his era, he returned the love with genuine respect.

Liszt was remarkably progressive in his belief in the power and potential of women. He taught and mentored dozens of female musicians, supported female musicologists and many of his closest friends were some of the most revolutionary and trailblazing women of their time. George Sand left her husband and wrote novels about social justice, women's independence and romantic freedom. She would dress in men's clothes and smoke cigars at her salon in Paris. Lina Ramann, his only official biographer, lived openly with her female lover, Ida Volckmann, and was part of the early German women's movement. Clara Wieck (later Schumann) may have had a love–hate relationship with him, but there is no doubt that they influenced each other as artists. His first long-term lover Marie d'Agoult may have been pictured swooning in wonder at his feet in the famous painting *Liszt at the Piano*, but she was also writing novels and ghostwriting quite a bit of his music criticism on the side.

Some people say that Liszt was always looking for his 'Beatrice' – a perfect muse who would guide and inspire him, like the Beatrice who leads Dante from purgatory to paradise in his favourite epic poem the *Divine Comedy*. Obviously, he never found her, but he had many female guides. Having had no formal schooling, much of Liszt's early education came from the *salonnières* whose gatherings he played at in his youth. Far from idealised, mystical visions of the eternal feminine, these were real women with intellectual and artistic universes of their own. Throughout his life, female mentors and collaborators would help him define his philosophy, refine his art and expand his intellectual world. Women were so central to his story that, in 1911, a musicologist called La Mara published a book called *Liszt and the Women*. It tells the story of his life through profiles of twenty-six women – from patrons and lovers to students and friends – who shaped his life and work. This is a serious, scholarly work, but she insisted on adding a little border of hearts on the title page, because why not?

La Mara's real name was Marie Lipsius, but she was forced to write under a pseudonym because it would have brought shame to her family for people to know she was a writer. She first met Liszt in the salons of Weimar when she was a teenager. He quickly became a life-changing obsession. Her female partner, Similde Gerhard, was the love of her life, but in her autobiography, she dedicated a whole chapter to 'Liszt, My Destiny'. Along with Lina Ramann, she helped lay the foundations for serious discussion of Liszt's work in his lifetime. Critics initially dismissed them both as *'löwenjägerinnen'* (lion hunters), the women who were said to flock around him hoping 'to gain favour, establish careers or simply experience pleasure through chasing the master'.[92] But the biographical methods they pioneered – interviews, surveys, archival research and having subjects review their own stories before publication – are standard practice today.

La Mara was prolific in her lifetime. She published dozens of books that often went through multiple printings, wrote about the great composers of her time, was the first person to investigate the unknown identity of Beethoven's mysterious 'immortal beloved' and made it her mission to tell the stories of dozens of lesser-known female composers and musicians whose stories might otherwise have been lost to time. The unique psychological and emotional depth of her writing generated mixed responses from critics, since it was dismissed as 'feminine writing' in her day, but Liszt himself praised her character study as one of the best things ever written about him.

In her biography of Liszt, La Mara wrote about his faith that 'the future tends to be a more just judge than the present'. Of course, she was writing as much about her own hopes as her hero's. During a period when her work was facing criticism, her friend (and Liszt's final long-term lover) Princess Carolyne zu Sayn-Wittgenstein wrote encouragingly: 'Continue your path firmly and courageously. You open it to women ... The future will thank you, dear woman, and believe me, its applause means more than that of the present. It is less biased, more enlightened.'

Rudolph Valentino and Agnes Ayres in *The Sheik* (1921)

3

DESIRE, HOLLYWOOD, 1926
THE LURE OF THE FLESH

He had fine Corsair's eyes, full of expression and determination, eyes that
could look love and bloodshed almost at the same time; and then he had
those manly properties – power, bigness and apparent boldness ... To be
hurried about the world by such a man, treated sometimes with crushing
severity, and at others with the tenderest love, not to be spoken to for
one fortnight, and then to be embraced perpetually for another, to be cast
every now and then into some abyss of despair by his rashness and then
raised to a pinnacle of human joy by his courage – that, thought Lizzie,
would be the kind of life that would suit her poetical temperament.
– ANTHONY TROLLOPE, *THE EUSTACE DIAMONDS* (1877)

On the afternoon of 6 September 1926, Peggy Scott left her friend Rosa's flat, just off Oxford Street in London's West End. She said she was going to the cinema.

Peggy, a 27-year-old actress, dancer and movie extra girl, had recently returned from the Continent, where she'd been on tour with a cabaret. With her bobbed hair, infectious gaiety and endless stream of disappointed suitors, Peggy had always seemed like the epitome of an emancipated modern girl. She liked fast cars, dancing all night and was often seen out partying with the champagne crowd. But since returning home from this latest trip to Europe, something in her usual carefree exuberance seemed to be off.

When she had appeared on Rosa's doorstep the previous day, in search of a room for the night, she explained that she was out of work, penniless and desperate. Perhaps today, after a good night's sleep, an afternoon at a picture show would lift her mood or at least provide a few hours' relief from the loneliness and shabbiness of real life.

As it turned out, Peggy's trip to the cinema would do precisely the opposite. When she returned home later that night, she seemed disoriented and unwell – 'sort of mad', Rosa said. Her eyes were glassy and vacant. Her breathing jagged and strained. Struggling to walk, she collapsed as she tried to get up the stairs. When Rosa rushed to help her up, she began grabbing and clawing at her. Through gasps and tears, she explained that she'd 'swallowed something' before collapsing again.[1] That was when the convulsions started: dark, violent spasms that contorted her whole body as if it were at war with itself. 'I'm dying!' she cried. 'Don't leave me!'[2] Rosa called for the doctor. By the time he arrived, Peggy was dead.

The suicide note was found in Peggy's handbag along with a signed movie photo. In her room were more letters, photos and clippings from movie magazines. 'Life is awful, I'm afraid of it,' explained the note.

> It is heartbreaking living in the past when the present is hopeless … Rudolph helped me carry on … With his death my last bit of courage has flown. I have been stretched for years like a piece of elastic. Perhaps it was only a matter of time before it snapped.[3]

The Rudolph of the letter was the movie star Rudolph Valentino.

Famed for his 'animal magnetism', tango skills and hypnotic stare (those eyes smouldered with ideas so outrageously inappropriate that some people dared not even put them into words), he had been the Great Lover of Hollywood. A few weeks earlier, the world had been shocked by news that this vigorous, athletic young man had suddenly died after collapsing at his hotel on Park Avenue, apparently the result of a perforated stomach ulcer (though some people whispered this was a cover-up: he had, in fact, been murdered by a jealous husband). He was just thirty-one. With his death, Hollywood mourned not only the loss of its most loved and adored male star but also a unique type of stardom in the cinema. This was a man who had built his entire career on the sexual and romantic fantasies of women.

Valentino had been the physical embodiment of desire. Ads for his films showed women hooked into heart-rate monitors spiking as they watched the kissing scenes of his historical love dramas. Now, it was the passion and wildness of his fans that would become the star of the show. The tidal wave of heartbreak and anguish that erupted around the world in response to his loss was dramatic and unprecedented. In the darkness of cinemas, women broke down in tears when news of his death flashed up on screens. Others wept openly in the street – 'and that is something that never happens here', said the Washington correspondent for *Variety*, 'not even for the death of a president'.[4]

From Los Angeles to Tokyo, tales of hysteria, grief-riots and suicides abounded: the housewife who shot herself in her kitchen on Halloween morning, the pair of schoolgirls who jumped hand in hand into a fiery volcano in Japan and the elevator boy at the Ritz in Paris, found dead on a bed scattered with photographs of his hero. Fearing similar events in Rudy's homeland of Italy, Mussolini put out a statement urging Italian women to become mothers and not suicides.

This Gothic carnival of heartbreak reached its peak on 24 August when 30,000 fans flooded the streets outside Campbell's Funeral Home on Madison Avenue where Valentino's body was lying in state. Tired of waiting and drenched in the heavy summer rain that had been falling all day, a riot erupted when the doors to the viewing chapel were finally opened. Windows were smashed, a car overturned and at least a hundred people, many of them women and children, were injured as mounted police charged the crowd in an attempt to hold them back from the doors. 'I must see him!' cried a young woman in tears. By the end of the day, a makeshift emergency room had to be erected in the reception of the funeral home. The scene was a war zone.

Valentino had always had a powerful effect on crowds. A few months earlier, at the New York premiere of his final film *The Son of the Sheik*, thousands of female admirers had torn at his clothes, stolen his hat and ripped off his buttons as he tried to make his way to his car after the screening. It took twenty policemen to finally clear the way that day, but the scenes outside Campbell's were madness on a completely different scale.

To some observers, this crazed mob was the culmination of two weeks' wall-to-wall press coverage that had whipped the general public into a frenzy. A dress rehearsal for future iconic celebrity deaths like Kennedy and Princess Diana, it was the first mass media event of the modern era. To others (by far the majority), it was Valentino's female fans who were to blame for the chaos. The 'middle-aged matrons' and 'hysterical women who prostrated themselves before his tomb' were symptomatic of a phenomenon that had been brewing and intensifying since the very earliest days of cinema: female film fans out of control.[5] It was a useful fiction. And a fitting one. Of all the actors in Hollywood, Valentino had always been the one who understood the power of inviting women to let go.

EVERY HUSBAND'S RIVAL

Stepping out of a creamy, freshly polished Rolls-Royce on Holly-wood Boulevard, sparkling in white flannel trousers, emerald-green sport socks and a grey tweed golf cap, Rodolfo Guglielmi di Valentina knew how to sell a fantasy. The car was borrowed. The outfit, one of many flamboyant ensembles calculated to attract the attention of casting directors and studio chiefs. He wasn't a star (yet), but if there was one thing that life had taught him so far, it was that greatness is the reward of those who are ready and willing to take the greatest risks. He was Rudolph Valentino now.

Ten years earlier, in Naples, eighteen-year-old Rudy had board-ed a steamliner with a second-class ticket, a $3,000 banker's draft and a tuxedo. Destination: America. Most of his fellow passengers, Italian peasants, were crossing the Atlantic in the hopes of finding work and building new, more prosperous lives, but Rudy was already comfortably middle class. His motivations for immigration were more visionary: he believed that Italy was too small for him. And apparently so was second class. The first thing he did upon boarding the SS *Cleveland* was sell his banker's draft (at a loss) and upgrade his ticket. For the next fifteen days – luxuriating in the opulent delights of his first-class cabin – he drank champagne, practised his English by flirting with beautiful, wealthy American women and learned the foxtrot. By the time he arrived at Ellis Island, he was broke.

Before coming to America, Rudy had imagined a land of boundless adventure and opportunity. What he got was the same dose of prejudice and hardship that was handed out to every other Italian immigrant fresh off the boat, regardless of education, background or charm. This was an America in the midst of a race crisis. The huge influx of Italian immigrants (1.3 million between 1900 and 1920), particularly from southern Italy like him, had led to heated political debate about who should and who shouldn't be allowed into the country.

Southern Italians, with their 'darker' complexions, were viewed as racially inferior to other 'whiter' immigrants from northern and western Europe, including those from northern Italy. Just marginally above African Americans in white old-world America's supposed pyramid of racial superiority, they were maligned as dirty, violence-prone peasants – too stupid and lazy to ever fully adapt to American life. There had been lynchings of Italians in the South. The nativists' greatest fear was sex and relationships between races, which they believed was now threatening to dilute, and eventually consume, the purity of the white American race.

With job prospects limited and initially refusing, for pride, to accept menial work, Rudy's first few years in the city were spent in an unhappy haze of poverty, odd jobs and frequent unemployment. When Julius Keller, the flamboyant owner of Maxim's Restaurant Cabaret, offered him a job as a dancer at one of his famous tango teas, Rudy jumped at the chance. It would be twelve more years before he arrived in Hollywood, but these early days in New York would define much of what was to come. He was now on a collision course with three of the most aneurysm-inducing moral panics of the 1910s and 1920s: dance, female pleasure and the future of the white American man.

In 1914, popular magazine editor William Marion Reedy announced that it was 'sex o'clock in America' – the country had gone dance crazy and (as with all the most popular and important trends in early pop culture) it was women who were leading the way.[6] Tango teas, or *thés dansants* as they were sometimes known, were afternoon events attended by ladies who were, for the first time in history, out on the town *unchaperoned*. Very little tea was drunk ('People wiggle much better on whisky,' said one waiter), but the name offered an air of respectability to what was, in essence, an excuse to meet, flirt and hopefully get up close and personal with members of the opposite sex.[7] The atmosphere at these events was hot and 'heavy with unleashed passions'.[8]

Keeping the pleasure of their female customers top of the agenda, clubs like Maxim's had taxi dancers on hand for women who didn't have dance partners of their own. These men could be hired at tea time but were also available to take women through the dance steps in more expensive private lessons. The exact content of these private lessons is a matter of debate, but the word gigolo was born on the dancefloors of these same events and increasingly used interchangeably with taxi dancer.

Rudy had no formal dance training but was handsome with natural grace. Within a few months, he was one of the most popular dancers at Maxim's. And within a few years, as his dance skills flourished, he had progressed out of taxi dancing into the more respectable career of exhibition dancer. But the stigma of his time at Maxim's would haunt him for the rest of his life. As men who 'lived off women' (whether through sex work or not), taxi dancers had a reputation as low-life social parasites who leeched on the daughters of the rich, manipulating and exploiting them for money. More derogatory terms for these men were tango pirates, lounge lizards or social gangsters.

Stereotyped as lazy, swarthy and lower class, most often from Italian or Jewish backgrounds, the tango pirates' good looks, sharp suits and sensuous, athletic bodies were said to be the tools of their nefarious trade in sexual and sensual seduction. 'The master of such passion-inducing dances as the tango and one step, the pirate held women in a spell they could not easily break,' wrote historian Lewis A. Erenberg, 'tightening his arms around her, dipping her, holding her, and in the tango from which he got his name, bending her over backwards in a perfect picture of sexual subjugation, the tango pirate was the master of all he surveyed.'[9] Look a bit closer, however, and this *pas de deux* of mastery and subjugation was not completely as it seemed.

The tango pirate did a great job of projecting masculine dominance on the dancefloor, but he had many supposedly feminine qualities as well. He was meticulous about his clothes and appearance. He lived for pleasure and luxury. And he had far too much leisure time on his hands (how else could he have become so skilled at the tango?). All this, apparently, in the service of catching and pleasing women, who were not only willingly being seduced but also apparently paying for the pleasure.

According to the rules of nineteenth-century masculinity, which most 'respectable' men still followed, men's lives were supposed to be about hard work, self-control and diligence. And if they wanted a woman, well, they could just go to a brothel (or buy a more respectable girl by lavishing her with gifts). Dancing, preening, leisure and luxury – this was the universe of women. But while the men of America were at work – slaving away in their offices and factories to buy women and things – their 'pleasure-mad' wives and daughters were swooning in the arms of dark-skinned, effeminate immigrants.[10] 'If the cabaret walls could talk,' said one newspaper, 'or the waiters tell all they knew, the state would have to open a few extra courts to keep up with the rush of divorces.'[11]

And so, the men of America began to worry. They worried that their wives would leave them for immigrants. They worried that their daughters would procreate with men of 'rotten ancestry' and therefore give birth to disabled, mixed-race children (this actually was the plot of an alarmist popular novel called *Possible Husbands*).[12] But most of all, they worried about what would happen to them.

If the pleasure-mad women of America wanted men who charmed them with sensuality and romance, men who fussed about their appearances and paid attention to their whimsical feminine needs, then what would they have to do to keep them? Would *they* have to start spending less time at work? Learn to dance? Invest in hair products? Face cream? And if they did that, then where would this hedonistic pursuit of pleasure and luxury lead? The inevitable conclusion, many believed, was that 'passionate women would lead men away from self-control towards the life of sensual expressiveness, men's concentration would be broken, their money lost and their businesses ruined .... They would lose their self-control and their identities.'[13] They would end up like the tango pirate: lost and adrift, living at the mercy of women.

Years later, at the peak of his Hollywood fame, these same anxieties would swirl around Valentino more directly. He was a too-pretty, too-swarthy man with a shady past who had tangoed the women of the world into believing that he was the lover of their dreams. But like the tango pirate, his cultural power did not come from deceiving women into believing a fiction. It came from his willingness and ability to bring female fantasies to life. Valentino was the inheritor of Byron's dark, brooding, sexually ambiguous mystique. But unlike Byron (a grudging idol), Valentino had been in the female entertainment business from the start. Those female dollars would keep him at the top of the box office. And it was powerful women in Hollywood who would make him a star.

June Mathis, the woman often credited with discovering Valentino, was living proof of the shining possibilities available to women in early cinema. Between 1900 and 1930, Hollywood had more female writers, directors and producers than at any other time in history. Cinema was still in its infancy at this point (Hollywood's first feature film, *Birth of a Nation*, premiered in 1915), but one thing was clear: it was women who dominated movie audiences. It made sense that they should be involved in writing, shooting and promoting them.

A hundred years earlier, it was restless young men who had flocked west in search of adventure and opportunity. Now, it was women who were arriving in their thousands, and it was the movies that brought them. 'Here was a vision of the West,' wrote novelist Margaret Turnbull in 1818, 'the West which spelled adventure, and the fantastic world of make believe, a picture studio ... and strange people, hers for the taking, and if God were good, the power to dream again.'[14] By 1920, Los Angeles was one of the few western cities in America where women outnumbered men. These were the women who built the motion picture industry.

Mathis began her career as a stage actress in New York. She was twenty-eight when she won a screenwriting competition in a Hollywood fan magazine, which landed her a writing contract at major studio Metro Pictures. There, she quickly moved up the ranks to become their first female film executive – writing, casting and overseeing productions from start to finish. She first noticed Valentino in *Eyes of Youth*. He was playing a minor role as a 'cabaret parasite'. Tired of exhibition tours (and fleeing the fallout of an East Coast divorce trial turned vice squad sting and then murder, for which he'd been a star witness – and some said the secret lover of the society woman accused), he'd come west to try his luck in Hollywood, but his 'foreign looks' were making it difficult to get work.

Hollywood may have been a place where women were beginning to flourish professionally, but it was still painfully traditional when it came to leading men. The biggest male stars of the day were either rugged, all-American swashbucklers like 'King of Hollywood' Douglas Fairbanks (more interested in swinging from chandeliers than getting the girl, though he somehow always got her anyway) or comedians like Charlie Chaplin. The best that a non-Anglo actor like Valentino could hope for was supporting roles as villains or heavies, as they were known. But something about Valentino's look – his fusion of intensity and grace – intrigued Mathis. She decided to stake her career on casting him as Julio Desnoyers, the playboy son of an Argentinian ranch owner, in her upcoming First World War epic, *The Four Horsemen of the Apocalypse*.

Julio is a classic Valentino role – the charmer you know you should resist, but the more you try, the more you can't. Of course, he promises unhappily married Marguerite that he'll behave when he invites her to drink tea at his art studio (he's a bad boy who also appreciates the higher things in life – painting, music, poetry). And he does behave… for about five minutes. But once he goes in for that first kiss, well, there's nothing she can do. As a woman who once danced with Valentino put it: 'Naturally I was scared to death. Who wouldn't be.' But then 'his arms supported me like a brace. I swung myself back, closed my eyes, breathed in the music and—'[15]

Mathis's bet paid off. *The Four Horsemen* was the second highest-grossing film of 1920. Praised by critics for its 'authenticity' (i.e. casting foreign actors in a film set in Argentina and Europe), it catapulted Valentino to overnight fame. The story of Julio's journey from lovable rogue to fallen war hero – all for the love of a woman – was a soul-saving fantasy for the modern age. And the tango scenes were smoking hot. The moment this beautiful, stormy-eyed man swaggered across the dance floor of a Buenos Aires brothel in his first scene – cigarette in mouth, smoke billowing, winking at the woman he was about to seduce before shoving her existing, painfully stilted dance partner out the way – sex in the cinema would never be the same again.

There was such a buzz in New York, said actress Constance Talmadge, who was there around the time of the film's premiere. 'The young women there could talk of nothing but Valentino.' They were 'wishing to each other that they would be lucky enough to dance a tango with that hero'.[16] And some were. When he was invited, as guest of honour, to a gala for professional women in New York, he charmed everyone by giving a tango lesson, and cooking Spanish omelette, for those who remained at the afterparty in the morning. Dancing and *cooking*? This was definitely not Douglas Fairbanks. Movie magazines were soon heralding the birth of a new type of star in the Hollywood firmament. Fairbanks may have been its king, but Valentino was its lover.

There was nothing particularly unusual about having a new leading man of the moment, so the press did what they always did: they packaged and promoted him. Rudy was 'the polished foreigner', 'the modern Don Juan', a 'champion screen love maker'.[17] They praised his acting and tango skills, but they had to be careful with his foreignness. They made a point of reminding readers that he was the 'good' type of European (more Library of Alexandria than brothels of Little Italy). But there was always a subtext of unease in the way they wrote about him – as if they didn't quite have the framework or even the words to explain him. 'He isn't so much melancholic as pensive,' said *Motion Picture* magazine. 'He has many friends, and very few. Books are his companions and dreams and memories.'

As an avalanche of fan letters flooded in, magazines found themselves inundated with questions about how to contact him, whether he was married and how to pronounce his name. In trying to promote their new star, the press had inadvertently stoked a fire they now realised they couldn't contain. 'My word! More Valentino!' wrote the exasperated letter editor at *Photoplay*.[18] 'I never heard of so much incense being burned for any popular hero. He has as many admirers as the president or the Prince of Wales. He may be addressed at Lasky Studios, Hollywood, California.'

The women of America were obsessed and for all the reasons they weren't supposed to be. Rudy was dark, brooding and Byronic. And – although no one was saying it directly yet – he was *sexy*, in a very physical, very naughty and dangerously foreign kind of way. For all the comparisons to highbrow heroes of classical literature – 'he has the indolence of Endymion ... the reverence of Dante ... the vitality of Don Juan ... the extravagance of Don Quixote' – those tango pirate rumours were impossible to suppress.

In an attempt to maintain respectability, many profiles now began reassuring readers that beneath the exotic surface, he was safe. 'First of all dismiss the idea of the sleek and insidious,' said *Photoplay*.

'There is nothing repellent, nothing unmasculine about Valentino, merely a heavy exoticism, compelling, fascinating, perhaps a little disturbing.' Those 'reassurances' weren't fooling anyone. The more they wrote and thought about him, the more hot and flustered they themselves – let alone their readers – seemed to get. 'His manner is always one of repression, repression, volcanic repression one thinks nervously,' concluded the article.[19] They were right to be nervous. To anyone in 1920 who thought *The Four Horsemen* was a sizzling tangofest of pure, unbridled animal magnetism and transgressive pirate eroticism, Rudolph Valentino might have quoted fellow Hollywood legend Al Jolson: you ain't seen nothin' yet.

ROMANCE, RED HOT

In February 1922, *Photoplay* did the unthinkable: they put a man on their cover. They'd been teasing they might do it for months. 'If we ever decided to have men on the covers … [Rudy] will be the first man,' said the editors.[20] No one quite believed they'd actually go through with it, but now here he was: Rudolph Valentino at his most unashamedly exotic: turbaned, kohl-eyed and absolutely smouldering. Were they finally ready to admit and accept exactly what it was about Rudy that made him so attractive? Or was it just that a movie this scandalous demanded a publicity stunt to match?

The Sheik, a big-screen adaptation of E. M. Hull's 'poisonously salacious' bestselling romance novel of 1919, is *hot*.[21] It's also painfully of its time. If it was produced today, it would have about ten minutes of trigger warnings scrolling across the screen and slowly disappearing off into the distance, like the text at the beginning of *Star Wars* films. This is my warning to you. The novel is the story of Lady Diana Mayo, a feisty young English woman who is kidnapped and raped by a handsome yet brutal Arabian chieftain, Sheik Ahmed, while on holiday in Algeria.

In classic romance novel style (think X-rated *Beauty and the Beast*), she eventually learns to love her abuser. This is aided by the novel's final twist. It turns out that the big bad Arab isn't even Arab at all; in fact he's a European aristocrat. This, of course, makes him so much easier to love and forgive for being a kidnapper and rapist. Diana, who's been wrestling her romantic attraction to Ahmed throughout the novel, is now finally free to admit and accept that Ahmed conquered her body and has now also conquered her heart. Luckily, he's fallen in love with her too – an emotion he didn't even know he was capable of. And so, they live happily ever after: re-spectably married but still having loads of ridiculously hot and wild Arabian sex.

Evidently, there's a lot that's problematic in there, but the un-comfortable truth is that – in much the same way that they were so fascinated and enthralled by Valentino's Otherness – white middle- and upper-class British and American women of the 1920s could not get enough of this. In England, where the book was first published, it became an instant bestseller. When it was published in America a year later, it went through fifty printings in its first year and stayed on the bestseller list for two. Its publication coincided with a post-war boom in sex novels written by women for women, as well as a fashion for all things 'oriental'.

The east had always had a mystical allure for westerners (this was part of what had made Byron's 'Turkish Tales' so popular), but *The Sheik* was one of the first times it became associated with female sexual fantasy. In the desert romance, as this genre came to be known, the exploration of the vast, mysterious desert became a metaphor for the heroine's more personal journey of sexual self-discovery. The fact that these fantasies so often revolved around violence and submission gives us an all-too-real window into the sexual politics of their day.

In theory, the women of 1920 had never had it so good. The war was over and new social and sexual freedoms (the vote, employment, rudimentary birth control and the advent of dating culture) were allowing them to experience and experiment with life in all kinds of new and empowering ways. But the war had left a heavy shadow over the world – one it was impossible to ignore since it had made its way back from the trenches, in the eyes of shell-shocked brothers and the fists of resentful husbands. Thousands of men had returned from the war mentally and physically ravaged by the horrors they'd seen. Many didn't return at all. Domestic violence rates were up. So were divorces. As soldiers struggled to adapt back into civilian life, both men and women were forced to confront the dissonance between their pre- and post-war identities and lives. What did it mean to be a man, or a woman, in the modern age?

New sexual freedoms were especially fraught with uncertainty and conflict. Was it OK for a woman to want and enjoy sex? Did sleeping with someone before marriage make you 'fast' or just modern? Who could, or should, make the first move? And where did love, or having children, fit into all of this?

In Britain, at the beginning of the war, a phenomenon dubbed 'khaki fever' had thrown many of these issues into the spotlight. Hundreds of young women – many, on paper, of 'good breeding' – were said to be flocking to army barracks to chase and proposition soldiers. 'Once I saw some young Colonials [American troops] running for their very lives to escape from a little company of girls,' wrote one journalist. 'One might have thought, to see them, that they had tigresses at their heels. Another day I saw some English

Tommies, who were being pursued by girls, spring into an omnibus for safety.' This writer acknowledged that the girls (keen to be involved in the war effort in some way) were likely just having a bit of fun. But in the eyes of most, they were playing with fire. These girls, 'by turn tempters and tempted', had apparently 'often ended up entangling themselves and their soldier friends in actual vicious conduct'.[22]

Soon, the newly established 'Women's Patrol Committee' were prowling the streets, intervening in situations where they believed young women might be 'at risk'. In 1918, for example, they visited a cinema in Hornsey where they found that 'a number of soldiers and girls were reclining in each other's arms, and that several acts of impropriety took place'. The girls were sent home. The cinema was prosecuted and fined.

The publication of Marie Stopes's bestselling sex and contraception manual *Married Love*, that same year, might have assured married women that female sexual desire was completely normal, healthy and to be encouraged, but on the whole, the rules on female sexual purity hadn't changed much since Byron's day. Thousands of young women, including Stopes herself just a few years before writing her book, still claimed (either in truth or modesty) to be clueless about even the most basic reproductive biology. Stopes first became interested in the subject when she began visiting libraries to try to understand why she'd been married for several years and was still not pregnant. She discovered that her husband was impotent and that they had never actually had sex.

This was the confusing and contradictory world that *The Sheik* was born into. And that's what made it so compelling to so many readers. Published on the eve of a decade in which female sexual desire would go from being dismissed as 'mainly a pretence' to becoming a national obsession – visible, debated and analysed – it's a hot mess of a novel that (in its own unique and slightly messed-up early 1920s way) celebrates female sexual agency.[23]

Set in an orientalist fantasyland, its rape-to-romance narrative allowed its unmarried heroine to have sex and like it, while absolving her of responsibility and guilt (the sexy foreigner made her do it). It also allowed female readers to 'treat themselves' to sexual and emotional fantasy by actively participating in the new economy of sex literature.[24] Derided as 'perverted', 'unnatural' and 'foreign' (even when they were set at home), these books provided a thrilling type of escapism.[25] They were also a safe way for women to explore more complex issues and tensions closer to home.

Diana begins the novel as a classic 'modern woman' – a tomboyish flapper who has sworn off marriage, preferring a life of adventure and autonomy. This is threatened when she meets Ahmed – the only man strong, handsome and violent enough to break her like the wild Arabian pony that she is. Her rape and captivity in the desert become physical manifestations of her fear of having to submit to the shackles of wifedom. According to romance scholars like the legendary Janice Radway, who has interviewed hundreds of romance novel fans, this plotline – a beloved staple of the romance genre – is particularly popular with women who want to be reassured that traditional gender roles and behaviours (including what we would now call toxic masculinity) are not incompatible with female fulfilment.[26]

By the end of the novel, Ahmed's violence and aggression are revealed to be the result of childhood trauma. Behind the bluster is a tender and loving man, who is on his own journey of self-discovery. Through sex, Ahmed teaches Diana that engaging with your womanly side isn't so bad. In fact, when you're sleeping with a sheik, it can actually be quite fun. Armed with this new power as a 'proper woman', Diana can now tame Ahmed into the monogamous, shockingly traditional relationship she finally understands she secretly wants. It's easy to see how this story would have resonated with women of the early '20s, grappling themselves with the question of how to square their newfound freedoms outside the home with the captivity of domestic life, many in relationships with traumatised men.

In casting Valentino as Hollywood's Ahmed, producer Jesse Lasky was playing on his existing star persona as a mysterious foreigner with passionate depths. His 'Otherness', previously played down by publicists, was now exactly the point – just tango pirate enough to get a lady's pulse racing, but just enough promise in those big brown eyes to reassure her that, ultimately, this was a reformable sheik. No one in the history of Hollywood had ever been more right for a role. The film was released in October 1921 in a sandstorm of publicity that sought to capitalise on the salaciousness of the book. 'Here is romance. Red-hot,' said an ad in *Photoplay*.[27] 'When an Arab sees a woman he wants, he takes her!'[28]

Unfortunately, viewers looking forward to explicit scenes were to be disappointed. Fear of censorship had led to a watering down of the characters and plot. The rape scene, for example, is left ambiguous. But what the movie lost in soft-core rape fantasy porn, it made up for in visual pleasure. Rudolph Valentino has never looked as spellbinding as he did in those hazy soft-focus close-ups normally reserved for female stars or strutting about in those billowy robes over modern western jodhpurs (strong Lord Byron in Albanian dress vibes). This Ahmed isn't so much the 'brute and a devil and a beast' of the novel as he is the boyfriend of your dreams, all dressed up and ready for your kinkiest role-play fantasy. Just look at those long lashes smothered in eyeliner. This is a man who wants to be looked at, fantasised over and to please – and not in a conventional way.

'We all saw ourselves in the role of Diana Mayo,' said Barbara Cartland years later (she was twenty at the time). 'We all longed to be abducted into the desert and to be forced by sheer violence into obedience by an all-conquering male.'[29] The infamous kidnap scene ('Lie still, you little fool!') shocked and thrilled audiences in equal measure. 'Why have you brought me here?' asks Diana. 'Are you not woman enough to know?' he replies.

The revolutionary thrill of *The Sheik* was that, by 1921, female film viewers *were* women enough to know exactly why Ahmed had brought Diana there – and to like it. They were also women enough to walk right into movie theatres to pay their own hard-earned cash to see it happen, women enough to talk about how much they'd loved it afterwards and women enough to make their own minds up about what type of man (and, in fact, what type of sex) it was acceptable to fantasise about.

Safe in their plush velvet movie theatre seats – gazing up at this beautiful man do unspeakably naughty things (but ultimately be brought in line by his girl) – *The Sheik* allowed female film audiences, like Diana, to engage with their wild sides. And – in classic desert romance style – they lived happily ever after. *The Sheik* was an instant blockbuster.

Nobody was prepared for the cultural phenomenon that would be *The Sheik*. 'We certainly did not expect to convulse the nation,' said studio founder Adolph Zukor.[30] But convulse the nation it did.

Within days, this movie had smashed all box office records in New York, where it was showing in just two cinemas. 'People are flocking in their maddest crowds to see it,' said the *New York Times*. 'They stand knee deep in Broadway, pressing fondly at the doors of the Rialto and Rivoli for entrance.'[31]

The clamour for showings in towns in cities around the country was so great that Zukor and Lasky soon announced 'Sheik Week'. In November 1921, *The Sheik* opened in 250 cinemas across America. This was nearly unheard of. So were the number of requests from international distributors. Within a year, *The Sheik* had grossed more than \$1 million (big money for 1921 and an incredible return for its budget of less than \$200,000). As 'Sheik Fever' galloped – wind in its hair, bareback astride an unbroken Arabian stallion – across the movie-watching world, it inspired copycats, parodies, fashion trends, tie-in books, jazz standards and eventually a brand of condoms.

Young men on the prowl for women were now known as 'Sheiks' (some did adopt Valentino as a style icon). Their girlfriends were 'Shebas'. 'Police declare war on "Sheiks" and "Shebas" in Parked Machines,' ran one newspaper headline (apparently a spike in in-car make-out sessions had led to a curfew in parks in Oakland). 'Spooners will be arrested if caught in tabooed places after 9 p.m.,' warned the article.[32] It was a losing battle. The veil had fallen, as F. Scott Fitzgerald put it – 'the Jazz Age was in flower'[33]. As the cocktails flowed and the music simmered, something about *The Sheik* (or more precisely, Rudolph Valentino as the sheik) had captured the mood and the knickers of a generation.

There was no denying it was Valentino and his romantic appeal to women that was responsible for the resounding success of *The Sheik*. 'Never in the history of the screen has the public fallen so

prostrate before an idol as they have before Rudolph Valentino,'
exclaimed *Photoplay*:

> On a pilgrimage from Coast to Coast I found the worshipers in
> awed and ecstatic attitudes. You would have thought the Pope
> had just passed by. They chanted fervently, none of his historic
> skill, but of his hair, his eyes, his lips, his smile … One votary
> spoke of the sturdy throat and another went so far as to admire
> his classic limbs as revealed in *The Sheik*. He is to school girls and
> virginal spinsters alike the personification of torrid romance. 'Ah,'
> says the elderly maid, 'to be swept off one's feet, despite one's
> good morals, by such a sheik!'[34]

Yes, there had been stars who had been the object of enthusiastic
fan love and adoration before. America's Sweetheart, Mary Pickford, and her husband Douglas Fairbanks had been mobbed by
well-wishers on their honeymoon. The great Matinee Idols of the
stage had, similarly, been hounded and sometimes even stalked by
fans. But the overt, libidinous aspect of the Valentino craze was
something new. So was the scale of the phenomenon. It seemed that
Rudy had become the phantom lover of every woman in America
– an embodiment of her fantasies and gunpowder for her desires.

Nearly overnight, his fanmail increased a thousandfold. Many
of these letters were, as one journalist delicately put it, 'missives
of which the intimate and tender nature may be guessed from the
request of the writers that the matter might not be dealt with by Mr
Valentino's secretary – especially if she is a woman'. His secretary (a
woman) was too inundated with letters to be able to comply with
individual requests. She told papers that reading Valentino's fanmail
had 'shown her life as it really is'.[35] But a question remained: had

Valentino and his uncontrollably potent animal magnetism been the key to unlocking these thousands of thus hidden and repressed kinky thoughts? Or was he actually responsible for creating new ones?

In 1933, sociologist Herbert Blumer set out to answer this question. He was commissioned by the Payne Fund (a group advocating for film censorship) to write a report on the social and psychological impact of the movies on American youth. In the nearly 20,000 interviews, questionnaires and 'motion picture autobiographies' he collected for the study, he found so many sexual and romantic references to Valentino that he dedicated an entire section of his chapter on 'Day-Dreaming and Fantasy' to teenage girls' responses to *The Sheik*. 'Some publicists and editorial writers have expressed their amazement at the overwhelming popular interest displayed in Valentino at the time of his death,' wrote Blumer. 'If American girls and women were affected to the extent to which many of the high school and college girls who contributed to this study seem to have been, then there is little occasion for bewilderment over the incident.'[36]

What is most striking about the Blumer fantasies is how physical many of them were. They are a testament to Valentino's magnetic star quality but also to the power of moving pictures in these very earliest days of cinema. Most female film fans had never seen or experienced anything like the passionate scenes of love depicted in *The Sheik* in real life, let alone up close and personal on a larger-than-life movie screen. It would be easy to underestimate, today, how it must have felt to sit in the darkness of a movie theatre and experience something so intimate and dramatic for the first time.

'After seeing *The Sheik*, I was in a daze for a week,' recalled a high school senior. 'His passionate lovemaking stirred me as I was never stirred before,' wrote another. 'I recall coming home that night and dreaming the entire picture over again; myself as the heroine, being carried over the burning sands by an equally burning lover. I could feel myself being kissed the way the Sheik had kissed the girl.' One young woman described imagining, in detail, what Valentino actually felt like: 'I often wondered what it would be like to be in his arms. If he gave wet kisses or dry ones, if he smacked his lips or merely held them tightly.'

Nearly all the fantasies, unsurprisingly, involved being carried off by a tall, dark, handsome stranger, skilled in the art of passionate lovemaking. 'For a long time afterwards, I couldn't think of anything grander than being kidnapped by an Arab,' wrote a high school student. 'Valentino had no more ardent admirer than I,' wrote another. 'At the time of his advent upon the screen, the feeling of sex consciousness was just awakening in me and Valentino stimulated it to the fever point ... I often imagined myself to be the object of his amorous lovemaking.' Some younger girls even described recreating the movie at home: 'My friend and I enacted the especially romantic scenes out under her mother's rugs, which made excellent tents. She was Rudolph and I the beautiful captive and we followed as well as we could remember the actions of the actors.'[37]

It wasn't just the girls dipping their toes into the steamy world of desert role play. If Rudy was what the girls wanted, then Rudy is what they were going to get. 'I studied his style,' wrote a young man whose experience was representative of many others:

I realised that nature had done much less for me in the way of original equipment than she had for the gorgeous Rodolfo, but I felt that he had a certain technique that it would behoove me to emulate. I practised with little success. My nostrils refused to dilate – some muscular incompetency that I couldn't remedy. My eyes were incapable of shooting sparks of fiery passion that would render the fair sex helpless ... The young lady who was trial-horse for the attempt is still dubious about my mental stability. Worse yet, she made a report of the affair to her friends. The comments that came drifting back to me left no doubt in my mind about the futility of carrying on any longer.

Taken together, the girls' and boys' responses to Valentino reflected a world in which gender and power dynamics were shifting. Rudy, the mysterious stranger from a foreign land, was perfect precisely because he was impossible. But as women began to talk, think and fantasise – as they began to wonder what it might be like to have a sheik of their own – they started questioning what they could and should want from the husbands and boyfriends in their lives. In fantasy and in reality, too, what made a man attractive to a woman was changing. As a result, a more essential truth was sliding into focus.

'As it happens, woman is just as much a human being as man', wrote Adela Rogers St Johns, the so-called 'Mother Confessor of Hollywood' and *Photoplay*'s most trusted chronicler of stars, in her analysis of the Valentino craze:

Deny it she will, submerge and repress it too often she must, but it's there. The poetry of the senses has its call for her too ... When she sees a man whose lovemaking is afire and aflame with that touch of madness that is called passion, he attracts her more than any other man in the world ... The lure of Valentino is wholly, entirely, obviously the lure of the flesh.[38]

PINK POWDER PUFFS

When June Mathis gave Rudy his big break, she was part of a whole generation of female filmmakers who believed the world was ready for a new type of male movie star.

The industry had long celebrated sassy, independent heroines, but their clean-cut, respectable male co-stars were struggling to keep up. Swashbuckling and chivalry were all well and good, but from flappers to Freud, sex was pretty much the only thing anyone in 1920s America was thinking about (except maybe where to get a drink). It had become such a universal preoccupation that, as Scott Fitzgerald noted, even happily married young mothers were starting to look into having affairs – not because they had anyone in mind but because it seemed 'sort of undignified' not to have had one by the time you were thirty.[39]

'American women have demanded equality, and they deserve equality,' exclaimed actress-producer Clara Kimball Young in *Photoplay*.[40] For her, as for many of these female power players, equality started in bed. They were looking for a man who understood that women had needs and (no pressure, boys) sex was art. Rudy, and the new archetype he had just smouldered into existence – the Latin Lover – was it.

Shortly after the release of *The Sheik*, Hollywood's resident sex expert and self-titled 'Tiger Queen', Elinor Glyn (the woman who invented the 'it girl'), made it official. She proclaimed that Valentino was the only man in Hollywood who had 'it': 'that strange magnetism that attracts both sexes', the quality seen 'in tigers and cats – both animals being fascinating and mysterious and quite unbiddable'.[41]

Glyn was a 57-year-old romance novelist who knew a lot about 'it'. She'd come to Hollywood from England after her older woman/younger man erotic novel *Three Weeks* (which culminates in a steamy sex-on-tiger-skin-rug scene) became an international bestseller. The American man 'could simply not make love', she said.[42] These good-natured big-brother and boy-next-door types could never satisfy a woman, since they treated them like sisters and aunts. The Latin Lover was the epitome of the antidote. Sensuous, sensual and seemingly psychic in his ability to intuit exactly what any and every woman wanted, this magical creature could mesmerise her 'into becoming a heroine who acted on her desires'. Glyn's dream was that 'under his imaginative tutelage, American men and women might learn to ignite a woman's sensuality so that, together, they could experience erotic bliss'.

As every studio in Hollywood scrambled to discover and sign a Latin Lover of their own, the women of America stood ready. 'In Rudolph Valentino, a girl sees a different lover,' gushed one of his millions of most spellbound fans:

> One who understands her; one who is different in every way from the average American man. And to us – girls who earn our bread and butter in the offices of New York, where there is nothing of romance, nothing of beauty, nothing of art – it is enthralling when in the evening we go to see a picture which is full of these; and when we see this man, this extraordinary Italian, we forget about the escort at our side, who is, beside Valentino, so commonplace. For then we know that romance is not really dead.[43]

At first, Rudy threw himself into his role as America's Sex Educator in Chief. In a series of articles in *Photoplay* (most likely ghostwritten by Glyn), he shared his philosophy of love, blamed American men for the restlessness and sexual dissatisfaction of American women and explained that 'a woman can never have a happy love affair with a man unless he is her superior'. His sheik-inspired theory was that a woman should be intelligent enough to appreciate being dominated but not so intelligent that she couldn't be. But more important than who was or wasn't pretending to be dominant or submissive was what was at stake: 'I have been won always by the woman who has great ability to feel,' he wrote. 'A reluctant woman, yes. But reluctant only as a flower is reluctant to bloom in winter. Place it in the hot-house of proper wooing – and it blossoms.'[44]

His fans didn't need much wooing themselves. The fantasy worked both ways and they were delighted to play along: 'Girls will love a fellow if he shows a little bit of life,' said one. 'Book me down for Rudolph Valentino any time, and I'll bet anyone he's some caveman. If in real life his eyes are like on screen, well that's enough for anyone to hear,' admitted another. 'I don't like the nicey nicey man who says, "Please dear." I like a real man who won't be ordered around.'[45]

It would have been unthinkable, even just a few years earlier, for women to be discussing their romantic fantasies and taste in men so openly, but fan magazines like *Photoplay* and *Motion Picture* had become the place for women to come together and debate everything from careers to marriage to love and of course sex. These magazines were packed with articles about the ins and outs of marriage, spicy discussions about 'sexual liberalism' and mutual sexual satisfaction in relationships, with many stars themselves jumping into the debate.

Valentino's sudden rise to fame was the perfect excuse for deep and meaningful discussions about romance and passion, but it also brought some other, even more unspeakable ideas to the surface: not everyone was onboard with the idea of a Latin Lover. Through the early '20s, the letters to the editor pages read like the most heated and sometimes vitriolic depths of social media today. They are a snapshot of a divided country wrestling with the realities of cultural change:

Won't someone please explain why our American public has picked that foreigner, Valentino, as the greatest screen lover? I think he's perfectly sickening! My mother says 'There's a man who thinks a great deal of himself.'

Personally, I like Rudolph Valentino. I think he is a fine actor. Surely it is our privilege to choose as we wish ... We are speaking of actors and their acting and not of intermarriage with them.

As for criticisms against Rudolph Valentino! Every man who knows perfection in a woman's heart will admit that Rudolph has attained it ... I don't think the old ladies who dislike him have ever tasted real life themselves.

I do not think the European lover sly. He is far more courteous than many American men I have known. However, I will say nothing more against my own countrymen. For myself, I prefer a frank, honest, American – even if he is not so skilled in lovemaking. But I would also like a little of the charm of the European lover. Most women crave for the romantic, though many of them do not say so.[46]

It wouldn't be long before the men themselves weighed in. 'I hate Valentino!' began a now infamous prose poem from Dick Dorgan, *Photoplay*'s resident cartoonist and Valentino-hater:

All men hate Valentino. I hate his oriental optics; I hate his classic nose; I hate his Roman face; I hate his smile; I hate his glistening teeth; I hate his patent leather hair; I hate him because he's the great lover of the screen; I hate him because he's an embezzler of hearts ... Ever since he came galloping in with the *Four Horsemen*, he has been the cause of more home-cooked royal battles than they can print in the papers.[47]

The article, titled 'A Song of Hate', was accompanied by two illustrations. One, captioned 'As the women see him', showed a handsome, smiling Rudy in fashionable evening attire. The other, 'As the men see him', showed a racist caricature in a tribal earring, gnashing his teeth wildly. It was one of many vicious takedowns of the star that had begun to appear since *The Sheik* made him Hollywood's first, true, male sex symbol. These cartoons, articles and film parodies like *The Shriek of Araby* persistently and very personally mocked Rudy's foreignness, questioned his masculinity and used his status as an 'idol of women' against him.

To his detractors, Valentino represented two of America's greatest fears packed into one criminally built body that looked way too good in skintight matador pants. First, and most obviously, there was his foreignness. Valentino's female fans might have called him a 'Latin Lover', but to his white critics obsessed with racial purity, he was the epitome of the foreign seducer. His obsession with 'romance' and 'pleasing women' made him the perfect embodiment of the race mixing they feared – a threat that, in their eyes, was getting so out of control that the women of America were leading the country to 'race suicide'.[48]

And what was most troubling about this 'foreign menace' was that women were so actively choosing him. This was no passive seduction. These love-crazed women were pursuing and openly expressing their desire for this man. When critics portrayed Valentino as savage and foreign, and his female fans as wild with desire, they were really expressing their terror at a new kind of woman – one who could vote, earn her own money and, most frighteningly of all, choose her own objects of desire. A shockingly lurid cartoon in *Photoplay* captured the problem in all its X-rated salaciousness. A blonde flapper stares, entranced, at a movie screen where a dark-skinned, highly orientalised Valentino holds a swooning, semi-orgasmic Diana in his arms. Her date sulks beside her in disdain.

The caption below, 'The Nordic sneered while his women folk thrilled to see this jungle python of a lover,' is as hateful as it is revealing.[49] Critics' obsession with Valentino as an exotic sex object was inseparable from the second threat he embodied: the fact that he was a 'woman-made man'. This sissy, effeminate, female fantasy of a romantic hero had been dreamed up on the pages of romance novels but was now making his way, through love songs and movie screens, into the living rooms and workplaces of respectable, everyday America. The fear, as it had been in the tango halls of New York, was that American culture was now well on its way to becoming 'feminised'.

'If it is true that man once shaped woman to be the creature of his desires and needs,' wrote Lorine Pruette in *The Nation*, 'then it is true that woman is now remodelling man. If it is true that this was once a man-made world, then it is a certain fact that the world is now fast becoming woman-made.'[50] As women gained more power as voters and consumers, men seemed to be pandering, with increasing intensity, to female dreams, demands and tastes.

In Hollywood, most male romantic leads like 'Handsomest Man in the World' Francis X. Bushman, 'The Screen's Most Perfect

Lover' Wallace Reid and even Matinee Idol John Barrymore, who had successfully made the transition to screen, were generally able to insulate themselves from potential accusations of being too 'feminine' or 'woman-made' by starring in films with enough action sequences to keep male viewers happy and to prove their manliness. They were praised for their acting talent – one of a number of strategies Hollywood had for dealing with (and deflecting from) the uncomfortable heart of the matter. These were men whose careers depended on their looks. They were objects of an actively desiring female gaze.

As Valentino continued to put out Latin Lover romances, he had none of these luxuries. His appeal was uncomfortably and undeniably *of the body* – a body that existed, and had always existed, purely as a vessel for female imaginings and desires. From the female fans whose daydreams and dollars sustained him to his tango pirate past and close professional relationships with powerful women like Mathis and Glyn – he was as 'woman-made' as they come. This wasn't helped by his love of luxury and fashion or rumours about his unconventional personal life. His ever-present platinum 'slave bracelet', a gift from his bisexual second wife Natacha Rambova, said it all. When he published *Day Dreams*, a book of love poetry, then signed a sponsorship deal with Mineralava face cream, he may as well have handed his enemies a loaded gun.

'Mr Rudolph Valentino is one of the hundreds of men and women of the stage and screen who endorse Mineralava,' said a full-page, full-colour ad in *Photoplay*. 'He was introduced to it by the example of his wife.' He may have been wearing his costume from *The Four Horsemen*, he may even have been selling out dance tour tickets with the promise of re-enactments of its sizzling tango scene – but his rosy cheeks and pink cherry lips in the ad spoke volumes. In the eyes of his detractors, the sheik had been tamed by his woman.

Rudolph Valentino was a beautiful trailblazer who arrived in Hollywood a hundred years before his time. His love of fashion, his artistic bravery and his willingness to engage authentically and unashamedly with female fantasy would have been celebrated today. Off-screen, he was a complex dreamer who longed for recognition beyond his looks, but his existence had become completely enmeshed with the dangerous exoticism of the sheik – a role he now believed he'd been forced to play 'like a patsy'.[51]

He tried to distance himself from the part. He gave interviews explaining he'd been forced to play Ahmed 'like an emotional Italian' when he should have been 'stolid' like an Englishman or 'dignified' like a real Arab. He spoke out against racism: 'People are not savages because they have dark skin. The Arabian civilisation is one of the oldest in the world.'[52] None of it worked. To the public, he was Ahmed, and Hollywood needed its dark, dangerous sex object. Some historians have even argued that some of the media hate was manufactured and stirred up by studios to boost his exotic mystique.

By 1924, exhausted by constant attacks in the press, Valentino decided to smash *The Sheik* myth. It was time to rebrand himself as an 'artist'. But the world had fallen in love with a body, not a brain. The two films he produced that year with his wife Natacha were praised by critics for their technical artistry (the sets and costumes were nice) but infuriated fans.

Period piece *Monsieur Beaucaire* (set in the court of Louis XV and brutally parodied by comedian Stan Laurel as Rhubarb Vaselino in

Monsieur Don't Care) may have given audiences their first ever look at Rudy's ripped, naked torso, but it mainly had him flouncing about in more face powder, rouge and ruffles than a nineteenth-century gigolette. 'You're trying to be too artistic,' grumbled a fan. 'I don't want to see Rudy turned into a hothouse flower.'⁵³ Wannabe swashbuckler *A Sainted Devil* didn't fare much better. 'They should have called it "Scented Devil",' said a cinema owner, 'because people could smell it out in the street. Terrible ... Lost me money? It sure did.'⁵⁴

'Something has happened to the Valentino of *The Sheik*,' mourned *Photoplay*. 'Rudy is trying to be an actor at the expense of the personality that made him a sensation ... He doesn't look a bit dangerous.' His fans wanted him 'wicked'.⁵⁵ Under the influence of Natacha (now being characterised in the press as the original Yoko Ono: meddling, influencing and filling his head with delusions of artistry), wicked he certainly was not. His most adoring fans stood by him, but it wasn't enough. Within a year, he was broke, divorced and resigned to his fate. There was nothing left to do but double down on what the women of America wanted from him. He accepted $100,000 to reprise his iconic rape-hero role as Ahmed and, through the magic of cutting-edge 'split screen' visual effects, play his wayward son as well. The sheik returns, with interest.

The Son of the Sheik was a money play for both Rudy and his new studio United Artists, but it was also a very personal opportunity for him to repair his relationship with male audiences. Superficially, agreeing to appear sweating and shirtless in a ten-minute scene where you're being flogged by a gang of men who have just kidnapped you might not seem like the obvious way to combat accusations of effeminacy. But Rudy believed that he could use this film to correct all the criticisms that had been levelled at his performance in *The Sheik*.

Luckily, United Artists were thinking along similar lines. They

wanted to make sure the sequel attracted just as many men as
women this time. For help, they turned to a Machiavellian publicist
called Victor Mansfield Shapiro who was put in charge of a top-
secret project called 'How to Make Rudolph Valentino More Acceptable to the Men Customers'. After a brainstorming session that
yielded ideas from the mundane to the ridiculous – these included
sharing photos of Valentino sparring with boxer Jack Dempsey,
playing polo with Douglas Fairbanks or being interviewed shirtless by female journalists (tagline: Men, why be jealous of Rudy
Valentino? You too can make love like he does. See *Son of the Sheik*)
– Shapiro decided it was better to tackle the pink fluffy elephant
in the room head-on. His big idea was to publish an inflammatory
anti-Valentino think piece in a newspaper and not tell Valentino
it was fake. This would give him the chance to get authentically
angry and then – with the eyes of the world watching – defend his
masculinity in some kind of big, dramatic publicity stunt.[56]

On 18 July 1926, as Valentino sat down to breakfast at Chicago's Ambassador Hotel, Shapiro handed him the *Chicago Tribune*.
On page ten was an editorial with the big bold headline 'PINK
POWDER PUFFS'. The 'anonymous' author was up in arms after
finding a face powder vending machine in a men's public toilet. He
knew exactly who was to blame:

A powder vending machine! In a men's washroom. Homo Amer-
icanus! Why didn't someone quietly drown Rudolph Guglielmo,
alias Valentino, years ago ... Do women like the type of 'man' who
pats pink powder on his face in a public washroom and arranges
coiffure in a public elevator ... Hollywood is the national school
of masculinity. Rudy, the beautiful gardener's boy, is the prototype
of the American male. Hells bells. Oh sugar.

As Shapiro had hoped, Rudy saw red. Within hours, he'd already sent his response (kindly pre-ghostwritten by Shapiro) to the papers. He called for the anonymous author of the article to come forward and meet him for a duel:

> You slur my Italian ancestry; you cast ridicule upon my Italian name; you cast doubt on my masculinity. I call you … to meet me in the boxing or wrestling arena to prove, in typically masculine fashion (for I am an American citizen), which of us is more of a man … I want to make it absolutely plain and clear that this challenge is not for the purpose of publicity.

The publicity stunt worked perfectly. When the writer failed to come forward, Rudy threw himself into a whirlwind of boxing matches ('That guy throws a punch like a mule's kick,' said Frank 'Buck' O'Neil, who was thirty-three pounds heavier than him) and manly photo opportunities like flexing at the gym ('Here's brawn, girls and boys! Rudolph, the Sheik, demonstrating that a man can wear a slave bracelet and still be a Goliath').[57] Best of all, what Shapiro called the 'continuous pink powderpuff imbroglio' in the press was attracting a new kind of crowd to these events. These were 'sporting' audiences known for their 'literary, dramatic, social and artistic distinction'. As he would later boast to trade papers, the campaign was generating 'millions of lines of free space all over the world' – publicity that would have cost 'millions of dollars if purchased at regular advertising rates'.[58]

But the drama was taking its toll. Rudy – clearly deeply disturbed by the article – was burning the candle at both ends. His entourage reported that he was chain-smoking forty to fifty cigarettes a day, eating and drinking far more than usual and spending his weekends at 'pleasure island' (man-about-town Schuyler Parsons's Long Island party retreat). Before long, his health began to suffer. He dismissed the persistent abdominal pain as heartburn or stress, but on 15 August, after a particularly boozy night on the town with Ziegfeld Follies girl Marion Benda, he collapsed at his hotel and was rushed to Polyclinic Hospital.

For all Rudy's anxieties about being washed up, the circus that descended upon the hospital in the coming days was a reminder of just how much his public adored him. The hospital was so inundated with phone calls (thirty-two per minute at one point, mainly from women) that they were forced to set up a 'Valentino Information Centre' on the second floor. Stacks of Bibles were sent in, along with one copy of *Bedtime Stories for Grown-up Guys* from a young girl in Chicago. A cabaret dancer who claimed to have known him back in his tango days arrived with a monkey called Pepy to cheer him up. So did hundreds more fans armed with flowers, gifts and prayers. 'Fight Rudy fight!' said a telegram from Matinee Idol John Gilbert, 'Millions need you.'[59] Eventually, his manager was forced to hire a private detective to stand guard at the doors. One fan still managed to get through. When she was told she couldn't see him, she was said to have gotten 'hysterical' and begun reciting poetry. 'Oh my beloved, I hope you get well,' she sobbed as she was escorted out.

Another fan, a boy, explained that he just wanted to kneel quietly by the bed and pray. But as a crowd began to gather outside the hospital, it was hard to know whether the draw was concern or sensationalism. The *New York Graphic* published fake photos of Rudy naked on the operating table, and his vitals were published in daily newspaper updates as if they were baseball scores. As he lay in bed after emergency surgery, wracked with pain but determined not to show it, it was still the article that was hurting him most. He turned to his doctor: 'And now, do I act like a pink powder puff?' he asked.[60]

'No, sir,' said the doctor. 'You have been very brave. Braver than most.'[61]

Rudy rallied just enough to dictate a message to his fans, thanking them for their support and assuring them that he'd be back on his feet in no time. He asked for his flowers to be distributed to the other patients. A few days later, however, he took a turn for the worse and descended into a delirium, muttering something about being lost in the woods. 'Don't pull down the blinds!' he said. 'I want the sunlight to greet me!'[62]

He died on 23 August 1926. According to the *New York Times*, the only people with him were two anonymous nurses. It was a stark reminder of how far he had fallen. But death is the ultimate makeover. This sad, quiet, lonely end was the moment he finally found the acceptance he had always wanted. As the grief that would culminate in the riot at Campbell's swept the nation, the industry that had once held him at arm's length finally embraced him as one of their own. Everything that had been abject or threatening about his foreignness and 'effeminacy' while he was alive was now miraculously forgotten – or, when it was mentioned, it was only to say how deeply he had been misunderstood.

The *Los Angeles Times*, which had never quite known what to make of him, now praised him as a man of grit. Even in his final hours, in his struggle with the grim reaper, he displayed a spirit 'worthy of the highest admiration', it said.[63] *Times* columnist Harry Carr went even further. He credited Rudy with single-handedly breaking down generations of prejudice against Latin men in English-speaking countries. 'When I was a little boy, it would have been almost unthinkable to represent an Italian in popular melodrama as anything but the arch villain,' he wrote. 'Overnight, Rudolph Valentino made the Latin the lover of the world.' Crediting his 'ability as an actor, for which he [was] seldom given credit', Charlie Chaplin called his death 'one of the greatest tragedies in the history of the motion picture industry'.[64] On the day of his funeral, every studio in Hollywood stopped work, flew their flags at half-mast and held a five-minute silence. Things that scare us are much less threatening when they are dead.

There was one person, however, who did not forget the painful reality of Valentino's life or death. H. L. Mencken, one of America's most trusted and feared cultural critics, was as far from Hollywood as you could get. He was famously suspicious of 'popular culture' and anything that would be considered a 'fad' – so disconnected from the film world that he had never even seen a Valentino picture. A few weeks after Rudy's death, in an opinion piece for the *Baltimore Sun*, he told the story of how the two of them had met at the Algonquin Hotel, after the actor contacted him a few weeks earlier in the hope of getting some advice on how to deal with the powder puff situation. It was one of those sweltering summer nights in New York – so hot that Mencken recalled how the two of them sat in shirtsleeves, mopping their brows with napkins and tablecloths as they debated what to do.

Mencken explained that, based on everything he'd heard, he'd been surprised by Valentino in real life. He found a 'curiously naive and boyish young fellow' with a 'disarming air of inexperience' sitting and sweating before him. Rudy seemed desperate to clear his name regarding the controversy. But as their conversation went on, Mencken began to understand that it was something much bigger and more endemic that was tormenting him. What he saw that night was:

The agony of a man of relatively civilized feelings thrown into a situation of intolerable vulgarity, destructive alike to his peace and to his dignity ... Here was a young man who was living the daily dream of millions of other young men. Here was one who was catnip to women. Here was one who had wealth and fame, both made honorably and by his own effort. And here was one who was very unhappy.[65]

THIS SIDE OF PARADISE

For years, on the anniversary of Valentino's death, a mysterious lady in black would visit the Hollywood Forever Cemetery to place roses on his grave. There was a beautiful Gothic romance to the scene, as if Rudy had been the last of those old-world Romantic heroes – one more suited to the foggy mists of time where Byron really had been a vampire and it was the music of the devil that was unleashed every time Paganini picked up a violin. It was also a yearly reminder of just how inextricably linked the myth of Valentino was with public displays of affection from his female fans.

Over the years, several women would come forward to claim the title of Lady in Black. We will never know who she really was, but the theatricality of her performance played out like a movie in itself. This was how Rudy's stardom had always worked. It was a real-life tango between actor and audience; a performance that was both artificial and deeply genuine. In life, Rudolph Valentino was a good man who found himself caught in the crossfires of some of the most vitriolic and dehumanising culture wars of his day. In death, he became an icon of nostalgia, longing and lost love, like early cinema itself – a flickering dream of a time or a person who is at the same time always there but always gone.

Fifty years later, in *From Reverence to Rape*, her classic history of women in the movies, film critic Molly Haskell mourned the brief moment in early cinema when Hollywood dared to put pure, unbridled female fantasy centre stage. 'Where are the romantic idols who built their reputations on their appeal to women?' she asked. 'They would rather be "real people" than actors, and would rather be "real actors" than romantic leads.'[66] Never again, after Valentino, would an A-list Hollywood leading man offer himself so willingly and so completely to the female romantic imagination.

On the evening of 2 September 1926, as Rudy Vallée's 'There's a New Star in Heaven Tonight' – hastily written and recorded in just ten days to honour Valentino – crackled on gramophones up and down the country, the newspapers turned their attention to Valentino's female fans. What was it about women that made them lose their minds in this way? The scenes of unrestrained hysteria surrounding his death had been shocking. To some, it was a sign that modern woman wasn't modern at all. They saw Valentino as the great 'revealer of realities' who 'smashed forever the illusion that "emancipated" woman is beyond the reach of the age-old mystery that made Eden a paradise'.[67] Women might talk about wanting equality and partnership, claim they saw men as 'comrades rather than lovers' and assert they had become 'sensible and a trifle hard', but their obsession with Valentino had exposed their 'true nature'.[68]

'It is not pleasant to think of these love-starved women', scoffed the *Sunday Sun*, 'hiding their emotional demands, indulging in the cinema, temperamental cravings for which life has furnished them no wholesome outlet.'[69] A few months later, the debate was still going strong. In an opinion piece headlined 'Idol Worship and Modern Girl', the *Sunday Mirror* reflected on the moral of the story of Peggy Scott, or 'The Valentino Girl' as she was now known.

Peggy was one of the few Valentino suicides that was more than a rumour or urban legend. An inquest into her death in London had attracted quite a bit of press coverage, and a stack of letters found in her room had added to curiosity about her story. They appeared to be *from* Valentino.

According to friends, the pair had met in Biarritz in the early '20s and stayed in touch. The letters – read out in court and excerpted in newspapers under sensationalist headlines like 'Secret of Valentino's Last Romance' and 'Letters Found in Girl's Flat Bare Secret Love – Sheik Turned Deaf Ear to Actress' Plea to be Near Him' – read like a romantic melodrama worthy of Hollywood itself. She dreams of coming to Hollywood to join him. He tries, repeatedly, to dissuade her – not because he doesn't love her but mainly because she has no talent. 'I wonder if you realise how much I have suffered,' he writes. 'I thought there could be no greater happiness for a man than to be united with his soulmate but I soon found out that marriage and the artistic temperament do not harmonise.'[70]

Whether the letters were real or fake or written by Peggy herself, we will never know and, as the judge at the inquest put it, did it really matter? However you looked at it, Peggy was a victim of romantic obsession. Like the rioting crowds outside Campbell's, she was a woman driven to madness by her infatuation with a movie star. 'Her real life having proved a failure, she dreamed a romantic life,' said the article. 'She found her ideal man in a film star whom she had never met. She surrounded herself with photographs and dreamed her delightful dream: and she became in the end the victim of her own inventions.'[71]

The tragedy of the female movie fan destroyed by her own delusions and fantasies was a story that would already have been painfully familiar to newspaper and magazine readers of 1926. Through the 1910s and '20s, this Movie-Struck Girl had become a stock character in conversations about women's potentially harmful relationship with the cinema. Obsessed with the movies and often in love with some screen star or another, she dreamed of coming west to make it in Hollywood. Like the Novel-Reading Girl and the Matinee Girl before her, she was endlessly immortalised in fiction and discussed and debated in the press. She was, as the general manager of Universal Pictures put it, 'at the same time the biggest asset and the biggest annoyance of the motion picture industry'.[72]

Women had played a critical role in the evolution of the movies from the start. 'DON'T FORGET HER!' ran one of many headlines in trade magazines advising cinema owners on 'feminine' marketing strategy. 'You must never lose track of the fact that the majority of your business comes to you because Mrs or Miss So-and-So says to the other half of the party, "I would like to see a picture tonight."'[73] With, but very often without, 'the other half of the party', movie theatres had become important social centres for women by 1915 – a comfortable place to rest after an afternoon shopping or long day at work, a palace of inexpensive luxury to meet friends and (most importantly) a window into a glamorous world of adventure, romance and becoming. On the big screen, in silent flickering close-ups, the movies took everyday people and turned them into gods.

By the time Valentino rose to fame, audiences were ready for animal magnetism, but in the very earliest days of cinema, the fantasy was more often about identification with female stars. The first fan favourites were actresses like Florence Lawrence, Pearl White and Mary Pickford – young women who charmed audiences with their adventurous spirits and every-girl authenticity. The press soon began to report incidents of young female movie fans disturbing the peace and quiet of cinemas with their fervent desire to participate.

'I wish to express my thanks to a young lady who assisted me while I was attending the picture show the other evening,'[74] wrote one 'Uncle Ira' in a parody thank-you card in the *Kansas City Star* to a girl he called 'Miss Chewgum Openface'. 'Being seated directly behind me, she read aloud all the announcements as they were thrown on the screen and described all the scenes in a loud clear voice.' There were other reports of girls arguing loudly about the identities of the actors and actresses on screen or screaming, swooning and sobbing as appropriate during the films. This 'attention seeking' was put down to vanity and self-centredness – these girls wanted to be the actresses on screen.

They weren't completely wrong. Fans were enthralled by tales of these glamorous modern women. They seemed to have it all, and their relatability made stardom feel attainable. Actresses were inundated with letters from Movie-Struck Girls, as these excitable young women were now called, asking how they, too, could make it in motion pictures. 'Some days after I have looked over all my mail, I do have a heartache for you girls ... who write to me and tell me what you long to do,' wrote Pickford in her daily newspaper column. 'I wish I were some kind of fairy godmother ... and could reach out and bring that look of happiness to every heart-hungry girl, just with a little love tap of a magic wand.'[75]

There was, as Pickford lamented, no magic wand that could make those thousands of movie dreams come true. But – to the delight of advertisers, journalists and marketing people – all that unrestrainable longing and ambition could be converted into dollars. The Movie-Struck Girl was the ideal consumer. Fan magazines, which had initially targeted both men and women, soon ditched the articles on bodybuilding and razor blades. They doubled down on advising women how to shop, dress, do their make-up, walk and talk like a star. They gave practical advice on breaking into the industry as well as travel tips for visiting Hollywood. The fantasy of stardom – or so the industry was learning – was just as compelling and lucrative as anything they produced for the screen.

The part that no one had anticipated was that so many Movie-Struck Girls would actually pick up sticks and make the journey to Hollywood. From 1915 onwards, inspired by rags-to-riches stories of actresses like Pickford and roused to action by an endless stream of magazine features with titles like 'How They Got In' or 'My Adventures as a Motion Picture Heroine', thousands of young women jumped on trains, in cars and on boats with just a few dollars in their pockets and stars in their eyes. This was spurred on by the press. Competitions like *Photoplay*'s 'Brains and Beauty' pageant promised to transform their lucky winners into motion picture starlets overnight.

When asked to explain, in their personal statements for 'Brains and Beauty', what being an actress meant to them, it was clear that for most girls, the dream of stardom had less to do with vanity or conceit, as it did with an overwhelming desire for experience and self-realisation. 'To me it is a deep thirsty call, like a lion pacing in his narrow house,' explained one participant. 'There has always burned in my veins a yearning for adventure,' said another. 'I don't want to sit on my hands and watch the world go by.'[76] 'Actress' was one of the few jobs available to women that required no prior training or experience.

And so, the story of the Movie-Struck Girl and her journey to Hollywood became an allegory for the wider migration of young working women to urban centres across America in the first two decades of the twentieth century. The city offered a glamorous alternative to the drudgery of life as a housewife or schoolteacher back home. And of all the cities in America, Los Angeles, with its sunshine and movie glow, was romantic in a way that was unlike anywhere else on earth.

'Were you ever filled with the desire to go straight through the screen and just see what is beyond it?' whispered a young woman to her friend in a *Ladies' Home Journal* article titled 'Behind the Screen'. 'I mean did you never want to go through the screen, just as Alice went through the looking-glass? What we see is nothing but shadow. Don't you realise that somewhere all those interesting and exciting things are actually taking place?'[77]

The women who came to Hollywood came for many reasons – work opportunities extended far beyond becoming a movie star. Pink-collar jobs were made infinitely more interesting and glamorous by their proximity to the movies, behind-the-scenes roles allowed women to express themselves creatively and life in the 'movie colony' offered many more social freedoms as well. Hollywood was a hotbed of bohemian life that supported a whole range of lifestyle choices and modern ways for a girl to be.

'Women can – and do – what they like,' explained *Photoplay*. 'They work, play, love and draw their paychecks on exactly the same basis as men.'[78] 'Are you married?', 'No I live in Hollywood' was a much-repeated joke of the time.[79] Some women lived with other women. Others did marry but experimented with new, more progressive dynamics within the home. Actress Marjorie Rambeau told *Photoplay* that her husband had agreed to do whatever was best for *her* career. His most important jobs in life were supporting her creativity and being her muse.

The idea of legions of single girls, in irregular employment, jazzing it up night after night in the 'real wild bohemian cafes' of Tinseltown or entertaining at home where male guests always brought the 'good stuff to drink' was too much for many, more traditional observers to take.[80] As the number of young, unmarried women arriving in Hollywood each week surged, the fairy tale of the Movie-Struck Girl began to sour. There simply wasn't enough work for this endless stream of unskilled, untalented, unintelligent girls whose main objective in life was 'to be admired and flattered', said studio insiders.[81] Most of the girls who swarmed the backlots and offices each morning, hoping and praying for that elusive big break, were not of the worldly wise, able-to-look-after-herself bohemian type you saw in *Photoplay*. They were instead self-absorbed, gullible, small-town girls lured to Hollywood by 'false profits and fake advertisements': easy prey for men of ill omen, at risk of exploitation, pregnancy or worse.[82]

The horror stories flowed. The 'haggard and hungry' girl, so desperate for a place to live that she agreed to 'share lodgings' with an actor. 'I guess I know what that means,' she told a friend, 'but I'm tired of being hungry.'[83] The screen hopeful found wandering the streets 'stupefied by liquor' after being 'betrayed' by a famous film director. She was 'kept confined to an asylum for the better part of a week after the incident'.[84] And, of course, the birth of the infamous casting couch. Rumours of the girls who would gladly and willingly 'give their all' for a part in a film ('Well, after all, we're just using what nature gave us,' said one actress. 'What's the difference between using this or using a voice the way the opera singers do?') were just as troubling as the police investigation into accusations from others who provided sworn statements detailing the 'liberties' that studio managers and directors had taken with them.[85]

The film industry was in a tight spot. Already straining under pressure from reformers who believed that too much sex in movies was corrupting America's morals, they worried about the optics of this ever-worsening 'Girl Problem'. With thousands of young women running wild through the city, flexing their newfound social and sexual freedoms and/or exposing themselves to the whims and desires of unscrupulous men, Hollywood believed that the censorship brigade would be given even more ammunition for their ever-strengthening case.

These anxieties intensified when comedian Fatty Arbuckle was arrested for the rape and murder of movie extra girl turned actress Virginia Rappe. Although he was later acquitted, it was the biggest and baddest of a series of sex, drugs and murder scandals involving some of Hollywood's most beloved names that, reformers argued, lifted the lid on the 'real' Hollywood – not as wholesome or as girl-friendly as it seemed. The solution to the problem was clear. The Movie-Struck Girl had to be kept away from Hollywood (back home, in her cinema seat, where she belonged) because young women's pervasive presence in the city now posed a serious threat to the longevity of the film industry.

Will Hays, the newly appointed motion picture tsar, tasked with cleaning up Hollywood, cracked down on the girls and ramped up the scaremongering. 'It is explained to me how many a disillusioned girl reaches home by acting as chaperone to a corpse,' wrote *Photoplay* reporter Ruth Waterbury in an epic, four-part special feature called 'The Truth About Breaking into the Movies'. 'The dead are not supposed to travel alone. So when a body must be shipped from Hollywood, the railroad lets the Chamber of Commerce know and some girl gets a free ticket for performing this job. Adventure cannot end more abjectly than this. Don't go to Hollywood!'[86]

The enduring image of the Movie-Struck Girl and her tragic romance with Hollywood became one of a long line of girls, each indistinguishable from the next, passively waiting to be discovered outside the studio gates. Shut out of the industry that had seduced her with its promise of adventure and becoming, she was a victim of her own self-confidence and aspirations. If the story stuck, it was because it put her – and kept her – back in her place. It also fit perfectly with the iconography of noir that would come to define Hollywood of the '30s, '40s and beyond.

With the arrival of the Motion Picture Production Code in 1930, the censors finally got their way. The free-spirited, sexually liberated world of equality and experimentation that had made Rudolph Valentino's stardom possible was soon replaced by a shadowy underworld of hard-boiled detectives, fallen angels and femmes fatales, where men solved mysteries and women were mysteries to be solved.

But before that era ended, there was one final act. And because this is Hollywood, there's a twist. On that rainy morning in New York in 1926, when tens of thousands of mourners began to gather outside Campbell's Funeral Home to say their final goodbyes to Rudy himself, another long line of female movie fans was distorted into myth. The press reported a 'terrifying, unruly mob screaming and rioting', but take a closer look at the newsreel footage.[87] There are just as many men as women in the crowd, and the atmosphere is more like a movie premiere than a funeral.

The outpouring of grief that followed Rudy's death was very real. Women did indeed swoon and faint before his coffin – one was so overcome she had to be helped away after falling three times, returning, each time for one last look. But his lying in state was just as much an opportunity for movie fans and curious onlookers alike to come together and take part in an unprecedented public 'movie event' as it was about paying their respects. The rare chance to see a movie star in real life (even if he was dead) was a big deal in 1926. Some women, clutching bunches of flowers, admitted, to the *New York Times*, that they'd brought them to make sure they 'got in'. Another paper spotted a crying girl accidentally drop an onion from her sleeve. They also noticed how quickly tears seemed to dry up and be replaced with smiles when girls were approached by photographers and asked to pose for the papers.

Superficially, the riot that broke out later that day confirmed every one of critics' worst fears about the dangerous influence of movies on the weak, impressionable minds of female movie fans, but even this was a carefully orchestrated performance. The funeral director, as it turns out, had made a deal with United Artists to gather a newsworthy crowd that would make Valentino's pictures 'more profitable and more popular than ever'.[88] They agreed to lock the doors to the chapel for twenty minutes every hour to make sure 'the crowds were kept at mob size and agitated'. The ensuing chaos was win-win for everyone. Campbell's got its name in the papers for days, *The Son of the Sheik* was a smash hit and film censors were happy too. The hysterical headlines were even more tangible evidence that both fans and movies were a threat. The only ones who didn't win were the girls.

Like the story of the Movie-Struck Girl, the image of the hysterical, love-crazed Valentino fan obscured the immense contribution that thousands of women back at home and behind those mythical studio gates made to early cinema, why they came to Hollywood and the profound impact that the female imagination had on shaping modern American life, first glimpsed, by many, in the mysterious shadow play of a flickering movie screen. A trip to the movies can be pure escapism – seductive and fantastical – a welcome break from, in Peggy's words, 'the loneliness and shabbiness' of real life.[89] But sometimes, somewhere in the fantasy, you see a vision of how real life could be.

Kissing the War Goodbye, Lt Victor Jorgensen (1945)

Source: Wikimedia Commons

4

ROMANCE, NEW YORK CITY, 1944
IT'S ALWAYS YOU

Nostalgia – it's delicate, but potent. Teddy told me that in Greek nostalgia literally means 'the pain from an old wound'. It's a twinge in your heart far more powerful than memory alone. This device isn't a spaceship, it's a time machine. It goes backwards, and forwards ... It takes us to a place where we ache to go again ... It lets us travel the way a child travels – around and around, and back home again, to a place where we know we are loved.

– DON DRAPER (1960)

Summer had come out for an encore. The thunderstorms had lifted and New York City was, once again, blanketed in a sweltering haze of blue skies and serenity. This was a day for shirt sleeves and sundresses, wide-brim hats, ice-cream carts and the crisp bite of cold seltzer. In the park and down by the ocean, couples strolled, children played and laughter drifted with the softness and lightness of a dream. There had been thousands of late summer days like this one – the type that lulls you into forgetting that anything, outside of sunshine and contentment, really exists. But there was something different in the stillness of the air that day. A note of melancholy. Could – or would – this peace and happiness remain?

This was 31 August 1939. As summer teetered on the brink of autumn, Hitler's army was gathering at the border of Poland. That morning, he'd issued an ultimatum: a long list of demands designed to strip Poland of its sovereignty. The Nazis' terms were clear: cede territories and allow German control or face invasion. The world watched, listened and held its breath.

In a dimly lit studio on 57th Street, Frank Sinatra cleared his throat and pulled the microphone closer. The aptly titled song he was recording that day was 'All or Nothing at All' – an achingly tender yet haunting love song of the kind that, even at this early stage in his career, he was becoming synonymous with. It's a song about a man who knows what he wants, what love is and – even in the face of looming uncertainty – is gonna put his all into going for it. Don't let the smooth delivery deceive you. This is a request for unconditional surrender.

Frank was twenty-three that summer but looked younger. At 5ft 7.5in., his slight figure and baby-blue eyes gave him a boyishness and frailty that was as disarming as it was strangely attractive, especially to women. A year earlier, he'd been arrested on a charge of seduction (sleeping with a woman under the false promise of marriage).

The now iconic mugshot, date stamped 11.27.38, tells us everything we need to know. Those eyes, framed by that trademark curl in the middle of his forehead, have this beautiful, almost wounded innocence. But there's a flicker of snark in the corner of his mouth – it's nearly imperceptible but it's definitely there: pure, base, New Jersey gangster. It's hard to say whether you want to sleep with him or mother him. Armies of psychologists would later theorise that it was, of course, a little bit of both.

Frank's girlfriend Nancy was crushed when local newspapers picked up the seduction story: 'Songbird Held in Morals Charge' screamed one headline.[1] His mother (a formidable woman) wasn't happy either. There was a lot of 'screaming and hollering' in the Sinatra household that Christmas, but the allegations were eventually dropped.[2] It turned out his accuser, ex-girlfriend Toni Della Penta, was technically already married. But listening to the achingly raw vulnerability of Frank's plea in 'All or Nothing at All', you get it. The thing about Frank was that – even despite your better judgement – he made you want to believe.

Twenty-four hours after the recording session for 'All or Nothing at All' wrapped, news reached American shores that Germany had invaded Poland. Shots had been fired. The world was at war. Over the course of the next five years, 10 million American men aged between eighteen and forty-five would be conscripted into the armed forces.

Frank, classified unfit for service on account of a ruptured eardrum sustained at birth, would be forced to stay home. But his voice would become the soundtrack to the war years for many. Big band ballads like 'I'll Be Seeing You' and 'Saturday Night (Is the Loneliest Night in the Week)' so beautifully and so soothingly captured the bittersweet mood of the time that Winston Churchill himself would eventually thank Sinatra for his contribution to the war effort. 'Young man,' he said, 'you belong to my people as well as your own. For yours was the voice that sang them to sleep during that infamous summer of 1940.'[3]

For homesick soldiers, dreaming of the lives and loves they left behind, every song on the radio was a comfort – a reminder of the everyday warmth of happy, ordinary days. But for many of the young women left back at home, lying awake, alone, in their beds at night with only the radio for company, *that* voice would be more than a comfort. It would be a revelation.

LUCK BE A LADY

Bob Weitman, the booking manager for the Paramount Theatre in Times Square, was not thrilled – at all – about the idea of having to drag himself all the way out to New Jersey to see some singer he'd never heard of, but Frank Sinatra's agent had been harassing him for days. 'It's the darndest thing you ever saw,' he kept saying. 'A skinny kid who looks strictly from hunger is singing over in Newark, and the she-kids are yelling and fainting all over the joint. You've gotta see it to believe it!'[4]

His curiosity was piqued. This was the height of the big band era. Swing music reigned supreme, and it was bandleaders like Glenn Miller, Benny Goodman and Tommy Dorsey who were known for sending the kids into paroxysms of ecstatic enjoyment – swing idols they called them. Dance madness had struck again. But this skinny kid, Sinatra, was a solo performer of love ballads. Not exactly a dance-floor filler.

Sinatra had begun his career singing with big band orchestras – he was a rising star, for sure. But a few months earlier (with a little help from his friends, the mob – or so the story goes), he'd controversially broken his contract with the legendary Tommy Dorsey. He believed that he could do better alone.

This was a risky move. The war had certainly ignited a trend for sentimental romance in music, and some of the highest paid performers in the business were vocalists, but they were a rarity. It was big band orchestras led by swing idols like Goodman and Dorsey who were guaranteed radio time, record sales and to sell out shows. For a singer to be successful, they really needed to team up with a band, not to leave one. Especially not one of the hottest bands in the country, as Dorsey's was.

Ten years earlier, maybe things would have been different. Crooners like Rudy Vallée, Russ Columbo and Bing Crosby had dominated the airwaves with the sound of their soft, sweet love tunes. But times were changing. Swing was king and even Crosby, the only crooner to have successfully made the transition, had evolved. With a string of hit records and Hollywood movies behind him and the release of 'White Christmas' earlier that year, 'America's Crooner' had cemented his reputation as the undisputed musical king of the nation's apple-pie eating, white picket fence-painting, fun-for-all-the-family hearts. He was so big there was hardly room for anyone else.

Frank adored Bing, but he disagreed. He was ambitious. He knew he was talented. And he had seen the girls – how could you miss them – there were more and more of them every time. There were the girls who would stop dancing – midstep – and be drawn, as if by some supernatural force, towards the bandstand every time he started to sing. There were the girls who had begun to gather outside his dressing room before, and especially after, performances. The girls who stopped and stared – sometimes even tried to follow him – or tucked perfume-scented love letters into the pockets of his overcoat in the street. And, of course, there were the girls in the front-row seats. They would press their hands to their hearts and sigh and whisper and giggle to their friends pretty much whenever he was on stage these days. And they were getting bolder. They'd started to shout, to scream and to make a whole lot of other sounds that he'd only ever heard in one other place.

Some musicians had started to complain that fans, on the whole, seemed to have become louder and more abrasive lately. Swing concerts were so filled with whoops and shouts from young men intent on joining in with performances that even 'King of Swing' Benny Goodman had taken to shouting at them to 'shut up!'[5]

It got so bad at Boston Symphony Hall once that critic George Frazier described how 3,000 fans had 'behaved so bastardly that some magnificent jazz was completely drowned out'. And in 1939, the usually cool Artie Shaw had snapped. He called his fans 'morons', before quitting at the height of his fame to get away from the 'hundreds and thousands of crazy people pushing and shoving and crowding and milling around in mobs, shrieking for your autograph, or your picture or something – or just plain shrieking for no reason'.[6] But when it came to the girls, Frank didn't mind one bit. In fact, he knew exactly what he needed to do to push them right over the edge, every time.

He'd never forgotten that night back in high school, when, singing at the school dance – out of nervousness – his voice had gotten stuck as he tried to hold a note for longer than he should have. He'd winced, bashfully lowering his eyes to the ground. When he looked back up, nearly every girl in the audience was gazing up at him longingly, as if she wanted to rush right up onto the stage, fold him into her arms and tell him that everything was going to be OK.

He'd learned a lesson that day. This help-me thing was an asset. And he knew exactly how they liked it now. 'Bambi with sex appeal' someone called it once.[7] One by one, he would look those girls straight in the eyes and take himself to the place where every line he was singing – every '*I thought my heart would break*', every '*in my frightened arms*', every '*I'm too romantic … don't make me fall unless it can all come true*' – really was true. And then he would stretch those notes right up to the edge of breaking point and watch as every one of those girls sighed and crumpled and melted and swooned. The girls were the canaries in the coal mine, he thought – every swoon was a sign that something big was on its way.

Unfortunately, when Weitman arrived in Newark to see what all the fuss was about, the place was half empty. In truth, he'd only agreed to come out that night because another band (one he had heard of) was playing too.

When Sinatra walked out – shoulders slumped, hazy-eyed and wearing this ridiculously floppy, almost comically oversized bow tie – he feared his worst suspicions were about to be confirmed. He seemed much younger than he'd even pictured him: 'Not much older than the kids in their seats,' he said. 'He looked like he still had milk on his chin.' Not a venue-filler, for sure. But as soon as that skinny kid in the floppy bow tie opened his mouth and started to sing, the girls, who – come to think of it now – made up most of the audience, completely and utterly lost their minds (as loudly and as masterfully as if they had known how much depended on it). 'They stood up and yelled and moaned and carried on until I thought – excuse the expression – that his pants had fallen down.'[8]

Two weeks later, on New Year's Eve 1942, Frank Sinatra arrived at the Paramount for his first solo show at the hottest music and movie venue in town. He was opening for Benny Goodman and although his name was right at the bottom of the poster under the title 'EXTRA ADDED ATTRACTION', there it was. Time Square, baby. This would be the litmus test of his decision to go solo. Was he worried? Yes. Did he show it? Well, he tried his best not to. Much later, as an old man, he admitted that he'd been 'scared stiff' by the magnitude of the occasion.[9]

Bambi needn't have worried, of course. With the help of the radio, his voice had preceded him. And it was the girls – ever the early adopters of cultural icons and trends – who had spotted its monumental greatness first. Comedian Jack Benny, who was emceeing that night, had barely finished announcing his name when a thundering wave of applause and screams erupted across the audience. 'Frankie!', 'FRANKIEEE!!!', 'I love you, Frankie!' Benny said it was like nothing he'd ever heard in his life: all of a sudden those 5,000 little voices got louder and louder and then merged into one: 'F-R-A-N-K-I-E-E-E-E-E-E!!!!!!!!!' The power and weight of the sound was as physical, and as terrifying, as an earthquake. 'I thought the goddamn building was gonna cave in.'[10]

For the next hour, the Paramount was a riotous symphony of girlish idolatry and love: girls running down to the stage, girls swooning in the aisles, girls screaming, girls crying, girls shouting for more. At one point, the balcony was shaking so hard it began to sway. Benny Goodman, who was conducting the orchestra, had his back to the crowd. 'What the fuck is that!?'[11] The American teenager had arrived, and she wanted Frankie. All of him.

Frank Sinatra's first solo show at the Paramount would go down in history as a watershed moment in the evolution of pop culture. Like the Beatles' first appearance on *The Ed Sullivan Show* or the night that Dylan went electric, it redefined pop music, stardom and the relationship between celebrities and fans.

'Like Byron, Frank Sinatra awoke one morning to find himself famous,' explained *Newsweek* a year later:

The son of a Hoboken New Jersey fireman decided to become a singer after seeing a Bing Crosby movie. He took no voice lessons then, nor has he since, believing that the words are the real essence of a popular song. 'I pick my songs for the lyrics,' he explained last summer. 'The music is only a backdrop' ... It was at this point that the word *swoon* re-entered the nation's vocabulary.[12]

From here on in, big band orchestras would be on their way out. Individual singers would be on their way in. And a performer's ability to forge an intimate personal and emotional connection with audiences would become a lynchpin of pop music stardom and success for decades to come. So would the visible and audible presence of young, adoring female fans. If Byron's fame had been founded upon the emotional authenticity of his writing, Sinatra's was rooted in his ability to step into the lyrics of a song and completely and utterly inhabit them. He brought romance to life. And thanks to the girls, these performances would, very often, be a two-way conversation.

'Of course he was smiling at ME,' wrote fifteen-year-old Peggy McShane, who was proud to have been there at some of Sinatra's earliest shows:

Listen, I know when a person smiles at me and when they don't. The songs were 'I Walk Alone'. *Puhleeeeeese, walk aloooooone* ('Don't worry, I will Frankie,' we screamed). *Till you're walking beside meeeeee, puhleeeese walk aloooooone.* Everyone assured him that he needn't worry, and we went onto the next number, 'Come Out, Wherever You Are'. *Where are you deeeeeear?* ('Here I am, Fuurraaankie,' waved every hand in the place).[13]

After years of sitting quietly and dutifully on the sidelines, the teenage girls of America were loved up and ready to make their presence and their feelings known.

The initial engagement at the Paramount was scheduled for two weeks, but sensing something big was happening, Weitman extended it to a month. Then two. This was a record for the Paramount.

Each morning, by the time the doors opened at 9 a.m., the ticket line, filled with schoolgirls in little white bobby socks and saddle shoes, oversized sweaters, hair ribbons and bow ties in every colour of the rainbow, would stretch all the way down the street and around the corner on Broadway. The press nicknamed them bobbysoxers. The moniker was literal (bobby socks were all the rage with schoolgirls in 1943), but it also became a shorthand for the unabashed girlishness of the phenomenon. This wasn't the sultry, guilt-ridden womanly fantasy of a Valentino picture. It was first love: optimistic and innocent, open-hearted and uninhibited.

Inside, the ecstatic scenes of that first New Year's Eve repeated themselves with exactly the same intensity and fervour – the screaming, swooning, shouting and fainting were, by now, so commonplace that both the Paramount management and Frankie's brand-new hastily assembled publicity team were factoring them into their planning sessions. The extra guards who were hired to attempt to control the crowd were issued with bottles of ammonia 'in case a patron feels like swooning' and outside the theatre, at all hours, an ambulance stood ready and waiting to transport the most severe cases of 'Sinatrauma' to hospital.[14]

According to the press, the girls swooned for all kinds of reasons, but it was particularly romantic song lyrics that seemed to have the most profound and dizzying effect. 'They would scream every time he sang a word like love,' said Frankie's guitarist Al Viola. 'I used to think, "Oh, here it comes."'[15] Sometimes the response would be deafening. At others, a hush would descend upon the crowd, as mystical and as sacred as if they had been in church. In those pure, deep, silent moments, girls would fall to their knees in wonder, in reverence, in tears. In the soft glow of that baby spotlight, there was something saintly about him, some mysterious secret in the air, in the space between the words and the body – a truth, like a prayer, that would remain unspoken yet deeply and profoundly understood by him and each one of them.

And whatever that magical secret was, it was great for business. Frankie's publicist George Evans branded him Frank Swoonatra and announced that more than 1,000 Frank Sinatra fan clubs with names like the Moonlit Sinatra Club, the Slaves of Sinatra, the Flatbush Girls Who Would Lay Down Their Lives for Frank Sinatra and the Frank Sinatra Mahjong Club were now springing up across the country. When the press seemed sceptical, Evans distributed highlighted copies of *Frank Fare*, the newsletter from the Sighing Society of Sinatra Swooners (a fan club in Newark, New Jersey): 'Cynical singers and orchestra leaders sneered at him at first, but we in the deepest of our hearts knew that our Frankie was straight and true and that some day he would be known and loved all over the world.'[16]

Back at the Paramount, Bob Weitman was learning, to his frustration, that too much love can actually be quite a bad thing. Frankie was packing the place out on a daily basis – he'd never seen anything like this in his life – but there was a logistical issue. Once the girls got inside, they were refusing to leave.

The Paramount was technically still an old-school movie theatre in those days. This meant the musical entertainment came on between the film screenings, but you could buy one ticket and stay for as many rotations as you liked. With Sinatra on the bill, girls came first thing in the morning and stayed all day long. This left hundreds, sometimes even thousands, of unhappy, potentially paying customers waiting outside. And those who did get in were so concerned about the idea that they might lose their seats in between performances that many refused to budge, even to take the shortest of bathroom breaks. 'That Sinatra really hit those kids in the kidneys,' reported a disgruntled usher. 'At the end of the day, there was more urine on the seats and carpets than in the toilets.'[17]

For the sake of both their bottom line and their carpets, management tried all kinds of strategies to coax the girls out of their seats. They created a new rule that lunch boxes had to be checked in at the lobby; the girls snuck food in their pockets or simply refused to eat. They tried showing films that were as boring as possible; the girls weren't there for the movies – they talked through anything and everything that wasn't Frank, so they hardly even noticed. Briefly, staff tried removing the ones who had been there too long by brute force. This was a mistake. They kicked and screamed and fought back until it was safer to give up.

This dogged determination to get as close to Frankie as possible, and to stay there, continued to cause chaos up and down the country as he graduated from his freshman tenure at the Paramount and stepped into his new role as the most adored and obsessed-over singer in the whole history of American song. 'Not since Rudolph Valentino has American womanhood made such unabashed public love to an entertainer,' said the *New York Times*.[18]

On Broadway, the windows to his dressing room had to be blocked out because the mere sight of him was causing traffic jams up and down the street. When he arrived in Chicago for a radio engagement, the windows of his train were smashed – and a priest was trampled – as the thousands of bobbysoxers who'd been waiting lovingly at the station stampeded to greet him. The younger ones showered him with whimsical love tokens: teddy bears, a loving cup, a key said to unlock a heart that he already possessed. The older ones threw their underwear, pulled down their sweaters and demanded that he autograph their bras. Girls would bribe hotel maids to let them sneak into his room while he was out. They would lie between his sheets, smoke his cigarette stubs and sometimes (if they were lucky) even get to sample his soggy breakfast cereal. When it snowed, girls fought over his footprints. The winners took them home and stored them in refrigerators. One girl wore a bandage on her arm for three weeks where 'Frankie touched me'.

Outside his family home in New Jersey, they set up a base camp. They would hide behind the bushes, try to steal his undershorts from the washing line and write love notes, in lipstick, on his garage door. When they were feeling brave, they would tiptoe up the driveway and peer in through the windows. 'I'd look out my bedroom window and there would be somebody's face,' said his wife Nancy. 'They'd sit out there on the lawn for hours. We tried asking them to go home, but they wouldn't leave ... Finally, I'd feel so sorry for them I'd send out doughnuts and something for them to drink.'[19]

'Sinatra's fans express their love in odd ways,' said E. J. Kahn of the *New Yorker*, who became so fascinated by the phenomenon that he published the first ever biography of Frankie (slightly prematurely) in 1947.

They sign letters 'Frankly Yours' or 'Sinatrally Yours' and they begin postscripts not with P.S. but F.S. They try, as nearly as is feasible for young women, to dress as he does. Once, after he had absentmindedly appeared in public with the sleeves of his suit coat rolled up, thousands of other coat sleeves were tortured out of shape.[20]

They pinned fan club buttons over their hearts and on their socks and sewed his name into sweaters and coats. One girl painstakingly inked the titles of 200 Sinatra songs onto the back of her jacket. Another tied her pigtails up with ribbons. One was labelled 'Frankie', the other 'Sinatra'.

This was a new type of fandom – a playful, expressive celebration of love that needed to be externalised. In decades and centuries gone by, romantic feelings for celebrities were primarily personal. They existed in the universe of daydreams and diaries, coming to life on the pages of magazines and fan letters. With the help of the bobbysoxers, it was becoming something more public and communal now. 'Forty years later, it might have been called "sisterhood",' reflected bobbysoxer Janice as a grown woman.

> The 'Sinatra thing' that girls shared was special; it didn't involve their mothers, brothers, or neighbours. This was an emotion shared only with their peers. They understood each other because they could express their feelings about Sinatra to each other. They wanted to assert their individuality while at the same time they longed to be part of a group.[21]

Janice lived in Philadelphia. When Sinatra came to play a USO (United Service Organizations) benefit at the Philadelphia Academy of Music, she wrote him a fan letter expressing her disappointment that she couldn't attend. On the day of the concert, she got a phone call from his press agent, George Evans, offering her two tickets for the show. 'Mr Sinatra received a lot of letters today, but he liked yours the best and wants you to hear the concert,' he said. Following Mr Evans's instructions, Janice and her best friend arrived at the side entrance of the Academy of Music promptly at 8:15 p.m. She announced her name, and the guard nodded. 'You're the one, follow me.'

For Janice, this experience reflected Sinatra's lifelong appreciation for the bobbysoxers. 'He never patronised them,' she recalled. 'He never found them a nuisance and always appreciated that their adulation was the key that opened the eyes of the rest of the world to his unique talent.' It also speaks to Sinatra's unique ability to make every one of his fans feel seen, even if she was one of thousands. Not every bobbysoxer got a personal phone call from George Evans, but when Frank Sinatra was on stage – or even just a voice on the radio – every girl got the feeling that she was The One.

SLAVES OF THE SULTAN OF SWOON

When Sinatramania first hit, journalists were quick to assert that it was only 'plain lonely girls from lower middle-class homes' and 'children of the poor' who were afflicted.[22]

In the years leading up to the war, with the hardships of the Depression forcing the country into survival mode, America had retreated to the safety of conservative family values more reminiscent of the Victorian era than the wild freedom of the Jazz Age. Gone were the riotous days of the 1920s when a young woman could drink, smoke, chase the men she wanted and still get every one of the wild and hot happy endings she could ever dream of. Through the Depression, with so many men out of work, struggling to provide for their families, the country had seen the return of more traditional gender roles.

Faced with the awkward spectacle of tens of thousands of young women wetting their knickers, screaming and moaning in the street and forming human ladders to lay lipstick kisses on posters of a young man's face, it was easier to dismiss the phenomenon as lower class. 'They are dazzled by the life Sinatra leads and wish that they could share in it,' wrote E. J. Kahn.[23]

This story was increasingly hard to believe. Sinatra's appeal wasn't limited to teenage girls: it cut across age, gender and class. At the upscale Riobamba Club, his next engagement after the Paramount, he effortlessly enchanted the wealthiest and most glamorous of New York's society elites. 'Those dames come in night after night,' said a waiter. 'When this guy sings, they actually swoon: we've got to bring them water to keep them conscious. It's plain wacky.'[24]

By the time a riot broke out outside the Paramount on Columbus Day in 1944 – echoing the chaos of the Valentino funeral – the ubiquity and scale of Sinatramania was irrefutable. The press looked on in wonder and bemusement. What was it about Sinatra that made grown women swoon and young girls descend into violence?

The theories came thick and fast: 'mass hypnotism', 'wartime loneliness', 'increased sensitivity due to mammary hyperesthesia'. Many psychologists, obsessed and bewildered by the way this 'skinny, practically voiceless kid with jug-handle ears and a golf-ball Adam's apple' seemed to be causing young girls to erupt in 'spasmodic imitations of sex convulsions', theorised that with all the boys away fighting, girls were making 'Frankie an image of their innermost desires'. And if not that, then perhaps his hollow cheeks and thin frame were triggering 'the womanly desire to feed the hungry'.[25]

'What yo-yos,' said bobbysoxer Martha Weinman Lear. 'Whatever stirred beneath our barely budding breasts, it wasn't motherly ... The thing we had going with Frankie was *sexy*. It was exciting. It was terrific.'[26] The adult world may have preferred to see the bobbysoxers as confused or deranged children, but Sinatra's rise to fame coincided with the birth of the teenager. Historians often cite the Columbus Day Riot in 1944, along with the launch of *Seventeen* magazine a month earlier, as its ignition point. This was the year that the word 'teenager' entered the popular vocabulary.

For centuries, people aged between thirteen and nineteen had been considered either children or adults. Now, they were beginning to be recognised as a distinct social group – one with its own unique tastes, behaviours and an increasing amount of cultural clout. It was teenage girls who were at the epicentre of this. As the fastest-growing consumer group in America, they were beginning to influence everything, from music to fashion to how one of their favourite subjects – romance – was imagined and sold.

As the world's first teen idol, Frankie was a new type of romantic hero – one whose tenderness and emotional sincerity spoke both to and for the complexities of teenage life. 'In everything he says and does, he aligns himself with the youngsters and against the adult world. It is always "we" and never "you",' said Bruce Bliven of the *New Republic*.[27] 'He is one of the greatest things that ever happened to teenage America,' explained one girl.

> We were the kids that never got much attention, but he's made us feel like we're something. He has given us understanding. Something we feel like most adults think we don't need any consideration for. We're really human and Frank realises that. He gives us sincerity in return for our faithfulness.[28]

His love songs gave voice to hopes, dreams and feelings that had, until then, felt impossible or out of reach.

The bobbysoxers lived in a world that was obsessed with love and romance but filled with heart-wrenching contradictions. Their mission in life, they were told, was to find a husband and become perfect wives and mothers. But the hardships of the Depression, followed by the upheaval of war, meant the boys they were supposed to be marrying weren't in a financial or even geographical position to settle down as early as they used to. This left teenage love and romance in a kind of limbo.

Teen culture – this new space that had opened up between childhood and adulthood – promised a brief window of freedom before it was time to settle down. But the price of that freedom was a snakes and ladders board of pressures and rules. Girls were now suddenly encouraged to date lots of boys at the same time, casually. The idea was that, if there were lots of them, you wouldn't fall in love with any one in particular.

Love was dangerous because it would probably lead to sex, which would destroy your reputation. And it was a slippery slope. Anything physical – even just kissing – could be the gateway drug. As Emily Post explained in an article called 'When Young Women Are Not Particular': 'Continuous pursuit of thrill and consequent craving for greater and greater excitement gradually produces the same result as that which a drug produces in an addict.' Even things like 'petting [mid-century teenager speak for second and third base, born at the petting parties of the '20s] and cuddling' might 'have the same cheapening effect as that produced on merchandise which has through constant handling become faded and rumpled ... and thrown out on the bargain counter'.[29]

To complicate matters, boys had their own separate set of rules.

They were being warned off love too, but for different reasons: 'No matter how infatuated you may be with an angel ... don't enter into that sad state of suspended animation known as "going steady",' explained an etiquette book for young men. 'Doing so cramps your style. Variety is the spice of life ... It sharpens your wits, teaches you how to get along well in spite of difficulties. Date many different girls, gaining experience ... You'll need that practical experience all through life.'[30] The result was an elaborate dance where boys were always pushing for 'experience', and girls – in quest of popularity – had to seem interested but not too interested, available but not too available, and more than anything had to protect their hearts (which were the keys to their pants).

Even Hollywood (still the nation's capital of love, lust and romantic fantasy) bombarded girls with warnings about the perils of fixating, romantically, on one boy in particular. *Gone With the Wind*, the most loved and romantic film of its era, is best remembered as the epic love story of Scarlett O'Hara and Rhett Butler (he definitely has a lot of 'experience'), but Scarlett spends most of the film pining after sappy, effeminate Ashley Wilkes, who's married to someone else. By the time she realises the error of her ways and the tragedy it's caused, it's too late. She's destroyed her reputation and her chance of happiness with the one man who was actually right for her. And to really bring the point home that it's delusions of romance that have clouded her judgement, Ashley is played by ultimate 'woman-made man', aging Matinee Idol Leslie Howard.

Scarlett's misguided obsession with Ashley was a cautionary tale for girls, but at least she got to have some fun – she was played by Vivien Leigh, an adult woman. Teenage actresses, on the other hand, found themselves stuck in much more basic plots. They starred in wholesome, saccharine films where they were forced to play sweet, innocent dreamers, forever singing about unrequited love and the bittersweet agony of waiting. But the girls watching these movies didn't want to stay innocent for ever – hell, they didn't even feel innocent now. They didn't want to be Deanna Durbin; they wanted to be Greta Garbo. They didn't want to be Judy Garland: they wanted to be Lauren Bacall, Joan Crawford, Bette Davis – sexy, snappy, sassy women who could hold their own in a man's world.

'My intellectual aspirations had quite a setback,' wrote one girl in her diary after seeing *To Have and Have Not* starring Bacall and her husband Humphrey Bogart. 'I began dreaming of myself in Martinique with a glass of rum in one hand and a cigarette in the other & a man like Humphrey Bogart to fall in love with. Oh Lord, what a life.'[31] When it came to male movie idols, the boyish stars who girls were supposed to be safely and innocently dreaming about, like the ultimately asexual Mickey Rooney, just couldn't compete with towering figures of romantic manliness like Clark Gable, Cary Grant or Errol Flynn: men who exuded power and danger – the type of charm that could sweep you off your feet, even as it loomed over you.

In real life, though, love didn't look like Clark Gable carrying you upstairs in a fit of passion or Cary Grant flashing that signature smirk. It looked like confusing signals, endless waiting and trying to decode the unspoken rules of attraction. 'Much depends on whether he is expressing a sincere fondness for you,' explained an etiquette handbook, 'whether he is merely curious to see if you will permit it, or whether it's just a casual habit of his … If in doubt – don't.'[32]

That was easier said than done. After seeing Laurence Olivier in *Wuthering Heights* in 1939, fifteen-year-old Rhode Islander Mary Lee Cantwell remembered standing, with her friend Ruthie, in front of the infinite darkness of the ocean at night, bellowing Heathcliff's name out across the waves. 'I'd love to live as wildly and fully as Cathy and Heathcliff did,' wrote a girl called Adele Mongan Fasick in her diary after seeing that same film in 1945.

> I worry about whether I can ever love a man as passionately as lovers do, or must I be content with a soft half-love. I don't care so much whether we should love or even if he loves me. I just want someone completely, and I'm afraid that maybe I never will. I want to be wild, strong, and fresh as the moors & I mean to become so and thus prepare myself for loving.[33]

And yet the transition from girl to woman wasn't seen as a complex process of self-growth and growing up – it was about crossing that invisible line from sexual innocence to availability: a moment girls were taught to both idealise and dread.

Teen girl romantic fantasies of the pre-war years echoed that same dissonance. On one hand, they gave girls a moment to dream, a rare place where romantic feelings were free to flourish. On the other, many subtly reinforced the unwritten rules that kept them in their place. Disconnected from boys their own age, dreaming of idealised older men who embodied the paternal authority of the era, they were reminded that true fulfilment lay in submission – learning to yield to your man. You only had to take one look at fifteen-year-old Judy Garland singing 'Dear Mr Gable' to a photo of 38-year-old Clark Gable in *Broadway Melody* to see that something was both missing and wrong.

As Garland, in her little white pinafore and ringlets, sits childishly at a desk in her bedroom, writing a fan letter to a distant, unresponsive photo of a man more than double her age, we see the problematic nature of teen girl fantasy in pre-war pop culture. Like that photo of Gable, sitting lifelessly on her desk, romance was something that teenage girls experienced from the outside looking in. At the movies, of course, you could imagine yourself into an endless stream of adult love stories. At home, too, you might dream of the romantic life of the woman you would one day be, but you were never quite there yet. The fantasy, you were told, was childish. It was something you needed to grow out of before you could ever actually get there.

When Frank Sinatra came along – so boyish and approachable, so sweetly and so earnestly singing all those dreamy, vulnerable, moonlit, sparkling words of love – it was a game changer. It was the musical equivalent of a more age-appropriate Clark Gable stepping right out of that scrapbook on Garland's desk, gazing into her eyes and showering every ounce of emotion and longing in that deep well of teenage love and idolatry back at her.

'Frank Sinatra sings like Clark Gable makes love,'[34] said actress Betty Grable. For girls who had, perhaps, never even been in love, or who were only just experiencing those first twinges of sexual and romantic feelings for the first time (and for many adult women too), this was a vision of a new type of intimacy. Frankie wasn't a mysterious, brooding, distant figure of fantasy like ultra-masculine Clark Gable slamming the door on Vivien Leigh in *Gone With the Wind*.

Frankie seemed kind, safe, familiar. He was the ultimate boy next door, except that – through the power of that big bad voice and those baby-blue eyes – he was able to express all the most secret, romantic, sometimes even painfully overwhelming feelings you felt in your own heart. He felt exactly the same way as you. This was reassuring. It meant that you weren't some lovestruck idiot who needed to wait until the moment when she could, or would, finally be ready to woman up. It also meant that there was hope – that some boys, maybe men too, maybe even love itself, could be just as kind, safe and familiar as it felt when Frankie tilted his head, leaned into that mic and confided that he was the one who needed *you*.

The inevitable response, the swoon that would become the defining word and gesture of Sinatramania, wasn't the wilting surrender of Garland pining away in her bedroom under the weight of an eternally unattainable dream. Frankie's boyish neediness and frailty – his ordinariness – inspired a swoon that was quite different.

Maybe it had been involuntary at first: a shudder, a sigh, a hint of electricity when you heard him sing something like 'I'll Never Smile Again' or 'The Song Is You' for the first time. All of a sudden, like magic, you could feel the words and the music in your body. But then, in the darkness of the Paramount – or even just sitting around the radio in your best friend's bedroom – when you knew that every other girl around you was breathless and joyful with amazement and wonder in exactly the same way as you, the swoon became something more deliberate. More powerful. The swoon was a statement of togetherness and belonging, of connection and joy.

'We loved to swoon,' said Martha Weinman Lear, who remembered skipping school to go to Sinatra shows at the RKO Theatre in Boston. And the swooning didn't stop there:

> We would gather behind locked bedroom doors, in rooms where rosebud wallpaper was plastered over with pictures of The Voice, to practise swooning. We would take off our saddle shoes, put on his records and stand around groaning for a while. Then the song would end and we would all fall down on the floor. We would do that for an hour or so, and then, before going home for

supper, we would forge the notes from our parents: 'Please excuse Martha's absence from school yesterday as she was sick.' We were sick alright. Crazy … In school they mocked us collapsing into each other's arms and shrieking, 'Oh-h-h, Frankie. I'm fainting, I'm *fainting*.' To hell with them.[35]

There are many stories about the birth of the swoon. Who swooned first? How and why did it catch on? Was it spontaneous or manufactured? According to myth, patient zero was a girl at the Paramount who was feeling lightheaded because she hadn't had lunch. She was so overcome with emotion when Frankie walked on stage that she fainted, which made the girl next to her scream, and the girl next to her and the girl next to her and so it went on – to eternity.

The more common story – the one Sinatra biographers most often tell – is that it was actually Frankie's publicist, George Evans, who planned and directed the whole thing. They say he'd pay girls to swoon at the start; take them down to the basement of the Paramount and audition them to find the best screamers, then get them to learn when to swoon at exactly the right moment. With a healthy dose of scepticism, Sinatra's most well-respected biographer James Kaplan tells the story of how Evans would give the girls 'precise cues when to yell, "Oh, Frankie! Oh, Frankie!" – not just during the loud parts, but whenever Sinatra let his voice catch', and how he coached Sinatra too, so the whole show would flow in and out of a call and response. 'Imagine that mike on its stand is a beautiful broad,' he told him. 'Caress it. Make love to it. Hold on to it for dear life.' Dreamy, I know.[36]

When Frankie sang about how he wasn't much to look at in 'She's Funny That Way', someone would shout, 'Oh, Frankie, yes you are!' When he got to 'Embraceable You', he'd open his arms and sing, 'Come to papa,' and all the girls would scream, 'Oh, Daddy!'[37] After that, Frank was supposed to mumble, 'Gee, that's a lot of kids for one fellow.'[38] Evans even, apparently, trained them to faint in the aisles. And yet, if these stories *are* true, then Evans was wasting his money. 'I used to bring binoculars just to watch that lower lip,' says Martha.

> The voice had this trick, you know that funny sliding, skimming slur that it would do coming off the note. It drove us bonkers … Harold Schonberg, the *Times*'s music critic, says that it must have been what is called *portamento*. Whatever it was called it was an invitation to hysteria. He'd give us that little slur – 'All… or nothing at allllll…' and we'd start swooning all over the place, in the aisles, on each other's shoulders, in the arms of cops, poor bewildered men in blue. It was like pressing a button. It *was* pressing a button.[39]

And it turned out the button was nuclear. By the end of the year, the swoon had become a law unto itself: an orgiastic insurrection of infatuation that was growing and multiplying as rampantly and organically as the number of new words that were having to be invented to be able to express and understand what the hell was going on. Among the new words in the American vernacular of the year 1944 were: Swoonatra, Swoonheart, Swoonology, Swoonatic, Swoonster, Swoonery, Sinatractive, Sinatrally, Swoondoggler, Sinatrance, Swoonism, Swoontrance, Sinatraless, Screenatra, Sinatrism, Sinatraphile, Sinatraphobe, Sinatraddiction and Sonatra.

What Evans did do, masterfully, was see and understand what it was about Frankie that was making the girls swoon – and give them more of it. George Evans was one of the first people in the history of pop music to take teenage girls seriously. Through the 1940s, Evans executed a swoontastic marketing campaign that managed to mirror all the feelings of intimacy and closeness that girls felt when they were listening to Sinatra's songs. He also shaved two years off his age.

His first order of business was to rewrite Frankie's biography to make him as relatable as possible. The fact he'd dropped out of school at sixteen was omitted. He became a football, baseball and track star who discovered his love of music in the glee club. He was a nice boy, raised 'poor but proud in the slums of Hoboken, narrowly avoiding mayhem at the hands of vicious street gangs'.[40] His overbearing, borderline abusive mother (the neighbourhood abortionist who ran a speakeasy) was now a Red Cross nurse. He'd married his high school sweetheart, Nancy, and off stage, he was just a normal average young suburban husband and father, mowing the lawn of his new home in Hasbrouck Heights and teaching his daughter, Little Nancy, how to play piano. His favourite colour was blue, and his favourite ice cream was pistachio (sometimes chocolate).

Next, and most importantly, Evans set up a centre of fan operations in his office at 1775 Broadway. In a cluttered cubicle stacked from floor to ceiling with fanmail, publicity stills and card files, his newly appointed secretary, a kindly middle-aged widow called Marjorie Divan, attended to Frankie's fanmail. Marj, as the bobbysoxers lovingly called her, was responsible for making sure fans felt that they were personally connected with Frankie and to connect fans with each other. Her dedication was absolute. 'People think it's strange that I take this business so seriously,' she said, 'but I've seen many things it does that go beyond the eye.'[41]

The majority of fans wrote to Frankie to ask for photos and

autographs and buttons from his suits. But they also used him as a sort of teenage oracle. 'A surprisingly large number of young people think Sinatra is omniscient', wrote Kahn, who was invited to observe the fanmail operation for the day, 'and thus qualified to answer such questions as "What does a girl do whose world seems to have come to an end?", or as a fourteen-year-old boy put his problem: "Do you think you should talk to your best girl about sex?"'[42]

Marj and Evans worked hard to make sure that every letter got a response. In fact, 'the most ticklish queries' were attacked by Evans himself – perhaps the only press agent on Broadway to spend an hour or so a day counselling young women on how to get over being wallflowers at dances.

This kindness and compassion would become a hallmark of Sinatra fandom. Marj once told a story about a girl from Alsace-Lorraine who, after a bad experience during the war, had become suspicious of all men except Frankie. 'Why, she wouldn't even trade stamps,' she explained.

After she wrote in, I got in touch with a 45-year-old male fan in Iceland – the serious responsible type – and had him write her a couple of letters. Five months later, she wrote Frank and asked if it would be alright if she wrote back to the man in Iceland, and I said yes. Now she's happy; she sleeps with his letters under her pillow.[43]

Being a Sinatra fan meant being part of something bigger. Many fan clubs published newsletters to share and communicate their devotion and connect with each other. These were homemade cut-and-paste numbers brimming with essays, movie and music reviews, personal writings and drawings. Fan club members could advertise for pen pals, or photoswaps, and of course share news and reports of in-person sightings of the great man himself. It was a way of ratifying their experiences, prolonging and celebrating them and sharing their feelings with their friends. 'Then he appeared', wrote Peggy McShane in her column 'I, A Bobby-Soxer – Or the Confessions of the Bobby Sox Brigade', and

> the screaming, squealing, fainting, swooning etc. ... was deafening before, but when that hunk of a song-man appeared. Oh brother! Oh give me credit, I was just as bad, if not worse than the rest of them. He looked ooooh, the word hasn't been made yet, but anyway, that's how he looked.[44]

These newsletters were testaments of love, but they also show how socially meaningful Sinatra fandom was becoming to fan club members. As a proud Italian-American who had experienced a fair amount of prejudice himself, Sinatra was a vocal advocate for civil rights. The bobbysoxers threw themselves behind his causes with the same passion. Between endless celebrations of his 'rumpled hair', 'dreamy stare', 'wistful smile' and 'gentle sighs' – most often in the form of poetry – they packed their pages with articles about racial equality and justice, urged members to skip ice cream sodas so they could donate to more humanitarian causes and (to the occasional dismay of Bing Crosby) made sure Frankie raised more money than any other star when he was involved in a bond rally or charity drive.[45]

This shamelessly passionate blend of thirsting and crusading was not only accepted – it was encouraged. What was most important to newsletter editors was engagement. 'Our thanx [sic] to those of you who sent in materials for The Voice,' wrote the president of the Slaves of Sinatra fan club in 1946. 'And now what about the rest of you? Those of you who haven't sent in any materials for our paper, what's the matter, don't you care? We always thot [*sic*] Sinatra fans were loaded with talent, so let's see some of it break into print.'[46] In line with Frank's ethos of inclusivity, everyone was welcome. One of the most prolific contributors to *Sinatral-ly Yours* was a young army private called John Martin. In one of his poems, 'Our Pin Up Boy', he offered an alternative to his unit's generic choices of barracks art:

> You guys can pin up Turner
> And Leys and Hayworth too,
> But we'll pin up Sinatra
> To beautify the view …
> He's dreamy eyes and handsome
> He's all that we desire
> His flame is growing brighter
> He has the world on fire
> The fire is burning deeper
> Into the hearts of we
> Who like to pin up 'Frankie'
> Wherever we may be.[47]

DEGENERATE SONG

Not all 1940s men were ready to join Private Martin in the swoon. One day in 1944, at the Paramount, a teenage boy stepped forward from the audience and pelted Frankie with eggs. The boy's name was Alexander Dorogokupetz. A few days later, under the headline

'Sinatra Egg-Tosser Tells All!', he explained that he'd hated Sinatra and his bow ties for two years already. 'How can you fall for a guy like that?' he raged. 'He looks starved.'

In his account of the incident, Alexander described how after his second egg hit Frankie in the chest, he'd found himself trapped. 'I spun around,' he wrote, 'but I couldn't move a step. Girls on all sides of me. I couldn't move. My God!'[48] The girls may have stepped in to protect their hero, but Alexander wasn't alone in feeling that enough was enough. The next day, a group of sailors stood outside the Paramount and pelted a poster of Sinatra's face with tomatoes. For many men, Sinatra was a suspect, effeminate draft-dodger who had connived to stay home seducing their women while the 'real men' were off fighting. The image of Frankie as a sickly, physically weak man who somehow still managed to send women out of their minds with love became a recurring joke in wartime pop culture.

In 'Rhapsody in Pew', one of several *Looney Tunes* satires, Frankie is played by iconic seducer skunk Pepe Le Pew. He's so skinny and frail that he disappears behind the microphone pole as he sings, needs an oxygen tank, plasma infusions and an iron lung just to make it through 'All or Nothing at All' and eventually an under-taker comes to measure him for a coffin. The female bunnies in the audience are so excited by all this that they scream, faint and bang themselves in the head, repeatedly, with whatever objects are on hand. Some squeeze barren trees so hard that they sprout leaves, while others blow kisses that hit the stage like bullets. The chaos culminates in a stage invasion, where the mob of lovestruck bunnies leaves Frankie flattened like roadkill.

'What does Sinatra have that I don't, besides a voice?' asks a sailor in Frederic Wakeman's 1944 novel *Shore Leave*. 'Oh, you've got shoulders,' explains his girl. 'We don't go for shoulders since Frankie came into our lives.'[49] Girls' reverence for Frankie and his decidedly unmanly qualities felt like a rejection of who and what these men were. When William Manchester reflected on this time in *The Glory and the Dream*, his classic history of America, he concluded that 'Frank Sinatra was the most hated man of World War II, much more than Hitler'.[50]

Sinatra wasn't the first male singer to generate this kind of hate or to be criticised for his supposed deficiencies in the manliness department (although, for the record, in case you were wondering, his manhood was another matter: 'There's only ten pounds of Frank,' said his notoriously foul-mouthed second wife Ava Gardner, 'but there's a hundred and ten pounds of cock').[51] From the troubadours of the Middle Ages, who rejected marriage in pursuit of the loftier, more spiritual pleasures of idealised and eternally unattainable courtly love, to the castrati of the eighteenth-century opera, male singers who spoke both to and for female feelings and fantasies had always complicated and challenged traditional ideas of heteronormative masculinity. And of all the singers in the long and tangled history of the love song, no one did it better than the crooners of the Depression era who paved the way for Sinatra's success.

When crooning first hit the airwaves in the late 1920s, America was reeling from the economic devastation of the Wall Street Crash. Radio, a new and rapidly growing medium, was an exciting and affordable form of popular entertainment. For the first time in history, music and voices could meet people where they were. A few years earlier, in 1921, at the height of Sheik Fever, Tin Pan Alley hit 'The Sheik of Araby' had women dreaming of Rudolph Valentino creeping into their tents and whispering all kinds of seductive naughtiness into their ears while they were asleep. Now, thanks to the radio, those daydreams didn't need Hollywood to come true. No longer confined to cinema screens, this next generation of dream lovers were creeping, over the airwaves, straight into the heart of American homes.

Years later, Sinatra would turn mic intimacy into an art form. 'Many singers never learned to use one,' he said. 'They never understood, and still don't, that a microphone is their instrument.'[52] Swinging it backwards and forwards, playing with distance and breath, he used the mic to add layers of intimacy and meaning to his sound. 'To Sinatra, a microphone is a real girl waiting to be kissed,' said E. B. White.[53] But before Sinatra and his mic, there was Rudy Vallée and his megaphone.

Vallée was the most iconic crooner of his day and the first true pop star of the radio era. Crooning had its roots way back in parlour singing and vaudeville but gained popularity in the second half of the nineteenth century (around the same time as matinee mania) when women began accessing public life in greater numbers. As producers started to target female customers, they noticed the ladies were particularly keen to see pretty young men 'in trousers tight-fitting and showing every muscle' singing love songs.[54]

In the days before microphones, old-school singers like Al Jolson had to belt songs out to be heard in the back rows. Crooners murmured, whispered and pulled their audience up close. It felt personal. Softly crooning into his trademark megaphone, Vallée could make a crowded theatre feel like a private conversation. And with the help of the radio, he brought that intimacy to millions.

Women adored Rudy Vallée. As a handsome psychology grad who styled himself as a London gentleman (and never failed to mention how much he loved his mother), he was particularly popular with college girls: songs like 'My Life Begins and Ends With You' and 'You Came, I Saw, You Conquered' were romantic in a way that felt both classic and modern. 'Rudy picks up a megaphone, stands quietly at the corner of the stage, and begins to sing,' wrote Martha Gellhorn in 1929.

> The audience holds its breath in joy, in adoration … His voice is an exquisite agony of waiting … He has chosen 'I Kiss Your Hand, Madame'… His voice is low, pleasant, natural … The words drift from the megaphone like a caress … He is their darling, their Song Lover. He's the best yet. Rudy Valentino wasn't it … Give us Rudy Vallée. Give us this tall, slender, simple boy, with his blond, wavy hair, his tanned face, his blue eyes, and his gentle voice that makes love so democratically to everyone.[55]

For women listening at home, the experience felt even more personal. The radio was just a few years old at this point. Just like early cinema stirred intense feelings for movie stars, the novelty of having these smooth, seductive voices right in your home amplified the emotions people felt. The best word that many fans could come up with to describe the feelings they were feeling was *love*. 'I'm just so in love with your voice,' wrote one fan. 'It just holds one in raptures when it floats over the radio.' 'I'm burning up,' wrote another.[56] It was intimate, familiar and weirdly physical – what a seductive new thrill to have a man's voice right there with you in your living room. Some fans even wrote to say they'd cancel their plans just to 'stay home, slip into a negligee, curl up with Lawson [the radio], and listen to you'. Radio pluggers soon dubbed Rudy Vallée 'the guy with the cock in his voice'.[57]

But it was about more than just sex. Crooners turned the rigid Depression-era expectations of men and women in love on their head. The heroines of their songs were strong and independent, while the men who loved them weren't afraid to show vulnerability and need. For married couples, often listening to the radio together, this new style of male sensitivity opened up new possibilities for intimacy in real life. 'Hubby and I just sit and hold each other tight while he is on the air,' wrote a newlywed bride. 'We just look into each other's eyes while he is singing.' Rudy's voice became a kind of romantic catalyst that helped couples get in the mood to experiment with the emotional and physical closeness that marriage manuals had begun to advocate. Even older couples wrote to thank him for helping them keep 'romance alive'.[58]

For a few glorious years in the late '20s, crooners ruled the airwaves. 'Remember, girls, Rudy's on tonight!' was the perpetual refrain on NBC.[59] It wasn't long before Hollywood rushed to catch up, except they weren't quite sure what to do with stars whose magic was invisible. In *Radio Rhythm*, they decided to go fully literal: a young woman sits smiling and stroking her radio, with Rudy and his band inside. Male film critics labelled these films impossible to review. 'New York gals, young and old, are nuts over this boy,' wrote *Variety*. 'Who can figure the feminine tangent? They threw flowers at him at the Riverside. So, upon that deduction, this release classifies as an oddity.'[60]

It didn't take long for the backlash to begin. One day, in January 1931, a male college student threw a grapefruit at Vallée while he was on stage at a concert in Boston. It was a symbolic moment that opened the floodgates to a deep well of anti-crooner hostility that had already been brewing for a while. Soon, moral crusaders were bemoaning the death of manliness. They claimed this new sound was reducing real men to lovesick boys. As one critic scoffed:

There are lots of things more pleasant in the world than hearing a masculine voice sobbing about 'you dear' and 'the day we met', and if crooners had any respect for themselves, they'd soon inform the song writers that there are plenty of interesting subjects in the world other than love.[61]

In a particularly vitriolic tirade, Cardinal William O'Connell, Archbishop of Boston, branded crooning 'degenerate' and accused it of promoting 'effeminate paganism'. 'No true American would practise this base art,' he wrote.

I like to use my radio, when weary. But I cannot turn the dials without getting these whiners, crying vapid words ... If you listen closely when you are unfortunate enough to get one of these, you will discern the basest appeal to sex emotions in the young. They are not true love songs – they profane the name.[62]

The moral panic about 'woman-made men' that had begun with Valentino was still going strong, except that crooners had taken it to a new level of degeneracy.

Throughout the Depression, with so many men out of work and unable to provide for their families, physical strength had become the ultimate proof of masculinity. What made crooners so disturbing was that, most of the time, they didn't even have bodies. As ethereal voices floating over the airwaves, listeners sometimes couldn't even tell if they were listening to a man or a woman. And yet they wielded real power: they could conquer and seduce without the physical virility typically associated with 'real men'. This was, as Gellhorn put it, a truly democratic type of seduction: the ever-present 'you' of their love songs could be anyone.

The press may have latched on to scare stories, thundered on about how the crooners were emasculating men, corrupting youth, turning women into hysterical, lovesick wrecks, but the crooners offered a softer and more optimistic story – a dream as enchanting as a love song – a vision of a world where tenderness and emotional expression could be a natural and whole-hearted part of what it meant to be a man.

Tragically, the world wasn't quite ready for this yet. By the mid-1930s, crooners were regularly attacked in the press, where they were painted as unmanly and immoral. The term 'crooning' itself became an insult, a spitting shorthand for weakness and effeminacy. Even Bing Crosby – by then the most commercially successful crooner who remained – felt the need to distance himself from the label. He sang in 'full voice', he said – none of that delicate falsetto business.[63] His films and songs reinforced his new image as the all-American family man: steady, patriotic and, most importantly, respectable. Who was he kidding? If he'd been nicer to his fans, I'd say mid-era Bing was still 10,000 per cent swoonworthy – in that aloof, slightly disinterested, dad-kind-of-way.

Bing had many female admirers, but he made it clear in interviews that he didn't approve. He told one fan magazine that these sorts of attachments were 'unhealthy' and encouraged fans to 'forget about him and instead to find a good man and start a family'.[64] By the time Sinatra rose to fame, America had put its gender trouble back in order – on the surface, at least. But when the girls started throwing knickers, and boys started throwing food, it was clear that the cracks were already beginning to show.

SONGS OF INNOCENCE AND EXPERIENCE

As the war wore on, Sinatra did his best to contribute to the war effort where he could. He performed at bond rallies with Bing and toured army bases, but the resentment from servicemen was still palpable. 'Hey wop, why aren't you in uniform!?' shouted a sailor at a USO performance.[65] While America's brave boys were knee-deep in mud and gunfire, Sinatra was back home, playing to sold-out crowds and out on the town with a who's who of Hollywood starlets. These were the same girls who, in their minds, should have been waiting faithfully for their boys to come home. The sight of Sinatra living a life of glamour and adoration, while they endured the brutal realities of war, threw their whole sense of mission and purpose into doubt.

For many servicemen, the purity and virtue of American women was central to the war effort. As historian Lewis A. Erenberg put it: 'The look homeward often assumed a nostalgic glow … and at the heart of that gaze was the American woman – representing everything worth fighting for.'[66] For the Sinatra-haters, Sinatra-mania was a troubling answer to the questions that were turning over in their minds as they lay lonely in their bunks or kept watch under starless skies. What might their women be doing while they were gone? Who were they with? Were those visions of all-American loveliness really worth fighting for?

Whether they liked it or not, life back home was changing. With husbands, boyfriends and fathers overseas, women were now stepping into jobs traditionally reserved for men – factory work, office jobs and even military auxiliary roles. During the day, they were earning their own money. At night, they were dancing, flirting and living in the moment. To many servicemen, the sight of thousands of teenage girls screaming and swooning over Frankie Sinatra felt like a slap in the face – yet another form of frivolous, carefree fun during a time of wartime sacrifice but magnified on a mass scale.

And the fun seemed to be getting less innocent by the day. Many women were experimenting with sex and having the time of their lives doing it. 'There was never a shortage of healthy bucks,' recalled one young woman. 'The bars were jammed, and unless you were an absolute dog, you could pick up anyone you wanted.'[67] As one teenage boy put it: wartime America was 'a sex paradise'.[68] But tales of spiking venereal disease (apparently spread by women, not germs) and the rising number of 'victory girls' and 'patriotutes' – women accused of using patriotism as a cover for promiscuity – triggered a crusade to control women's behaviour.

'The greater social freedom of women has led to more sexual laxity,' explained a marriage textbook from 1942, 'a freedom that strikes at the heart of family stability. When women work, earn, and spend as much as men, they ask for equal rights – including the right to misbehave like men.'[69] Women were warned not to lose their femininity, which was apparently critical to the war effort. From here, a series of ridiculously contradictory messages emerged. Women were encouraged to do their bit for the war effort by keeping themselves pure for returning veterans, obsessing about their looks (give 'em something to fight for!) and posing for sexy pin-up photos (no sweetheart or husband to send yours to? Any serviceman will do!). Men's promiscuity was excused as natural – necessary for victory, in fact – but when women did the same thing (or less), it was condemned as 'the decay of established moralities'.[70]

In a move that would soon become standard practice in handwringing about female independence and autonomy, no one came under more fire than our darling teenage girls. Scrutinised in public, vilified in the press, it was as if the whole of wartime society had decided to dump all its pent-up adult-world problems onto their vulnerable shoulders. With fathers away and mothers at work, they were labelled reckless or immoral for having too much fun or experimenting with freedom and accused of everything from juvenile delinquency to everyday selfishness.

Soldiers were told to watch out for girls – the diseases they might carry, the reputations they might ruin or the way they might manipulate them into marriage to gain pensions or money – as if they were the threat, not the wandering hands that pleaded for affection, the cat calls in the street, the footsteps in the park. Girls as young as eleven found themselves having to fend off unwanted attention from servicemen on leave in town.

In New York City, *Wuthering Heights* fan Adele Mongan Fasick couldn't even spend an afternoon with her friends, feeding birds and squirrels in Central Park, without being followed by a group of merchant marines. Mary Lee Cantwell remembered her little sister coming home in tears because she'd been propositioned by a soldier. And yet the philosophy of victim blaming was so entrenched in wartime psychology that Mary Lee was unsympathetic to her distress. 'Walk faster and quit drifting the way you always do,' she told her.[71]

This framing was everywhere. 'Don't Be Her Pin-Up Boy' warned one public health poster. It showed a young woman in a tight dress and heavy make-up, sitting on a bed, gazing dreamily at posters of a sailor, a soldier and an airman. In the corner of her top, embroidered like a name tag, sat the words: 'venereal disease'. The subtext was clear: girls' excessive, obsessive consumption of pop culture – movies, music and the romantic fantasies that many of them held so dear – were a threat, yet another manifestation of this dangerous, predatory form of female desire that was spiralling out of control. There was a glaring double standard, of course. Men had their pin-ups – Betty Grable, Rita Hayworth and countless more. This was celebrated: their fantasies were patriotic. But when girls pinned up Sinatra, indulging in their own form of fantasy and escape, it became at best a joke and at worst something to rage against or control. Some young women even felt the need to 'give up Sinatra' when they got engaged.

It's dangerous to generalise. There were approximately 6.5 million teenage girls in America by the time the war ended in 1945, each as complex and unique as teenage girls are today. Some experimented sexually; others didn't. Some longed for excitement; others feared it. Some were disappointed when no one grabbed them and kissed them on V-J Day; others – like the nurse being kissed by a sailor in the iconic V-J Day Times Square photo – felt violated when they did. What was universal to all of them was the frame: the epic, chaotic, confusing, intense and often lonely firestorm that was the backdrop of their coming of age. And in the middle of all that chaos and uncertainty, confusion and noise, for the bobbysoxers, there was Frankie. Sweet, gentle, untouchable Frankie.

Frankie gave girls 'an opportunity to concentrate on something else', said Janice, 'someone else apart from family separations and potential danger'.[72] He was someone on whom

> fantasies could be focused: yet he was safe because he was un-attainable ... Troubling situations with boyfriends were absent in this crush ... You could explore romance from a distance, daydream about his romantic songs, attach the lyrics to the love of the moment, but dismiss the realities that the boy next door might present.

When a radio station in New York held a 'Why I swoon for Sinatra' essay-writing competition, the winning girl framed him like a lighthouse: 'If lonesome, he reminds you of the guy away from your arms. If waiting for a dream prince, his thrilling voice sings for you alone.'[73]

Just as soldiers pinned up photos of movie stars and pin-up girls as a reminder of what they were fighting for – a fantasy of feminine beauty and the promise of home – Frankie provided comfort, fantasy and a hopeful vision of the future for America's wartime girls. George Evans's masterpiece Frankie Sinatra, family man, the loving husband mowing the lawn in his suburban home, was a vision of domestic bliss that felt so real, and so attainable, that they could nearly reach out and touch him.

The newspapers may have scratched their heads that girls screamed so hard when he fiddled with his wedding ring or even the fact that they were so obsessed with this married man at all. But to them, the very existence of Nancy and the kids was weirdly satisfying – like the happy ending of a movie, except (unlike in Hollywood) this movie included relatable young people like them. The Sinatra family became a comforting symbol of everything these girls craved: romance, yes, but also safety, warmth and belonging – a world where all those tentative daydreams of polka dots and moonbeams blossomed into a stable, loving, happy home. And they didn't just love Frankie; they loved Nancy and the kids too. They knitted booties for the babies and wrote letters to Nancy. 'I wish Frank were twins,' wrote one girl, 'one for me and one for Nancy.'[74]

It may seem frustratingly backwards, in hindsight, that amid signs of social change and new freedoms and opportunities for women what these girls longed for – more than anything – was a home, a dependable husband as provider and the ideal of domesticity. But for the bobbysoxers, it was a comforting fantasy that represented a return to normalcy. That kind of life was also the only place (or so they had been taught) where all that desire and longing in Frankie's voice could be given true expression. Stephen Holden put it beautifully in the *New Republic* when he described how this 'quasi-religious romantic ethos engulfed movies and pop music in the '40s'. Here, in this 'fantasy world of tender rapture', faith in romantic love and the sanctity of marriage promised 'ineffable sexual ecstasy' as the 'ultimate reward for postponement'.[75] 'True love' was the happy ending everyone was coaxed into anticipating.

Beauty can be truth – it was for the bobbysoxers, anyway. But truth isn't always beauty. In those wee small hours, when the bobbysoxers were lying alone in their beds dreaming of Frankie and Nancy's universe of tender rapture (and future Frankies of their own), Nancy – the one girl in the world who was actually living those dreams – was sitting at home just as lonely as they were. She would cry herself to sleep most nights. She would pull herself together in the morning, clean the house, feed the kids, do all the things a good wife is supposed to do. But the loneliness was crushing, and there was nothing any Sinatra record could do.

Frank's cheating had started early, even before they were married, and apart from a few fleeting moments of fragile hope and half-hearted resolve, it had never really abated. Later in life, he would describe himself as an '18-karat manic depressive'.[76] Well, he was a 24-karat womaniser. Nancy knew it. She had always known. But her deep love for Frank and her devout Catholicism meant divorce was unthinkable. As she told a newspaper in a rare interview in 1950: 'I have something too fine and precious to give up.'[77]

The bobbysoxers were NOT HAPPY when the Sinatra divorce was announced. Neither were their parents. 'Lana Turner must be proud of herself to break up a nice little family like the Sinatras,' wrote an outraged mother.

> I hope the bobbysoxers will stick together and put him on the skids ... All that ballyhoo about him being such a wonderful husband and father makes me sick ... He ought to know Lana Turner will grab the next pair of pants that goes by. Marriage vows mean nothing to people like her, in my estimation it is just glorified legal prostitution. I am sick and tired of the whole mess, and anybody who pays money to see trash like that is a fool.[78]

The irony, of course, is that the actress who ended Nancy and Frank's marriage wasn't Lana Turner – it was Ava Gardner (although, I suppose, most 'glorified prostitutes' are interchangeable). In keeping with the romanticised notion of love as a kind of religion, the story most often told is that Nancy made the ultimate sacrifice at the altar of 'true love'. She stepped aside so that the man she loved could marry the woman he loved. But to the outraged bobbysoxers and their parents, this so-called new love felt less like romantic destiny and more like a deep betrayal.

For the parents, the divorce stung because it seemed to set a dangerous example for their children. The screaming and swooning had been worrisome, but at least Sinatra – the focus of all that chaos – had represented a respectable model of love and family. Now, that idealised image had been shattered. For the bobbysoxers, it went deeper. Frankie's fall from grace felt personal, as if they too had been deceived. The dream family they had invested so much love and attention in was a lie.

'I am not a young schoolgirl with foolish ideas,' wrote a 21-year-old woman (this would have made her fifteen in 1944).

My husband and I are avid listeners to the Sinatra program, but now whenever we hear 'Frankie', we think of Nancy Sr, Jr, and Frank Jr … She's a wonderful woman, and if I were her, I doubt I would have been able to put up with so much for so long … I'm just happily married and want everyone else to be.[79]

Slowly, the screaming grew quieter, the flood of fan letters started to slow and the fervour that had once seemed endless began to fade. Something had changed. The bobbysoxers were growing up and the world around them felt different too. The innocent excitement of swooning for a voice on the radio was giving way to the realities of life, and that kind of devotion just didn't feel the same anymore.

Most of the older girls were busy with families now, and the younger ones had new teen idols like Johnnie Ray, Frankie Laine and Perry Como to obsess over. Soon, they would have Elvis. Sinatra was thirty-five. It would have been a bit creepy for him to be crooning boyish love songs to teenagers while inching closer to forty. And they weren't even interested anyway. One day, Frank's buddy Sammy Davis Jr was in New York. He described spotting Sinatra walking in Times Square one afternoon, right around the corner from the Paramount, 'alone and unrecognised'.

I would love to tell you the story ends there. That – in the face of all that deception and heartbreak – the bobbysoxers managed to put that egotistical love rat 'on the skids'. Women, collectively, did – briefly – but it was still a man's world.

As the swoons faded, Sinatra's career began to crumble. The loss of the bobbysoxers, combined with his spiralling personal life, hit him hard. His second marriage to Ava Gardner made the Byron–Caroline drama look like *Pride and Prejudice*, except this time *he* was the one calling *her* up, bawling his eyes out – hysterical – in the middle of the night with a gun to his head. He lost his record deal, his movie contract and then, one day in Vegas, struggling, under the weight of three years of drama and chaos, to reach those high notes, the man nicknamed 'the Voice' lost his voice.

'Of course, all life is a process of breaking down,' said Sinatra's favourite writer, F. Scott Fitzgerald. 'There are the blows that do the dramatic side of the work – the big, sudden blows that come, or seem to come, from outside.' This was Ava's secret abortion. That first empty front-row seat. Losing it all. But 'there is another sort of blow that comes from within – that you don't feel until it's too late to do anything about it, until you realise with finality that in some regard you will never be as good a man again'.[80] This was 1952.

By the end of that terrible year, Frankie was dead. Frank had known real heartbreak now, and it didn't feel like the nostalgic melancholy of his early songs, where all that desire and longing is really just the promise of a sweet and rapturous future. It felt like loss, regret and the weight of the thousand things you didn't say and you don't even understand why. That type of pain will change you. But because we all – and I mean all of us, from teenage girls to men in grey flannel suits, exasperated parents and battle-hardened veterans – need a good fairy tale now and then, Francis Albert Sinatra of Hoboken, New Jersey, did the impossible. He rose from the ashes.

Fifties Sinatra is the Sinatra most people remember today – fedora, cigarette, raincoat slung over shoulder, whisky in hand, mood: indigo. It's 3 a.m., and it's just you and me – so pour me another. His voice on the radio is different now: worn, weathered, knowing, but the ghost of Frankie is still in there somewhere.

If you're awake, like tonight, sitting at the kitchen table while everyone else in the house is asleep, he understands you like no one else does – because he's been there, trust me. And it feels good to know someone out there gets it. To know that after turning it on each morning – putting on the show – masking all those little cracks and bruises with a smile and a steady voice, someone out there knows the truth.

And at the bottom of his voice, in that place where, in a heartbreaking and haunting kind of way, Frankie still exists, there's a bittersweet ache, a reminder of something you thought you'd lost, but here – just for a moment – you can feel it again. And if you can feel it, there's hope. There's just one difference now: you're not a bobbysoxer anymore; you're a mom. And these days, more often than not, you're Dad.

Sinatra's male fans of the 1950s didn't scream or swoon. But it's not that Sinatra didn't affect them just as spiritually or as deeply as he did the bobbysoxers. The war had hardened them, broken them in places they didn't know how to repair. And they were struggling, trapped between the expectations of post-war masculinity – stoic, unemotional, dependable – and the feelings they couldn't quite suppress.

On the surface, they wore the mask of dutiful fathers and husbands, reliable workers, pillars of their communities. But in their hearts, there was a quiet, unspoken yearning for something softer – for tenderness, for understanding, for connection. They were trying to balance the burden of responsibility with the quiet ache of loneliness. And in Sinatra, they found a mirror – a way to feel understood without having to say the words out loud.

People often try to draw a line between Frank and Frankie: before and after the fall, high romance vs lapsed romanticism, the teen idol vs the true artist. But maybe these were two sides of the same thing. 'This was a generation who inculcated the idea that males did not display emotion, that only women loved with all their hearts, that only women suffered when love was lost,' reflected bobbysoxer Janice years later. Frankie's 'poignant portrayals of desire and longing perhaps helped, in some way, to pave the way' for the bobbysoxers 'when they were mature, to have expectations of intimacy and emotion on the part of men that heretofore had remained dormant'.[81]

Now, in Frank, you saw the other side of that same dream of emotional connection. Yes, there were contradictions – Rat Pack-era Frank is a trashcan fire of conflicting signals about sex and gender. On the surface, he played the role of the suave, unapologetic playboy – the kind of guy who could charm women effortlessly, break their hearts and walk away without ever looking back. But he carried it off like a Byronic Hero – regretfully flawed, hoping upon hope each time that things could be different. His vulnerability and heartbreak proved that 'males, even young boys, could show pain at the dissolution of a love affair or the fruitless quest for one'. This, 'coming from a very masculine, sexual man, gave males permission to be emotional about love'.[82]

Some revolutions start with a bang, others with a whisper. Frankie was never a two-dimensional figure of romance for the bobbysoxers in the '40s. His voice stirred deep, complex emotions and became a safe space for them to explore intimacy and desire at a distance. By the '50s, he was doing the same thing for men: helping them connect with the vulnerability of emotions like longing and heartbreak without having to confront them directly. Sinatra's capacity to evoke raw, universal feelings – love, loss, hope, desire or even despair – touched something fundamental about the human condition. Let history never forget it was the bobbysoxers who saw it first.

Years later, the feelings were just as fresh. 'Ah, Frankie everlovin',' wrote Martha Weinman Lear (of the after-school swoon sessions) in a review of a comeback gig he did at Madison Square Garden in 1974. He was nearly sixty by now:

> Here we are ... dancing cheek to cheek and the lights are low and it's oh so sweet. We haven't been this close since the old days when I played hookey from school to come see you ... You re-member me, don't you? ... Lord, what that man meant to me. If you didn't go through it, you wouldn't believe it. Look at him now, what do you see? A paunch, a jowl, a toupee. What could have driven me so crazy – the cuff links? ... We were all grown up and our swoons were memories, but I tell you, the gravity was as powerful as ever.

Martha had grown up to be an entertainment journalist, but in that moment, she was transported back to those giddy afternoons of innocence. A few years later, at the afterparty for a film premiere, her husband rushed over to tell her that Sinatra had just walked in. 'Wham! A child again, beguiled again, zooming backward through time and space,' she wrote. 'I stood there shaking like a thirteen-year-old, hands clasped right behind my back and wailing, "No, I can't." (And didn't.)'[83]

Maybe it was better to keep him perfectly imperfect that way, a figure suspended in the gravity of first love. That old Sinatra magic was something too precious to give up now. And maybe it really had been love, in a way. Once, when asked to explain the bobbysoxer phenomenon, Sinatra put it down to 'a kind of mutual adoration'. 'Every time I sing a song, I make love to them,' he said.[84]

Elvis Fan in Her Bedroom (1957)

© Bettmann / Getty Images

5

SEX, MEMPHIS, 1954
SACRED AND PROFANE

What a sweet lady. Sing lady, sing!
Of course, she wakes the dragon.
Love always wakes the dragon and suddenly
flames everywhere
I can tell already you think I'm the dragon,
that would be so like me, but I'm not. I'm not the dragon.
I'm not the princess either.
Who am I? I'm just a writer. I write things down.
I walk through your dreams and invent the future
– Richard Siken, 'Litany in Which
Certain Things Are Crossed Out'

Jumping on a Greyhound bus in her hometown of Dallas, Texas, Kay Wheeler didn't have time to think. There was no time to breathe, let alone think. But rock 'n' roll doesn't want you to think. It wants you to move. It wants you to do. It wants you to jump up, grab onto that crazy feeling and hold on tight because it's gonna be a wild ride, but that's what being sixteen in 1955 is really all about.

The dress she'd picked out (the sexiest she had) was sticking to her body in the heat – she didn't care – and she'd kicked off those high heels (the highest she had) for now. They were hurting her feet. Out the window, the fields of America: rolling. In the sky, the clouds: restless, shifting. And in her head, the driving bass of 'Trying to Get to You' playing over and over. His voice, even in her imagination, was so urgent and true. Not long now.

The whole thing had started as a joke. She'd been hanging out at the radio station one Saturday and the DJ (a friend of her aunt) had a new record. Some hillbilly kid from Memphis with a silly name. 'Nobody will ever get anywhere with that name,' he said.[1] She nearly died. Every girl in study hall was already talking about him – how there was this singer down in Gladewater who was shaking his legs and singing these songs and how he was the best-looking thing anyone had ever seen.

'He's gonna be a huge star,' she said, 'don't you worry about that', and then – typical her – she'd blurted out that she loved him so much she already had a fan club (she didn't). But anyway, the DJ had announced her name and address on the radio for anyone who wanted to send fanmail. When her mother came running into her bedroom the next day to tell her about the mountain of letters on the porch – all addressed to her – and she'd gone down to see for herself, her eyes had popped right out of her head. And now here she was: bang slap in the middle of all of it.

There weren't many sixteen-year-old girls whose parents would let them cross the state, alone, to go to a rock 'n' roll show, but her mother loved him too. She said he seemed like a nice boy. The whole fan club thing had been her idea, actually. She had told Kay that when she was young, all the kids started Frank Sinatra fan clubs and sometimes they got invited to special events. 'Maybe you'll get to meet him,' she said. Kay had never in a million years thought it would actually happen, but it had been worth a shot.

When she arrived at the Municipal Auditorium in San Antonio, his road manager Tom Diskin met her at the stage door where she showed him the telegram from Colonel Parker's secretary. It was like waving a magic wand, she later recalled, because before she had time to think, he was whisking her down a corridor, backstage, around corners, another corridor, another corner and then, at the end of the final corridor, there was a door. 'He's in there – go on in,' said Diskin, like it was the most normal thing in the world. That was when reality hit, like someone had just pulled an amplifier out of its socket. The electricity was gone. She was frozen. The hallway felt cold and endless. The only sound was her heartbeat – too fast – pounding. For a moment, time stretched out to infinity. Diskin looked at her. 'Go ahead,' he said, 'open the door.'

Well, there was no going back now. Kay Wheeler, age sixteen and a quarter, 200 miles from home, standing 5ft 8in. in her highest heels and sexiest dress, took a deep breath, gripped the door handle and turned.

BORN UNDER A BAD SIGN

Kay always used to say that – whether they knew it or not – the teenagers had been waiting for Elvis Presley, but there's no point going into the usual 'rise to fame' story. Sure, there's that shy boy in a pink shirt and slicked-back hair who wandered into Sun Records one day to cut a record for his mama – but that's not how it felt. That's not how it happened either. For anyone who lived through it, there was only before and after. Elvis didn't rise – he arrived, like a thunderbolt. Like love at first sight. Like Lucifer crash-landing on earth and waking up to realise he had become Satan. Like a messiah of movement and electricity preaching his new gospel of sound and sex to a raw, thumping backbeat, blues riffs twisted into something wild and a guitar that howled like it had been set free. The only backstory worth mentioning feels like myth.

Once upon a time, in a tiny two-room house in Tupelo, Mississippi, a woman goes into labour just as a storm is breaking. She gives birth to twins. Jesse and Elvis. That very night, as the storm rages, Jesse dies. Elvis lives. And so, he takes on the unlived life, and the weight, of the brother who never drew breath.

His destiny? To love his mother twice as hard, to live his life twice as fast, as loud, as large and – because he will grow up to be a good boy with a bad boy inside him (or maybe it's a bad boy with a good boy inside him – no one has ever been able to say, with certainty) – for his body to become a battleground. A place where the eternal struggle of good and evil will play out in real time with such intensity and force that the world will never be the same again. Eventually, he will die for our sins.

Whether it really was the battle of good and evil, or whether it was just that he was so beautiful and that no one had ever seen a man move as obscenely as that in public, no one would ever forget where they were when they saw Elvis for the first time.

For the girls at the Overton Park Shell on 30 July 1954, it was a physical experience. They'd come for music. What they got was something more primal. As Elvis stepped out on stage, in all his raw, untamed glory, and hit the first bars of 'That's All Right', they saw it, and felt it, before even he did. He didn't understand why they were screaming until Scotty told him after the set – it was something he was doing with his legs. Elvis was only shaking because this was his first ever paid performance and he was nervous, but he understood now.

When he came back on for his encore, he was ready, leaning into it. He let the music and the girls take control – gave his body over to them. He didn't even know what was happening, but the girls could feel it, their voices and bodies were reacting to his in a way that was completely new. He could feel it too. It kind of looked like he was being electrocuted. No. That hip shaking, thrusting, grinding was unmistakable. Ten years earlier, all that swooning for Sinatra had been sweet, but that's not what this was. As Lester Bangs put it: 'Elvis kicked "How Much Is That Doggie in the Window" out the window, and said, "Let's fuck."'[2]

It would take a while for both Elvis and the girls to process this chemistry. With Sinatra, it had been enchantment – studied and deliberate – an achingly sincere enactment of courtly love, the pleasure of wanting and dreaming. With Elvis, it was the Real Thing – sparks flying, sweat dripping, bodies moving – too fresh and electric for either of them to fully comprehend, to begin with anyway. But make no mistake: this wasn't that – in the face of some love God – the girls were losing control. It was that they were beginning to understand how much of that raw, wild, untameable electricity was in them too.

The revelation of Elvis and the girls at the Overton Shell in 1954 came in the wake of the explosive Kinsey Report, which had shocked the nation by exposing the reality of sexual behaviour in America (apparently things were much steamier behind closed doors than the tidy world of Rotary Club meetings and neighbourhood pot-lucks wanted anyone to think). But the scenes of rapture that played out at the Shell – and again and again in cities across the south that summer, with Elvis describing it as a dream and hoping he wouldn't wake up – were in direct opposition to what people had read in the report.

'Kinsey largely portrayed women as repulsed by men's bodies and sexually mutant,' reflected a fan years later.[3] '[He] told women it was unusual for them to be easily or rapidly aroused. Presley showed them it wasn't. The sexual mutant lie couldn't work anymore. Kinsey was a false prophet of the Old Guard.' It was near-on impossible to see Elvis – the wiggle, the snarl, the overt sexuality all wrapped up in that pretty mama's boy body that made you think of Sunday service, first kisses in haystacks and the smell of summer rain – and not feel something. He was turning women on in new and revolutionary ways – and in public. But as Rudolph Valentino would say, it takes two to tango.

If Elvis was the light, he was shining on something that was already there. And it was the girls at Elvis's shows who were bringing it into the open. They were making female sexual desire visible in a way that could no longer be ignored. If they were 'out of control', as many in the press were saying they were, then, as historian Joel Williamson put it, 'it was only in the sense that the rebels who staged the Boston Tea Party during the American Revolution, or stormed the Bastille in 1789, or sat-in, rode-in, and marched-in during the civil rights movement in the early 1960s were out of control'.[4]

Through 1954 and into 1955, Elvis and the girls laid siege to the repressive gender norms of the mid-1950s. There were a few boys in the audience, but his shows, at this time, were overwhelmingly female. This was a whirlwind romance that doubled as an insurrection: a secret world where – for a few ecstatic hours – anything and everything was all right, mama: screaming, shouting, dancing, jumping, pushing through barriers, losing control, twisting and rocking, grinding and rolling because the music was in you, and it felt good.

Elvis was the one on stage, but this performance was a collaboration. In the heat of the moment, he moved and they responded, but then he would respond back to them. It was an exchange of energy, a shit-hot feedback loop that intensified as the show went on, and it was the girls who were in the driver's seat. From that very first moment at the Shell, when their screams drowned out the music, they had shaped Elvis into what they wanted and needed him to be: a visceral, visual articulation of *their* feelings and thoughts. If you had walked into an Elvis show in 1955, you would have seen it and heard it immediately: his body, their voices. The screaming was so loud that his band used to joke that they had to watch Elvis's ass just to keep time with the music.

The press had no idea what to make of any of this. It was so bizarre and so new that they struggled to even put it into words. Some described Elvis as a wild animal who 'slunk panther-like across the stage', while others said he 'strutted like a duck' with 'a masculine version of Marilyn Monroe's wiggle in every jerking step'. Many thought his 'continual flexing of the hands, gyrating of the knees, and facial expressions' made it look like he was suffering from some kind of illness – acute appendicitis maybe.[5]

'He's the kind of child that other children are traditionally not allowed to play with,' sneered one reporter, 'a sullen, ill-kempt-looking youth. If he was my kid, I'd smack that sneer off his face and send him out for a haircut.'[6] But it was the blatant sexual give-and-take that truly baffled and concerned them. 'The singing did not seem to be what the teenagers particularly were interested in,' complained another reviewer, 'for every time the sultry side-burned singer would bump his lip the frenzy would mount.' His performance was 'the most disgusting exhibition' – 'the male counterpart of a hoochie-coochie dancer in a burlesque show'.[7] As the

San Francisco Chronicle concluded: 'If he did that same stuff on the streets, we'd lock him up.'[8]

And then there were the girls. Unable to deal with the fact that young women might have been actively choosing this, they were portrayed in the press as mindless mobs under the control of an evil master. Their 'air raid siren screams' became battle cries as their hero 'worked himself into an orgiastic rhythm, losing himself to the savage beat'.[9] In a particularly dark allusion to wartime punishment (French women accused of collaboration with the Germans had their heads shaved), one newspaper described the sound of an Elvis concert as 'like 12,000 girls having their heads shaved at once'.

'It is a frightening thing for a man to watch his women debase themselves,' said the *Vancouver Sun*. 'If any daughter of mine broke out of the woodshed tonight to see Elvis Presley in Empire Stadium, I'd kick her teeth in.'[10] The *Miami Daily News* couldn't have agreed more: 'We might suggest a gift for these fourteen thousand Miami girls who, as if it were a fetish, are vocally and mentally genuflecting to Elvis Presley: A SOLID SLAP ACROSS THE MOUTH.'[11]

As the media frenzy continued, it became clear that the girls' behaviour was more than alarming. It was framed as an invading army: an unstoppable force, so wild and reckless that even Elvis himself was at risk. 'A girl got past the police, bounced up on the stage, and hugged and kissed her panting crocodile,' recounted a review that read more like a horror movie in the *Kansas City Times*.

A policeman got her off again, but the signal for the avalanche was on. As the cool cats would say, they were determined to get really with him. They poured over the front and over the sides of the stage. They surrounded their almost prostrated hero, reaching for buttons, a piece of his shirt, a lock of his ducktail or anything they could grab. The Presley gyrations stopped suddenly. He was immobilised.[12]

The association, in the American popular imagination, between teen girl sexual desire, violence and danger had been building since the war. With more women than ever joining the workforce, rising numbers of unmarried women living alone and the explosion of dating culture, the social and sexual autonomy of teenage girls had become a flashpoint for much bigger anxieties about changing gender roles. 'What's the Matter with High-School Girls?' asked *Good Housekeeping*. 'They are shrill. They talk too loud and giggle too much in public places. They travel in groups. They take possession of a bus, pushing, crowding, calling across defenseless strangers.'[13]

Nowhere was this increasing boldness and taking up of space more visible than in dating culture. For centuries, parents had been warned to protect their daughters from the lustful thoughts and advances of men. Now, with girls feeling more confident to look, flirt and even pursue the boys they liked, parents were being urged to protect their sons. 'Boys by nature, facts and statistics prove it, are a lot less aggressive than girls,' explained a 1948 sex education manual called *The Stork Didn't Bring You*. 'They don't get "fresh" unless a girl provokes a "pass".'[14] The real anxiety was that girls and women seemed to be adopting traditionally male behaviours and roles in both romantic and everyday life. The inevitable conclusion, as the increasing number of horror films featuring sexually aggressive teenage girls warned audiences, was that this gender inversion would lead to the complete destruction of society as they knew it. In *Blood of Dracula*, for example, an evil science teacher at a girls' boarding school creates a weapon of mass destruction by harnessing the sexual energy of teenage girls.

The good news was that it was only some girls that were the problem, and they were easy to spot. The bad girls were the ones who smoked like chimneys, ran around with ne'er-do-wells and 'did not conceal their physical attractions or restrain their awakening sexual interests' – until Elvis came along.

Now, under the influence of the wiggle, it was impossible to know which girls were good and which ones were bad. Sonny West, who would later become one of Elvis's bodyguards, described attending a show on a date with a 'quiet, corn-fed Southwestern girl' in her Sunday-best dress 'whose demeanor and looks suggested that when someone invented virginity and apple pie, they must have had her in mind'. Upon meeting up with him, she was clear that he could 'scrap any thoughts of ever scoring' with her that night. Half an hour later, however, when Elvis took to the stage, he watched in amazement as she became, in his words, 'totally out of character', behaving 'like a sex-starved little nymphet'.[15]

At first, he was quite pleased: he thought it meant he might actually get some action later. 'If someone had grabbed that lady right there and then and dragged her off to bed, it would have happened there and then,' he said. To his dismay, after the show, she simply returned to her previous self. Sonny concluded that Elvis was some kind of magical wizard and 'all that carrying on' was for Elvis and no one else. This was still a 'nice girl', he told himself – he took her return to her 'normal self' as all the evidence he needed.

The truth was that being good or bad wasn't binary. Most teenage girls of the '50s were leading double lives. One of the most shocking findings of the Kinsey Report had been that 50 per cent of American women were not virgins when they got married. No one would admit they were one of those girls, but in the secret language of jukeboxes and record players, hidden between the rituals of prom night and going steady, stolen moments behind the bleachers and whispered promises at school dances, teen girls were already testing the waters of 'teenage love'.

Sex was a serious matter. Your virginity was sacred and you had to protect it with your life, but before that there were still lots of interesting things you could do. By the time Elvis rose to fame, getting a bit hot and heavy at the drive-in or 'petting' in the backseat of a car were unspoken but accepted parts of teenage life. More than that, in fact, it was part of becoming yourself – discovering who you were, becoming a full, experienced person in the world. 'I couldn't stand the idea of a woman having to have a single pure life and a man being able to have a double life, one pure and one not,' wrote Sylvia Plath.[16]

There were just three rules. One: you had to pretend you didn't want it. Two: whatever you did do, you didn't talk about it. And three – and this could not be emphasised enough – you resisted going 'all the way'. Being branded a bad girl could ruin your life. It meant social death and, worse, that no one (possibly even your boyfriend) would want to marry you. But whatever you did or didn't do, told yourself you were doing or tried not to do, the call was always there. Shimmering. 'Real life was sexual,' wrote Joyce Johnson.

> Or, rather, it often seemed to take the form of sex. This was the area of ultimate adventure, when you would dare or not dare. Sex was like a forbidden castle whose name could not even be spoken around the house, so feared was its power. Only with the utmost vigilance could you avoid being sucked into its magnetic field. The alternative was to break into the castle and take the power yourself.[17]

When Elvis arrived, the magnetic field exploded and the keys to that castle manifested instantly in the hands of every girl who saw or even just heard him. Not only was he the first male celebrity since Valentino to fully embrace being the object of pure, unbridled, bodily girl-lust, but he seemed to completely love and get off on it himself. Here, strangely and miraculously, was a way for girls to experience many of the things that seemed so exciting about the idea of sex – the power, the intensity, the abandon – without any of the consequences.

In the earliest days of his celebrity, while Elvis and the girls were enjoying their secret honeymoon in small music venues across the south, the threat was mostly tolerated. Like teenagers hiding in their bedrooms, it was hard for parents to know exactly what was going on in there (aside from bizarre and only slightly alarming press reports), but it was inevitable that, eventually, they would have to come out. When he was beamed into millions of American homes in a series of TV appearances in 1956, most infamously on *The Ed Sullivan Show* (where he was only shown from the waist up), they were forced to go public. Everyone wanted to see, with their own eyes, what all the fuss was about.

In a flash (or, in fact, in the flicker and crackle of millions of 1950s TV screens all turning on and tuning in, in anticipation, at exactly the same time), that beautiful body – so sweet and wild, so dangerous and irresistible, so restless, so charming, so unlike anything anyone had ever seen before – arrived, pouting and grinding in 8 million living rooms. And in the background: the screams. It wouldn't have been an Elvis show without the girls.

As open-mouthed parents turned to their children in shock or bolted from their sofas to turn off their TVs, the normal everyday moral panic that had been quietly simmering in the background suddenly exploded into full-on DEFCON 1. Ten-year-old Priscilla

Beaulieu (the future Mrs Presley) remembered peeking through a crack in the living room door as her parents watched in disbelief. The first words out of her mother's mouth were: 'That's disgusting!'[18]

By bringing his bump-and-grind routine into thousands of 'nice' middle-class American homes, Elvis had crossed the public decency line by about a million miles. But the negative reviews in the press the next day were just as incensed by the 'jungle rhythms' of his music as the obscenity of his 'striptease with clothes on'.[19] The *New York Times* called his performance 'sheer voodoo acrobatics', while the *Oakland Tribune* described his band as 'three young men blaring a jungle rhythm', with girls screaming 'like banshees' in response.[20] The racially charged undertones of these comments were impossible to miss.

Elvis had grown up in the south and was deeply influenced by African American music and fashion. What white middle-class America saw that night was a white boy with a Black haircut, dressed in Black clothes, exciting their daughters with Black music and Black dance moves. Elvis was sexy but not in a clean-cut, wholesome, white-bread Hollywood way – he was sexy in the raw, earthy way they associated with Black male sexuality. The fact that this was exciting their daughters so much made him terrifying. It was him, of course, but it was also about what the reactions of the girls meant – the terror and shock that it was his 'Blackness' that seemed to excite and fascinate them so much.

This was 1956 – the height of the desegregation era – a year that had seen some of the most violent resistance to integration across the south. Two years earlier, the Supreme Court had ordered the desegregation of high schools, sparking mob violence and school closures from those desperate to keep young Black and white people apart. But the levees were bursting. Even when young people weren't physically mixing Black and white, they were culturally mixing Black and white. Music and youth culture were bringing them closer than they had ever been before.

On dance floors, pirate radio stations and in record stores up and down the country, rock 'n' roll was fast becoming teenagers' shared language of freedom and rebellion, and – as Elvis and the girls reminded everyone who saw and heard them – the sound, the dance moves and even the name itself were undeniably sexual (rock 'n' roll was originally an old African American euphemism for sex). Behind all the histrionics about Elvis's hoochie-coochie show was a deeper fear: that as young people began sharing spaces and culture, they might start 'rocking and rolling' in the original sense, with each other. A publicist at Elvis's record label actually once described rock 'n' roll as 'a giant wedding ceremony' with 'two feuding clans brought together by marriage'.[21]

As rock 'n' roll continued to gain momentum, fangirl love and adoration became one of the most visible and irrepressible signs of segregation crumbling. Memphis radio DJ Rufus Thomas described seeing 'a thousand black, brown, and beige teenage girls' taking off 'like scalded cats in the direction of Elvis' after a show. He wondered how and why 'cullud girls would take on so over a Memphis white boy ... when they hardly let out a squeak over B. B. King, a Memphis cullud boy?' His conclusion gave voice to the thing everyone was wondering or already knew: that perhaps girls' reactions to Elvis revealed 'a basic integration in attitude and aspiration which has been festering in the minds of most of your folks' women folk all along'.[22]

And this was bigger than just Elvis. Black rock 'n' roll heroes like Fats Domino, Chuck Berry and Little Richard were gathering large, enthusiastic mixed fanbases just the same. Berry described white girls rushing the stage after shows, 'mingling with and hugging performers' with a 'friendliness' that went 'beyond normal musical appreciation to wanting to personally meet and associate with the singers'. In a segregated society where even accidental physical contact could be dangerous – could get someone killed – this kind of intimate, enthusiastic mixing was unprecedented. Berry said it was something he 'never expected'.[23]

Rocking and rolling in the eye of this storm, Elvis became a cultural lightning rod. As a white boy steeped in Black culture, making girls of all colours of the rainbow scream with dance moves that were so sexy they were borderline illegal, he made all the fears and anxieties of his day visible at once. The backlash was swift and brutal. Records were burned. Shows were banned. In some states, Elvis haircuts were outlawed. And I hate to break it to you: even Frank Sinatra weighed in. He called Elvis's music 'deplorable, a rancid-smelling aphrodisiac … The most brutal, ugly, degenerate, vicious form of expression it has been my displeasure to hear.'[24]

The hysteria reached its peak in August 1956 when Elvis arrived in Jacksonville, Florida, and was met by Judge Marion Gooding with a pre-emptive arrest warrant for impairing the morals of minors. He told Elvis he would send him straight to the slammer if he performed any of his signature gyrations on stage. That morning, a congregation of girls in the front rows of Trinity Baptist Church had led prayers for the salvation of his soul after their reverend declared that he had 'achieved a new low in spiritual degeneracy' (though he also warned them that Elvis might already be beyond salvation).[25] That night, as he took to the stage, flanked by policemen ready to arrest him, the whole city held its breath. He lifted his hand and wiggled... his little finger. The screams were deafening.

[S]HE'S A REBEL

The night Elvis appeared on *Ed Sullivan* for the first time, something changed. When the music was over and the TVs were off, the sound up and down America was the thud of millions of bedroom doors slamming. 'My aunt told me how foolish I was to sit screaming with joy at the spectacle of that vulgar singer on TV,' said Maureen, who was thirteen at the time. 'It was then I knew that she and I lived in different worlds.'[26]

If the teenager had been an idea before that moment – an age group, a transition phase, a culture – it was something even more tangible now. An identity. Half secret society, half religion, being a teenager was about the music and movies you liked – fervently. Of course, it had been that way for a while. But now it was also about what you believed. Adults didn't understand. How could they? Their world was built on work, order, appearances – layers of phoniness and pretence. Their reactions to Elvis only confirmed their ignorance.

To add insult to injury, for his next TV appearance, on *The Steve Allen Show*, he was forced to endure the humiliation of having to wear a tuxedo and sing 'Hound Dog' to a dog in a top hat, as if in penance. 'They tried to get him to go away,' says singer-songwriter P. F. Sloan. 'They tried big time, but he wasn't going ... For many of us, he was the first opportunity [we had] for self-exploration. We didn't have to be what they wanted us to be.'[27]

For boys like P. F., the idea of self-exploration – and the example set by Elvis – was cataclysmic. But it wasn't difficult to embrace. The holy trinity of 1950s teen rebellion – Elvis, James Dean and Marlon Brando – were young men just like them. From the moment Brando coolly rode into town on his motorbike in *The Wild One*, teenage boys had a new model for expressing their inner struggles. 'What are you rebelling against?' asks the waitress in the diner in the movie. 'Whaddaya got?' His nonchalant reply became a rallying cry. Leather jackets, aviators, being moody and leaning against walls had never felt as powerful, or as deep and meaningful, as they did in the hands of the boys who saw themselves in these men.

When James Dean died in a car crash in 1955, it felt like the inevitable conclusion to the myth he'd created on screen. His mangled Porsche, 'Little Bastard', was carted around high schools as a grim warning against dangerous driving. When the garage it was being housed in caught fire, and then it fell off its pedestal outside a school and nearly broke a student's arm, everyone decided it was cursed. Dean was a martyr, and that made the car a holy object. Fan letters poured in long after his death, teenagers made pilgrimage to his hometown of Marion, Indiana, and fragments of the car were eventually sold off as relics. 'Come back, Jimmy! I love you! We're waiting for you!' screamed a girl at a film screening.[28]

'He seemed to express some of the things they couldn't find the words for,' explained a documentary two years later, 'rage, rebellion, hope, the lonely awareness that growing up is pain.' But this same film drew a stark contrast between how boys and girls were understood to be idolising and imagining him. For boys, it was deadly serious. 'Because he died violently, every boy could use him as a warning to his parents – "If you don't start understanding me, I could go the same way."' For girls, it was dismissed as a crush: 'Because he died young and belonged to no one, every girl could feel that he belonged to her alone.'[29]

There is no doubt that James Dean was dreamy in that classic 1950s rebel boy kind of way – restless and wild but child-like and almost holy in his innocence at the same time. He was the kind of boy who needed you as much as you needed him, but more than ever before, male stars like Brando and Dean gave girls a richer, more layered form of identification and idolatry. 'It seemed to me that James Dean was a free-spirited person,' reflected one girl.[30] 'Then and now I wanted so much to be that free, to feel that free.' Barbara, who turned sixteen in 1950, saw a similar expansiveness in Brando. 'He was called the Valentino of the Bop generation ... But we loved him because he kept shaking the stardust off,' she explained. 'Uncouth and dignified, sensitive and rebellious, he was the poet-buried-in-the-animal ... with beautiful, brainy, muscled Brando, you got it all – Zen and Freud, talk and action, sex and sensibility.'[31]

These men symbolised the possibility of something bigger for their girl fans. In an era when every aspect of a girl's life was oriented toward one future – marriage, suburbs, children, laundry – no one wanted to be branded a bad girl. The cost was too high. But there was a loophole: fantasy. Daydreaming about the wrong kind of boy became a form of rebellion in itself. These weren't the steady boyfriends who would lead to washing machines and wedding cakes. Dating – or even just dreaming about – rebels, rockers, bikers and beatniks was a way to imagine a completely different kind of life for yourself.

Seventeen-year-old Sheila Rowbotham pieced together her 'ultimate man' from fragments of Dean, Brando and Beat poets like varsity football player turned philosopher turned poet turned vagabond – mad to live, mad to talk, mad to burn, desirous of everything all at the same time – Mr Swoon of the Highway himself: Jack Kerouac. She imagined this 'ultimate man' to be 'a man of few words but intense emotions, expressed through a grunt or a flick of the eye'. Her fantasy was that 'such a friendly psychopath' would notice that under her 'remarkably healthy exterior', she was just as intense and adventurous as him. He had 'holes in his pants and holes in his T-shirts and holes in his jeans', she said, 'but the biggest hole of all was in his heart'. Hearts, she decided, were 'expendable' – they belonged to 'slushy pop songs' and the domestic future she wanted to escape.[32]

Rowbotham would go on to become one of the most influential feminists of the 1960s – she was one of the founders of the women's movement in Britain. In her book *Woman's Consciousness, Man's World*, she reflected that these teenage fantasies weren't really about the men at all – they were about replacing the world of careful planning and reasoned choices with one of pure feeling and immediate experience. Books, films, music and magazines became secret maps to this wilder way of living. And Sheila wasn't the only one. 'I wanted wildness, originality, genius, rapture, hope. I wanted strength, not tea parties,' wrote Pulitzer Prize winner Annie Dillard, recalling her teenage years in Pittsburgh.[33] 'I was raised in Texas,' said Janis Joplin. 'I had all these ideas and feelings I'd pick up in books ... but there just wasn't anybody, man, in Port Arthur. Nobody. I remember reading about Kerouac in *Time* magazine and thinking, "Wow!" So I split.'[34]

As the countercultural Beat poetry scene flourished in Greenwich Village, a steady stream of young women arrived, copies of Kerouac's *On the Road* in hand, in search of what Joyce Johnson called Real Life – 'dramatic, unpredictable, possibly dangerous' – the antithesis of the 'bourgeois respectability' waiting for them back home. 'With her seat at the table in the exact centre of the universe,' she wrote,

that midnight place where so much is converging, the only place in America that's alive ... As a female, she's not quite part of this convergence. A fact she ignores, sitting by in her excitement as the voices of the men, always the men, passionately rise and fall and their beer glasses collect and the smoke of their cigarettes rises toward the ceiling and the dead culture is surely being awakened. Merely being here, she tells herself, is enough.[35]

Yes. These women had fled convention only to find that paradise had its own, very similar, set of rules. They got all the romance of cramped apartments and having no money for food by the end of the month, wrote poetry and novels and explored sexual freedom. But they also found themselves cooking and cleaning while the men set off on Benzedrine-fuelled road trips in search of enlightenment. 'Naturally, we fell in love with men who were rebels,' Johnson reflected. 'We fell fast, believing they would take us along on their journeys and adventures ... We were very young and we were in over our heads. But we knew we had done something brave, practically historic. We were the ones who had dared to leave home.'

In the '50s, being a rebel boy was a right. For girls, it was risky enough to get you locked away in a mental institution or strapped down for electroshock therapy like Sylvia Plath in *The Bell Jar*. As a consequence, the beatnik women of Greenwich Village were an avant-garde minority. Back home, in the suburbs, their younger sisters were still grappling with the good girl/bad girl dilemma. For more mainstream girls, rebellion took the form of arguing with parents over watching Elvis on TV or defiantly buying his records and hiding them under their beds – small acts of resistance, even if they didn't fully realise it at the time. What they did know was that something about him affected them. The energy, the excitement, the intensity: the freedom to be exactly who and what he was. One eleven-year-old girl, Cherilyn, described seeing him on *Ed Sullivan* as a lightning bolt: 'I was a goner,' she said. 'I loved the way he sang and the way he looked. In some strange way, I felt he expressed who I was.'[36]

Cherilyn, who grew up in Sharp County, Arkansas, described herself as 'a tomboy, but a girlie girl too'. She liked to sing and she was in the school choir, but she had a low voice that didn't quite fit the usual mould. She never seemed to fit neatly into one category, and when she saw Elvis, what struck her most was that he didn't seem to, either. This was reassuring. 'Well, this is just who I am,' she thought.

After *Ed Sullivan*, most mothers in Sharp County 'shrank in revulsion' and forbade their children from buying his records, but Cherilyn's mom appreciated his music. She thought it was pretty good and even bought two tickets for a show when Elvis came to town. Cherilyn was ecstatic. She got her hair cut especially. 'I was so crazy,' she recalled, 'I hoped he would notice me.' When he walked out in a gold suit and the girls started screaming, she didn't completely understand why. 'I wasn't quite sure about the sexual part,' she admitted, 'but I was just fascinated.' She even asked her mother if they could stand on their chairs and scream, and they did, but she couldn't keep her eyes off him. Her heart, mind and imagination were racing. 'My mom was yelling and laughing, and I projected myself up there. It didn't make much difference what sex he was.'

Seeing Elvis, first on TV and then in person, was a defining moment for Cherilyn. It felt like a sign that she didn't need to fit neatly into categories or be defined by them. He also helped her realise what she wanted to do with her life. Ten years later, she would be standing on stages of her own as a folk musician, and by the 1970s, she would become one of the bestselling female artists of all time. By then, the 'Goddess of Pop' had shortened her name. The world would know her as Cher.

As Cher – even at eleven – understood: of the three rebel boys in the 1950s' holy trinity of teen rebellion, Elvis most overtly defied gender norms and was the one girls identified with most deeply. As Elvis scholar Erika Doss puts it, much like 'Rudolph Valentino, Elvis helped destabilise conventional understandings of masculinity'.[37] In doing so, he invited girls and women to ask questions about femininity as well. From the very earliest days of his career, he radiated a magnetic type of sexual ambiguity. His movements, behaviour and personal style were expressive and uninhibited. They screamed blatant defiance of social conventions, like a big middle finger to everything that was expected of him as a performer and as a man.

Nowhere was this more visible than in his fashion sense. Some days, he wore blue jeans and leather jackets; others, it might be black pin-striped pants with a pink frilly shirt. He'd been wearing eyeliner since long before he was famous. He dyed his hair (originally blond), as well as his eyelashes and eyebrows (depending on who you ask, either to look more like actor Tony Curtis or as a tribute to his mother). And his favourite colour was pink. This was a long way from the stultifying, conservative conventions of what a 'masculine' man in the 1950s was supposed to look like (see Sinatra circa 'helping men in grey flannel suits tentatively learn about vulnerability' for details). For many fans, it sent a strong message about freedom and individuality. It was especially meaningful to girls because it made it easy to imagine themselves in his body. 'I have big blue eyes, pretty lips like yours,' wrote one girl. 'All my friends tell me I look as much like Elvis as a girl possibly could. I even wiggle like he does,' wrote another.[38]

'Elvis loved his body,' says Doss.[39] 'And he loved intimating what he could do with it, especially with the fans who wanted to do it with him too.' But, like Cher, for many girls, it wasn't about sex like that. It was about harnessing all that raw, wild, sexual power for themselves. Like the boys who had begun to dress like Marlon Brando when *The Wild One* was released, thousands of girls now began to style themselves like Elvis. In 1957, *Life* magazine reported that 1,000 girls in Grand Rapids, Michigan, had chopped off their ponytails and were now wearing their hair 'slicked back with a lank hand over the forehead and a graspable tuft in front of each ear'.[40] Tens of thousands more traded in their poodle skirts for jeans, rolled up their T-shirt cuffs and stood in front of the mirror, curling their lips and practising their swaggers.

Whether they were enjoying the sexy spectacle of his rebel moves on TV, screaming and shouting at a concert or becoming him in real life, Elvis's girl fans of the 1950s were, in the words of sociologist Wini Breines, making 'tentative forays into alternative notions of femininity'. For many girls, she says, Elvis fandom offered an escape from 'boring and stressful courtship rituals' and the 'wholesomeness of their futures'.[41] These were three-minute pop songs that cracked open a space for freedom and experimentation. Like dreaming of boys from the wrong side of the tracks, it was a way to take advantage of the small spaces on offer in teen pop culture for exploration, escape and protest.

When fifteen-year-old Janis Martin, the 'Female Elvis', burst onto the scene in 1956, it was a sign that the music industry might finally be beginning to take note of teen girls' desire to see and hear their own full, powerful authentic selves up on stage.

There would be a few 'Female Elvises' in the 1950s: Wanda Jackson with her rockabilly growl, Alis Lesley with her slicked-back hair (she's the girl holding a guitar, with Little Richard and Eddie Cochran, on the cover of Bob Dylan's *The Philosophy of Modern Song*) but Martin was the original and the best. Her lyrics and her voice – bouncing between good girl sweet and bad girl sass – were rebellion perfected. If Elvis's wiggle expressed all the things that many girls were thinking and feeling, Janis said them out loud, with words. Her first single 'Will You Willyum' was a hand grenade to the idea that a girl should ever have to, or need to, hold back.

'Martin's lyrics made a radical statement in the 1950s,' says historian Susan K. Cahn. At a time when 'experts portrayed women's sexuality as passive and responsive, that is, as primarily oriented around male pleasure', here was a young woman who was 'singing about her own sexual desires, satisfactions, frustrations, and fantasies'.[42] And as the stuff that so many teen girl fantasies of the 1950s were made of, Elvis made direct and indirect appearances in quite a few of her songs. Most famously, in 'My Boy Elvis', he is both an object of identification and love. It's joyful. It's playful. It's a love letter to Elvis. But most of all: it's a love letter to the power of music and fandom themselves.

Like millions of 1950s girls, Janis's relationship with Elvis is a fantasy, and she knows it. But there's freedom in that. This is her Elvis – one she's created for herself, shaped by her desires and imagination. He exists to please, entertain and empower her and only her. That was the magic of Elvis. He was a beautiful, infinite, blank canvas onto which girls could begin to paint a picture of their own dreams, identities and ambitions. But as rock 'n' roll emboldened them to start expressing those feelings and desires more openly, for some, the fantasy just wasn't going to be enough.

THE TENDER TRAP

By the late 1950s, the Memphis police had a new protocol. If a teenage girl went missing, the first place to look was outside the gates of

Elvis Presley's sprawling Graceland estate. Girls had always gathered wherever Elvis went – backstage at concerts, in hotel lobbies, outside his childhood home – but Graceland became a mystical focal point. With its grand gates, manicured lawns and gleaming white columns, it radiated a kind of quiet majesty. Even its name – Graceland – sounded like a little piece of heaven.

For the 'gate girls' who stood outside day after day, rain or shine, the chance of catching a glimpse of him was worth the wait, and Elvis was always good to them. As he came and went, he would stop to pose for pictures, answer questions and sign autographs. There were also whispers that, on some nights, a chosen few might be invited inside.

From the very earliest days of pop culture – especially when young women began to gather in large groups like this – the fear had always been that female fans might start spending time with their heroes behind closed doors. In the nineteenth century, at the height of the Matinee Idol craze, the nervousness was so prevalent that actor Charles Cherry felt compelled to issue a reassurance to parents. 'Those who worshipped the Matinee Idol did so in perfect safety,' he said. He assured them that 'he could never make the mistake of offending their best instincts of good manners and morals'.[43]

In those days, the idea that girls' attraction to their heroes might be, in any way, physical would have been so scandalous that no one talked about it. Fans described their feelings as 'rapture' and said they were interested in their hero's 'spiritual beauty' and 'aesthetic charm'.[44] But behind the scenes, the reality was often quite different. Years later, the daughter of a famous Matinee Idol admitted that while her father, Richard Bennett, was 'overbearing and puritanical about the women in his own family, he exercised no such restrictions with his fans. His matinees were mobbed by flushed, agreeable ladies who fairly quivered in his presence.' He was 'often extremely charitable in rewarding their attentions, individually, and the demand was never more than he could supply'.[45]

The idea that these men were simply responding to their female fans, giving them what they were relentlessly asking for, was common backstage gossip. Actress Michael Strange recalled hearing, from an older actress, that Matinee Idols were often warned to beware of Matinee Girls. With their incessant 'worshipping, writing, and waiting', it was impossible for even the most virtuous of men not, eventually, to surrender to the 'impassioned vitality of their hunters'.[46]

Even Lord Byron frequently framed himself as a helpless victim of female desire. When seventeen-year-old Claire Clairmont – a vivacious, guitar-playing 1950s rebel girl 200 years before her time – pursued him relentlessly, he said he found it increasingly impossible to resist. As his biographers love to remind us: she repeatedly 'offered herself' to him. 'He took advantage of her offer but he never loved her.'[47] A few months later, he wrote to his sister: 'Now don't scold, but what could I do? ... I could not exactly play the Stoic with a woman – who had scrambled eight hundred miles to unphilosophize me ... I was fain to take a little love (if pressed particularly) by way of novelty.'[48]

That 'novelty' would result in the birth of a daughter, Allegra. Byron initially questioned whether the 'brat' was even his but eventually conceded it was.[49] He had her removed from her mother and sent to be raised in a convent in Italy, where she died at the age of five. Claire spent the rest of her days unmarried and heartbroken, working as a governess in Switzerland. Haunted with regret over her misspent youth, she wrote damningly of Byron and her brother-in-law Percy Bysshe Shelley (with whom she was also said to have had an affair) in her memoirs. Shelley famously advocated for 'free love'. As a young woman, under the influence of this 'doctrine and belief', she said she had seen 'the two first poets of England ... become monsters. What evil passion free love assured, what tenderness it dissolves; how it abused affections that should be the solace and balm of life.'[50]

History likes to cast Romantic poets like Byron and Shelley as the rockstars of their day. This (as I was recently informed by a tour guide at Byron's ancestral home, Newstead Abbey) makes women like Claire and Caroline Lamb nineteenth-century groupies. It's the same story of helpless male celebrities and predatory female fans that history had been telling since the very birth of celebrity, but Claire's words remind us that the truth was often darker. These were relationships that hovered in the no man's land between empowerment and exploitation. When fantasy became reality, it rarely played out the way these women had imagined or hoped. From there, the moral dilemma was often not just about what to do but about how to remember it.

Twenty-five-year-old Eliza Francis didn't pursue Byron romantically, but when she met him at the height of his celebrity in 1814, she met a side of him she had not anticipated. She'd called on him with the hope that he might pre-order her new poem *The Rival Roses* (you needed 'subscribers' for your work to be published and having someone like Byron could encourage others to do so). When he agreed to see her, and he invited her to return several times, she even began imagining that perhaps he might become a kind of mentor. Her words were 'guide my life'.[51] She nearly fainted when, during one of their meetings, he began making advances and kissed her. 'Perhaps had we met much oftener, our adventure might have ended as most adventurous do,' he said.[52]

Of course, she 'made an effort to get away' immediately. She felt 'ashamed', she said, but reflected, looking back, that what tortured and confused her most was her own inability to leave.[53] Her account reads like *Romeo and Juliet* meets *The Sheik*:

'Don't tremble, don't be frightened – with me you are safe,' said he, and throwing himself into an armchair, he drew me towards him. For a moment I clung to him – I loved for the first time … he had drawn me down upon his knee, his arms were round my waist, and I could not escape.

When, with difficulty, she finally got to the door, she described turning to 'gaze once more at that Being I was resigning forever' before she 'flung herself into his open arms again'.

Eliza's story, written years later for a Victorian anthology of recollections of Byron, is as dramatic and romantic as something from the 'Turkish Tales' – tortured hero, noble resistance, heroine torn between virtue and her soulmate. Maybe that was the only way to make sense of an encounter like this. Or maybe that just *is* what it felt like. We don't know. What we do know is that this is how she wanted us to remember it – how she wanted us to remember her. Not as a victim or as yet another conquest in the story of the infamous Lord Byron, but as the heroine of her own Byronic adventure story. When your life fleetingly crosses paths with a legend, you want to write yourself into their myth on your own terms.

Over a century later, very little had changed. When Kay Wheeler jumped on that Greyhound bus to meet Elvis, she wasn't going into it as innocently as Eliza (she was feeling quietly confident about how much she looked like his mother, which was apparently his type), but she was still shocked by what happened when she

opened the door to his dressing room. 'He came at me like Godzil-
la,' she said.[54] A few minutes later, at a press conference, he pulled
her against him for the cameras – half lover's clinch, half human
shield – while reporters fired off questions. 'I was on the same page
with him,' she said. 'We were both young and riding the rock 'n'
roll wave.'[55] But in the pictures, she looks awkward, like a sixteen-
year-old girl trying to maintain coolness and sophistication in the
face of a hurricane. 'Elvis, will you ever get married!?' shouted a
reporter.

His reply, delivered with his arms casually draped all over this
sixteen-year-old girl he had known for exactly twenty minutes,
startled her. 'Why buy a cow when you can get the milk through the
fence for free?' He laughed. So did the reporters. At that moment,
Kay vowed that she would never be one of those girls. And yet,
a few months later, she found herself sitting on a bed in a hotel
room, waiting. When you're summoned by The King, it's difficult to
say no.

Of all the male celebrities who came before or after, Elvis is one of
the most complicated in terms of fans and sex. He carefully constructed his image and performances to turn women on. And it
worked. From the first time the girls saw him at the Overton Shell,
long lines of them – as many as 300 at once, apparently – would line
up outside his motel room every Saturday night. His sex life was
so entwined with his stardom that he actually lost his virginity to
a fan. But the '50s were still an era of strict moral codes, and Elvis
understood the power of playing both sides.

The myth of Elvis, as written by the male rock critics who were

the gatekeepers of rock history for decades, is the story of 'an incredibly virile super-stud that women were powerless to resist'.[56]
David Marsh of *Rolling Stone* described how 'the pure fuck-me
splendor of his movements ... began to strike sparks. Boys became
as hostile as their girlfriends became aroused.' His real-life exploits
seem to back this up. 'Elvis could score whenever he wanted,' said
producer Horace Logan. 'He screwed around with so many girls
he'd never seen before and never saw again that I'm surprised he
didn't catch something and die.'[57]

Tales of these early backstage encounters – like the rumours that
surrounded Matinee Idols – framed him as supplying a select, lucky
few with exactly what they'd come for. 'For a man who was pawed,
groped, scratched, and had his clothes ripped away by women for
his entire twenty-three-year career, [he] demonstrated a remarkable
tolerance for his audience,' says biographer Alanna Nash.[58] Pre-1954,
he'd been a nice boy (you know, the faithful marrying type). Once
he realised the effect he had on women and how good being with
them made him feel – in the same way that he would with food and
drugs in the 1970s – he gorged. He didn't limit himself to the fans
who actively pursued him, either.

Elvis's sexual magnetism was said to be so great that he could
pretty much walk up to any girl he wanted and, 99.9 per cent of the
time, she would acquiesce – agree to go on a date with him later,
drop what she was doing and come with him right now or even
just let him kiss her then and there (Elvis loved kissing). *The Kiss*, a
photograph taken backstage at the Mosque Theatre in Richmond,
Virginia, in 1956, captured one of these moments (Diane Keaton
once called it 'the sexiest picture ever taken in the whole world').[59]
Earlier that day, a girl called Bobbi Owens had phoned Elvis's hotel
room on a dare. She didn't expect to be having lunch with him a few

hours later, let alone hanging out backstage that night at a show, but when Elvis wanted something, he got it.

'Right off the bat, he kept trying to embrace me and kiss me, and he kept telling me to kiss him,' she recalled.[60] 'I told him "no".' Elvis persisted playfully. This was his MO. On stage, he was all swagger and snarl, but off stage – when that guitar was safely packed away in its case – his approach to seduction often took the form of this overgrown lost-boy puppy-dog thing (he was a big fan of pillow fights and tickling). Eventually, Bobbi stuck out her tongue, which he touched with his. That's when the photo was taken. It's a pure, stolen moment of carefree intimacy. Forget anything that happened on *Ed Sullivan*: if you want to understand the relationship between Elvis, women and sex in the 1950s, this, right here, is the Rosetta Stone.

On the surface, *The Kiss* is just a boy and a girl sharing a personal moment in a stairwell. What makes it so sexy is its lightness: the tips of their tongues barely touching, his hands on her waist, leaning in almost respectfully. Except – you can see that these two are so completely into each other that this respectful distance won't last many seconds longer. The whole photo is a ticking time bomb of desire and anticipation. And it's all about the girl. Elvis is the centre of attention – we can hardly even see her face – but this is her moment. She looks powerful. In control. Arms wide, as she leans casually against the railing, it's as if she's saying, 'I've got you exactly where I want you.'

This would be hot if it were any random couple, but it's not. It's Elvis Presley and down that stairwell is a screaming crowd of thousands. Soon, he'll be on stage wiggling for the world, but right now, in this moment, he's just a boy, standing in front of a girl, letting her decide how far this goes. For many of his girl fans (who let's not forget made up his largest fandom in the 1950s), Elvis didn't just represent sex because, as Lester Bangs put it, 'he alerted America to the fact that it had a groin with imperatives that had been stifled'.[61] What made him so goddamn irresistible was the duality we see in this picture – the way he could transform from rockabilly rebel to nice mama's boy in an instant. He was the boy who could make your mother faint but would then rush and fetch the smelling salts and charm her when she wakes up.

As a teen idol, Elvis's good boy/bad boy persona was essential because it spoke to the good girl/bad girl conflict young women felt in themselves. They had to find ways to connect with the freedom and power of 'bad' within the bounds of 'good'. He looked mean, like a hood, but he admitted, 'Just being near girls makes me kinda nervous and tingly all over, like getting shocked, but I like it!'[62] If Sinatra was Bambi with sex appeal, Elvis was the thug who, deep down inside, was secretly Bambi. The way he reacted to them – performed *for them* – reminded them how much power they really had. The fantasy lived in that sweet spot between abandon and control.

People sometimes forget about the music, but it's all there. Lie on your bed, close your eyes and listen to the feral neediness of ballads like 'Blue Moon' or 'I'll Never Let You Go' on his first album *Elvis Presley* and you're reminded that Elvis has a lot more in common with Sinatra than you might think (they did team up for a duet once and, yes, it was the most adorable moment in the whole history of television).

Elvis's voice, in these early love songs, is almost more compelling than Frankie's ever was because he strips everything right down to the naked, aching bone. There's no pretence here. No polish. What there is, is pure, desperate, unfiltered longing. He sounds like a baby animal in pain. Like Marlon Brando in *A Streetcar Named Desire*, falling to his knees in tears and a ripped T-shirt, wailing for his girlfriend outside her window, it's the fusion of brute masculinity and unrestrained neediness that made Elvis so sexy. It's also what made him so dangerous. As Sinatra would say: that's the tender trap. Because how do you resist a devastatingly beautiful man who is both the king of rock 'n' roll and a little boy with a bottomless well of loneliness and need? That dead twin is never coming back.

There were a lot of women in Elvis's life, and apparently, he'd slept with at least 1,000 of them by 1960. Many of these women knew what they were doing. The 'road girls' who sat in the front rows with no knickers on and flashed him while he was trying to sing were in on the game. So were his Hollywood co-stars. Even Bobbi, with her daring spontaneity, was an experienced and knowing girl. As she lay with him in the bunk of his sleeper train after the show that night – and finally let him get that kiss – she knew her limits, oh, and she also had to get back to her boyfriend.

But here's the tragedy: for all the revolution that Elvis represented on stage, he didn't seem to like women who were empowered or in control. He liked girls who were young, adoring and innocent, preferably aged around fourteen. He may have effortlessly flitted between good and bad, rebel and mama's boy, but he did not extend the offer of that same freedom to the women in his life. Like the world his music was disrupting, he sorted them into neat categories: the good girls and bad; home and away; virgins and whores. I'm not sure the girls who got categorised saw the division so neatly.

One of the men responsible for helping Elvis sort girls was an agent-in-training at William Morris fittingly called Byron. His unofficial job was to go down to the gates of MGM, or wherever they were, and supply Elvis with girls who were his type and to take them away when he was done ('It's time to go now, honey, Elvis needs his sleep').[63] He described a steady stream of girls coming out of Elvis's room 'in tears or hysterical that he didn't love them'. He'd try to reassure them as he ushered them out. 'I'd say, "No, that's not true … He'll call you again." Of course, he almost never did. But with some of the younger ones, he'd be like the tooth fairy, slipping hundred-dollar bills in their schoolbooks.'[64]

The image of a teenage girl sitting in class, opening her school-book to find that hundred-dollar bill, with everything it implied, is disturbing. And yet, accounts like these from Elvis's staff seem to conflict with the memories of many young women themselves. 'When you were in that room, you wanted to shut out the whole world for the rest of your life,' explained a girl called Gloria, who was fourteen when she and her friends Heidi and Frances became frequent fixtures at sleepovers.[65] Elvis was (and continues to be) such a massive cultural icon that he seemed to exist beyond the metaphysical boundaries – and therefore rules – of the real world. What was left was devotion, awe and the surreal sense of being one of the lucky girls who had been chosen to be part of his world.

The thrill of being chosen, of walking through those mystical music-note gates, of sitting in that famous pink bedroom with Elvis Presley records spinning on the turntable while the beautiful man himself sat right there in front of you, must have felt like a dream come true. Perhaps this helps explain why so few of these women – who were young teenagers of fourteen, fifteen and sixteen while Elvis was in his twenties, thirties and forties – have anything negative to say about these treasured memories, even in hindsight. When asked whether she would let her own fourteen-year-old daughter or granddaughter spend time alone at a man's house like that, Jackie's response was telling: 'I probably wouldn't like that,' she said, 'but then again, they wouldn't be Elvis.'[66]

Jackie was thirteen when she first met Elvis. One of the first things he did was stick his tongue in her ear. When she recoiled, he told her mother, who had brought her and was sitting in the living room with them, that she needed to take her to a doctor because she 'wasn't normal'. This cognitive dissonance – the ability to understand that something is inappropriate in general while making an exception for Elvis – appears repeatedly in women's recollections of their time with him. Elisabeth Stefaniak, who was nineteen when she lived with him while he was stationed with the army in Germany, is one of the people who have articulated it best: 'It was painful – I had feelings,' she said, 'but I knew how it was – that if I complained or said anything I might as well pack my suitcase and leave.'[67]

Like many of Elvis's 'girlfriends', Elisabeth was a fan first. The night she approached him for an autograph, he ended up walking her home and kissing her goodnight. A few months later, she agreed to move in with him, under the guise of helping manage his fanmail. She would sleep in bed with him most nights, but he would have other girls in his room before that. 'There would be at least a couple of girls each week, more on weekends,' she explained. 'Although I resented them, I knew they were not staying … I did not let him see me cry [and] all the time I was telling myself how lucky I was.'[68] This was a pattern that would repeat, with different women, throughout his life. 'She was completely in love with Elvis,' said his friend Rex. 'It was deflating and degrading for her to spend all day answering his love letters, only to hear his muffled moans with others through the walls.'

One of Elisabeth's sources of consolation was the fact that he probably wasn't actually having sex with these girls. For a man who was the perfect image of raw, untamed sexuality, one of the biggest ironies of Elvis Presley was that he wasn't actually that interested in sex. The story goes that his mythic status as the ultimate sex symbol had given him so much anxiety about his ability to perform in real life that he preferred kissing and everything else – especially with the younger girls, the ones he categorised as 'good'. In fact, his obsession with these girls was born in part from the fact that they had no experience and therefore no expectations.

It's easy to imagine how, for these young women, raised in a world where virginity was the thing you needed to protect, Elvis's insistence on 'being good' only confirmed the romantic fantasy of a bad boy with a tender heart. They quote his catchphrase – 'fourteen will get you twenty [years in prison]' – as proof of his moral good character.[69] But it doesn't mean he wasn't getting what he wanted out of the situation, because let's be honest: when your pants are off and you're touching each other, sex, as Alanna Nash puts it, is really a matter of semantics. Even with fourteen-year-old Priscilla, who he would later marry, he was said to have maintained this fiction of 'technical' virginity for years.[70]

This manipulation of what 'counted' as sex kept these young women emotionally invested while letting him maintain plausible deniability. In many ways, it's the ultimate microcosm of post-war teenage girls' relationship with sex: an alluring, mysterious world that promised both fulfilment and power but was ultimately controlled and defined by male pleasure and male standards – a world where only certain acts 'counted', while the emotional and physical realities for women were largely ignored.

Today, most of these women dismiss the sexual things that happened as 'teenager stuff' and describe Elvis more as a friend or first love than an idol – a boy-man who seemed almost like one of the girls.[71] They describe slumber parties that stretched until dawn, pillow fights that left them breathless and carefree days at the fairground, eating endless Pronto Pups and crashing in the dodgem cars. In these moments, Elvis let his guard down, they said, laughing and teasing like a peer. He felt safe with them, as if, in their presence, he could shed the pressures of fame. And they felt safe with him too.[72]

Except that he wasn't one of the girls. He was a grown man – one who was used to getting his own way and whose mood could easily turn. This was the realisation that began to dawn on sixteen-year-old Kay Wheeler as she sat waiting for him in that hotel room. She described a sudden, unsettling feeling that she shouldn't be there. Just as she'd decided to leave, she caught sight of Elvis in the hallway. He ran after her, pinned her to the wall and finally, for the first time ever, it was just the two of them. She looked into his big blue eyes and felt the urge to say something meaningful, something that would differentiate her from all the other girls.

'Elvis,' she said, 'what do you think life is all about?' He kissed her. This was a moment she had imagined a thousand times, but it didn't feel right now. 'He got really rough with me,' she said.

> He grabbed me and kissed me so long and hard I thought I was going to suffocate. He wouldn't get off my lips. Then he threw me against the wall and started grinding his pelvis, pushing on me really heavy. It was exactly what he did onstage, his whole performance.

He was scaring her. 'I was not old enough for what he had in mind. And it really disappointed me, because I wanted moonlight and roses. It was one of the biggest letdowns of my life.'

Kay felt a strange sense of power as she walked out of the hotel that night. On her way out, she passed a group of girls in the hall-way, who she guessed had been sent up the same way she had. 'I'm not one of you,' she thought. 'He'll remember me for not doing it.'[73] But it wasn't as simple as agreeing or not agreeing to do it. There were plenty of girls who did it, plenty who didn't and plenty more who must have found themselves stuck in a confusing, in-between place – unsure of what they wanted or what they were ready for, unable or unwilling to disentangle the truth from the dream, the man from the myth, their personal feelings from what it meant to be chosen.

AMAZING GRACE

Behind closed doors, Elvis's complicated relationship with women would continue for the rest of his life, but for the vast majority of fans, he existed only in the mythical glow of carefully man-aged public appearances, TV slots and magazine interviews. Stars are not people; they are symbols. And as a symbol, who Elvis was in 'real life' has very little to do with what he came to rep-resent to his fans. His body had always been a battleground of ownership and meaning, and this only intensified as his career progressed.

On 3 March 1960, Elvis sat at a press conference table looking new. Fresh from two years in the army, stationed in Germany, the rebellious young man who had once scandalised the nation had been transformed into a clean-cut all-American hero. The King was dead; long live The King.

Some people said that Elvis's military reset had been orchestrat-ed by his manager, Colonel Parker, in an attempt to rehabilitate his public image. The colonel had never been a fan of rock 'n' roll. He saw it as a stepping stone to much bigger, more lucrative things, so he'd been strict about the rules of Elvis's time away: no recordings, no concerts, no public appearances or interviews. The press were itching to see what would emerge from this chrysalis.

In his absence, fans, who had gone into mourning the moment he left, waited patiently for his return. They rewatched his movies, bought every one of his pre-recorded EPs and wore their 'Ladies in Waiting' necklaces distributed by Kay's fan club. On the back was engraved: 'Let's all remain faithful to Elvis while he is gone to prove to the adults that we're not fickle.' The crowds that greeted him upon his arrival back in the States, and everywhere along the road on his journey back to Graceland, left no doubt of their devotion in anyone's minds.

They did wonder about its longevity, though. With scandals like Jerry Lee Lewis's career-ending marriage to his thirteen-year-old cousin and Chuck Berry's arrest for transporting a fourteen-year-old across state lines for immoral purposes, rock 'n' roll itself seemed to be gasping its last breath. Clean-cut, white-bread teen idols like Frankie Avalon and Fabian were taking over the charts now.

'Elvis! Do you feel that you're a little old for the teenagers now?' jibed a reporter at the press conference.

That famous lip curled slightly (thank Satan it was still there).

'That's the first time I've been asked that one,' he replied. 'I don't know. I don't feel too old. I can still move around pretty good.'

'Are you apprehensive about what must be a comeback?'

'Yes, I am,' he admitted. 'I have my doubts. I'm not gonna commit to saying I'm gonna do this or that because I don't know. The only thing I can say is that I'm gonna try. I'll be in there fighting.'

But he wasn't naive. He'd seen what happened to Sinatra when the bobbysoxers grew up. Elvis knew that if he wanted to stay relevant, he needed to evolve, so he was headed for Hollywood. Taking a leaf out of the Sinatra playbook, his plan was to reinvent himself as a movie star and prove he could be more than a musical heart-throb. He'd always dreamed of being a serious actor like Brando and Dean: this was his moment. Unfortunately, Hollywood had other plans. Elvis would spend the next ten years starring in a never-ending string of frothy, formulaic, feel-good family films that capitalised on the nice mama's boy side of his charm.

At best, 'Elvis films' would be breezy hits like *Blue Hawaii* and *Viva Las Vegas*. At worst – and there were more worsts than bests – they would be cringe-worthy spectacles like *Kissin' Cousins* (Elvis plays twins, one of whom is trying to sleep with his cousin), *Clambake* (he's a millionaire oil heir pretending to be a waterski instructor, who sings a song about how much he likes barbecued shrimp) and *Live a Little, Love a Little* (he's a photographer who's waiting for his seventeen-year-old girlfriend to turn eighteen so he can 'finally kiss her').

Expressing the frustration and heartbreak of countless young male rock 'n' rollers who had deified Elvis as the ultimate symbol of male sexual dominance and rebellion, *Rolling Stone* writer Langdon Winner described this as the moment 'Elvis sold out to the girls'.[74] Seeing him serenade a puppet, dress in drag for a cheap laugh and sing 'Old MacDonald Had a Farm' had transformed the angry young bull of rock 'n' roll into 'a masturbation-fantasy object for adolescent girls', he said. Elvis had 'stopped threatening and begun pleading'.

You only have to hear the titles of some of these films to understand the extent of Elvis's '60s sellout. But let's get one thing straight: Elvis didn't sell out to the girls. He didn't need to. For better or worse, Elvis and the girls had been in a hot-and-heavy, codependent relationship since 1954. Elvis had always gladly and willingly been an object of teen girl fantasy and desire, and from Marion Keisker, Sam Phillips's secretary who first spotted his talent and saved his contact details to Kay Wheeler, whose fan club mobilised tens of thousands of devoted adorers, to the girls at his earliest shows, it was women who had made him a star.

Now, as he transitioned to Hollywood, many girls (and plenty of boys, too) were so in love with him, they would have paid to watch him read the phone book. And because he was Elvis, I'm sure that still would have been wonderful. 'Elvis gives me years of pleasure and delight, and I am sure he will continue to do so in the future,' explained a fan writing in to *Elvis Monthly* magazine.[75] 'Be it through his records, his films, or just reading the articles written about him. Nothing, but nothing, will match Elvis!' Plus, seeing *that face* on a forty-foot movie screen was quite spectacular: 'OUR GREAT STAR-ELVIS! NEVER SO: UTTERLY CHARMING, BEAUTIFUL, APPEALING, BOYISH, CUTE, GORGEOUS, SEXY, SWEET, INCREDIBLY HANDSOME! ... WHAT A DOLL.'[76] Except, that the himbo on screen wasn't really Elvis. It was Hollywood's fantasy of what women wanted – or should want – him to be.

In their quest to appeal to the widest possible audience, Hollywood stripped away everything androgynous and dangerous about Elvis and rebuilt him in the mould of Rat Pack-era Sinatra. Hollywood's Elvis personified the 'swinging 1960s bachelor', says Erika Doss, 'slick and charming, very Palm Beach. He was *Playboy* sexy,' and his films 'almost always revolved around his apparently irresistible, swaggering stud image' surrounded by hundreds of 'curvaceous babes intent on wedding and bedding him'.[77] These were films written and directed by men that reasserted all the conservative, patriarchal gender roles and family values that Elvis's early star persona had threatened. If he sold out to anyone, it was actually Hugh Hefner.

New Elvis – the 'official poster boy of the patriarchy' – was 'safe' not because girls wanted a safe fantasy but because this sanitisation allowed them to experience and enjoy him while keeping him traditional and heteronormative enough to placate and entertain the parents, husbands and quarterback boyfriends of Middle America. Even fans themselves seem to feel conflicted. They didn't waver, but articles with titles like 'THAT OLD BLACK MAGIC: Why has it disappeared?' and 'THE AGONY AND THE ECSTASY OF BEING AN ELVIS FAN' made consistent appearances in fan magazines.[78] 'We Elvis fans are honest enough to admit that some of his recent films have not maintained the standard that is expected,' wrote the editors of *Elvis Monthly*. 'This, we feel, is the fault of the producers and not of Elvis. One must remember that Elvis is only human, and cannot be expected to hold a film together single-handed.'[79]

For some fans, as time went on, the idea of Elvis as a playboy bachelor began to present a moral dilemma, especially as Women's Lib began to emerge in the late 1960s. Sue Wise, for example, discovered Elvis at eleven. She would spend hours scrapbooking and listening to his records in her bedroom. But as she got older and feminism became an important part of her life, she began to wrestle with her affection for him. Eventually, she felt the need to disown him. It wasn't until he died in 1977, and she was overcome with an unexpected wave of very real grief, that she decided to re-evaluate what he had meant to her.[80]

Leafing through her old scrapbooks and copies of *Elvis Monthly* magazine, she realised that her Elvis had very little to do with the

Hollywood himbo, cock rocker or even the tender trap heart-throb of the popular imagination. He was a 'teddy bear' – a dear friend who she didn't have to share with anyone else. 'As an adolescent I had been a very lonely person,' she wrote, 'never feeling that I fitted in anywhere, never "connecting" with another human being. In later years I understood this in terms of my early awareness of being gay, but at the time it was just confusing.'

Elvis became both an absorbing hobby and a constant companion:

In my own private Elvis world I could forget that I was miserable and lonely by listening to his records and going to see his films. Some people who feel so alone in an alien world turn to religion or to drink or to football teams to give their lives purpose. I turned to Elvis; and he was always there and he never let me down.[81]

Like Sue, millions of Elvis fans created Elvis in so many different ways. For some, like her, he was a friend and confidant or even an honorary family member. For others, he was someone to look up to: a 'blue-collar guy in blue suede shoes' who proved you could achieve the American dream without losing your soul.[82] 'Although I am not a religious person I am drawn to Elvis almost as though he was a disciple of God,' explained one woman.[83] 'I suppose it is as close to religion as I will ever get.'

Many fans, even today, talk about how Elvis's own personal difficulties and suffering gave them strength and hope in their own lives, and this only intensified after his death. He was 'a miracle', 'a healer', 'an angel', they said. 'Elvis is an emotion that entails everything we are capable of feeling,' explained one woman. 'It cannot be captured. It cannot be bought. You cannot draw it. You cannot write it. You cannot take a photograph of it. You cannot explain it. YOU HAVE

TO FEEL IT – IT MUST BE FELT BECAUSE IT COMES STRAIGHT FROM THE HEART!!'[84]

Elvis, like his fans, understood how real and how sacred that connection was. A profile in *Life* magazine once described his habit of tearing up his fan letters after he read them. When asked why, he was as protective as if they had been prayers: 'I've read them,' he said. 'It's nobody else's business what's in 'em.'[85] In many ways, the distance created by only being able to see him on screen helped cement this more mystical bond. It gave fans the space to imagine and fantasise even more deeply, but something essential had been lost – the ecstatic togetherness of in-person shows.

From the moment Colonel Parker began managing Elvis in 1955, he'd begun pushing his wholesome, all-American vision for his boy. An essential part of this transformation had been to steer Elvis away from live events. The colonel believed the combination of screaming girls and Elvis's unpredictable behaviour on stage was a liability. However sweet and polite he was in interviews, he seemed to go full Dr Jekyll and Mr Hyde under the influence of a live audience. By 1956, the moral panic had gotten so bad that the FBI began compiling a dossier on how he might be endangering American youth.

Once Elvis made his TV debut in 1956, Parker began scaling back his in-person shows. These went from 230 performances in 1955 to a big fat zero by 1958. By confining his boy to the screen, the colonel believed he could both make Elvis more mass-market and control his unpredictability. While this did, as he'd hoped, catapult him to superstardom, it came at a cost. Fans, particularly the girls, lost their gathering place to externalise their deepest feelings and take joy in shared rituals. As one critic put it: 'Television, in effect, burned their churches and dispersed the faithful.'[86]

In 'Girls Just Want To Have Fun', their seminal essay on Beatle-mania, Barbara Ehrenreich, Elizabeth Hess and Gloria Jacobs de-scribe the 'hysteria' of early Beatles fandom as an embryonic surge of feminist energy – an outburst of sheer female adolescent libido that shook the foundations of post-war sexual norms. 'To abandon control – to scream, faint, dash about in mobs – was, in form if not in conscious intent, to protest the sexual repressiveness, the rigid double standard of female teen culture. It was the first and most dramatic uprising of the *women's* sexual revolution.'[87]

This energy wasn't new – Valentino and Sinatra had stirred ver-sions of it – but Elvis and the girls created its clearest and most radical blueprint. The speed with which the fever dream of their love was suppressed and contained only proved how potentially powerful it really was.

The tragedy wasn't that Elvis had been tamed. It was about all that raw, transformative energy being redirected into something so much smaller than what it could have been. And what made this even more heartbreaking was that by the late 1960s, the world was too busy to even remember. With the sexual revolution, civil rights movements and counterculture in full swing, the memory of Elvis the rebel was fading into the background. Music itself was a form of protest now. James Brown was rallying Black Pride across the coun-try, the Beatles were singing about revolution and Bob Dylan was the prophetic darling of transcendental discontent – you don't need a weatherman to know which way the wind blows. Elvis seemed so disconnected that even his most loyal fans were beginning to lose faith. 'Please, Elvis,' pleaded one of them, 'if you have any regard for your career and fans, get out of this rut and establish yourself right back at the top where you really belong.'[88]

When Elvis agreed to do the *'68 Comeback Special*, a one-hour

TV event on NBC, it was a last-ditch attempt to pull himself out of that rut he'd fallen into, to see if that fire was still burning inside him, somewhere. The plan was simple: no clams, no twins – the centrepiece would be the epic 'Guitar Man' song and dance sequence. It would trace his journey from small-town boy to stardom, sin and ultimately redemption. Before that, it would be just him and his guitar in front of an intimate studio audience on a stage that looked and felt like a boxing ring. Packed into a black leather jacket, matching trousers and sleek, pointed-toe boots (and that was literally it), he was about to perform live for the first time in nearly ten years.

Backstage, he was visibly shaking – anxious for it. But as he began the seemingly endless walk from his dressing room to the sound stage, the doubts began to creep in. Would they remember him? Would they care? Or worse, would they see through him? The producers hovered, nervous that maybe he was too far gone – he was sweating – maybe the nerves, or the years, had taken their toll. As he stepped onto that stage, there was a hush – a breathless, hanging silence. But then there it was, soft at first, like a secret gathering force, filling the air, pushing the walls, swelling until it was overwhelming and unmistakable: applause. And after that – because it wouldn't be an Elvis show without them – the screams.

For the first time in ten years, it felt like coming home. He was singing all his old songs from the '50s, but this wasn't the old Elvis coming back now – it was something new. It was Elvis at his most Elvis in years because he was hungry and he needed this so badly and you could see it – you could see him coming alive again with every chord, every twist, every growl. The first time he snarled (involuntarily), he actually burst out laughing. 'Hold it. I got my lip hung. You remember this, don't you? They did twenty-nine pictures like that, baby.' It was pure joy. But it was also kinetic, electric, devastatingly human. He'd fall to his knees in front of individual girls, and they'd scream with delight. He'd borrow their handkerchiefs to wipe the sweat off his face, and they'd melt. Between takes, he'd flirt and joke with them. But most of all he gave *himself*. He'd been holding the animal in for ten whole years, and it felt so good to finally remember who he was. Not to mention how much he'd missed and needed *them*.

When they wrapped, the producers worried that the footage was so wild and unkempt it was unusable, but biographer Peter Guralnick described it perfectly: 'Everything that everyone objected to – the sweat, the hair falling down his face – that was the blood and guts of the show, that was what people liked.'[89] Elvis was back.

In the 1950s, part of Elvis's appeal had always been his status as an outsider. It wasn't just the wildness; it was the tension between vulnerability and bravado – the neediness that existed in the heart of the swagger. As a boy from the wrong side of the tracks, one who had driven trucks for a living and embodied both working-class America and elements of Black culture, he spoke to teenagers, especially young women, who felt marginalised and unseen themselves. Now, it was that same duality that made him so compelling again. He was the biggest star in the world but somehow still an outsider. As Ehrenreich, Hess and Jacobs said of Elvis in the '50s: 'He acted arrogant, but he was really vulnerable, and would be back behind the stick shift of a Mack truck if you, the fans, hadn't redeemed him with your love.'[90]

That push–pull between power and need – between giving and taking – between Elvis and his fans, was exactly what had been missing all those years in the wilderness of Hollywood. The *Comeback Special* was a turning point. Elvis realised he needed the intensity of a live audience, but watching him prowl the stage night after night at the International Hotel in Vegas in the '70s, it's hard to know what to think. This is the Elvis the impersonators love: cape, rhinestones, flash, karate kicks. He's so trashy he's become holy again. Who knew that Franz Liszt's vision of musicians as 'apostles and priests of an invisible religion, elected by celestial force' would be reborn in the form of a middle-aged man convulsing in a rhinestone jumpsuit.[91] But more importantly, look at the audience: Elvis and the girls are back together again.

Every night, when he gets to the instrumental break in 'Love Me Tender', he jumps down from the stage and walks through the crowd, bestowing kisses on any woman who wants one. It's like the seven ages of woman – or maybe the seven stations of the kiss – quick pecks on the cheek, sweet, tender, weirdly intimate ones. Sometimes he holds their faces in his hands: they close their eyes and completely give over to it. Other times they step forward but are nervous: 'Are you afraid of me?' The screams rise and fall as he winds between tables. 'Hang loose – I'll be with you in a minute!' Some women reach out just to brush his sleeve, others press napkins into his hands. It's become a ritual now. He takes them, wipes his brow or (if they're lucky) his chest and hands them back. They squeal, 'THANK YOU!!!' He's Elvis. He'll always be Elvis – the most beautiful, bodily man who ever lived. Of course they want to touch him. Of course they want to kiss him. This is communion.

During one of these 'Love Me Tender' walkabouts, Elvis kneels down to take the hand of a little girl who looks no older than about ten. She's blonde, with a big blue bow in her hair that makes her look like a doll. As he takes her hand, she starts laughing with nervous excitement. She isn't really sure what to do. And for a moment, Elvis doesn't know either. They just stand there, holding hands, looking at each other slightly awkwardly. Then, all of a sudden, she pulls him towards her, throws her arms around him and lets out this bloodcurdling, almost primal scream of 'I LOVE YOU!' Her mother and sisters rush in to pull her away, but she holds on fiercely.

Elvis, mildly shaken, eventually manages to extract himself from the girl and moves on to the more age-appropriate hottie in a pink dress and Jackie O bouffant at the next table. 'You wanna get serious or just play a bit?' he asks. I'm not sure she's even heard the question, because her response – without even waiting for him to finish – is an emphatic 'Yes!' She grabs his face, and suddenly, it's a full-on make-out session. The rest of the audience sip their martinis and look on in amusement.

But I've always wondered about that little girl – who, or what, was her Elvis? Teddy bear? Romantic? Rebel? God? Whoever he was, I like to think that, in that moment, it was the spirit of '54 that moved her – that wild, mysterious power that wasn't exactly sexual but tapped into something intense and elemental. Something that felt big and important that she knew she needed to express, even if she didn't quite understand why.

Beatlemania in New York City (1964)

6

REVOLUTION, LIVERPOOL, 1963
FROM ME TO YOU

every man / every woman carries a firmament inside
& the stars in it are not the stars in the sky
w/out imagination there is no memory
w/out imagination there is no sensation
w/out imagination there is no will, desire
history is a living weapon in yr hand
& you have imagined it, it is thus that you
'find out for yourself'
– DIANE DI PRIMA, *REVOLUTIONARY LETTERS*

On 18 June 1965, seventeen-year-old Luci Johnson, daughter of President Lyndon B. Johnson, hosted a dance party in the East Room of the White House. As the bright harmonies of the Beatles' 'Twist and Shout' echoed through the marbled hallways of power, the photos taken that day captured a new generation of young people twisting and jiving, laughing and mingling amid the stately decor – youth and authority clashing and merging in a single frame.

This was a year brimming with change, captured in a series of iconic images, like this one, that would come to define an era of revolution and defiance. Marchers, led by Martin Luther King Jr, link arms as they face down police on that bridge in Selma. In Lewiston, Maine, Muhammad Ali stands victorious, fist raised over Sonny Liston, while girls in miniskirts proclaim the victory of their rebellion in style on Carnaby Street. At the Newport Folk Festival, Bob Dylan wields his electric guitar, defying folk tradition. And as the violence escalates in Vietnam, protesters flood streets and gather before monuments from London to New York. But outside Buckingham Palace that October, no single image could contain what was happening.

As the gates opened and a Rolls-Royce cut through the crowd, the scene was a riot of movement and sound – girls streaming in from all sides, chasing the car, climbing the fences, waving banners and throwing their bodies against the gates. There must have been thousands of them running, jumping and waving. Hundreds of policemen linked arms, straining to hold them back, but the girls laughed and pushed. Some of the younger ones, no older than about twelve, hung off the policemen to get a better view. The screams were perpetual, more like one long scream with no end than thousands of individual ones.

Inside the palace grounds, those lucky enough to press their faces up against the back gates might have caught a glimpse of four mop-headed boys in four matching suits – recognisable even from a distance – giving a final wave to the crowd as they made their way into the ceremony.

If you knew who they were you probably knew which one was which too. John: always a bit wild-eyed and cocky, striding about like he owned the place. Paul: such a charmer, turning to flash a smile at the crowd more often than the others. George: mystery and depth, hands in pockets like he was holding back secrets or maybe just keeping his distance so he could size up the whole scene. And Ringo. Well, Ringo just being Ringo – bouncing along a step behind the others all cheeky and adorable, as if he was still just amazed to be here at all.

Seeing these four grinning, irreverent boys emerge from the front door a few hours later, proudly showing off their MBE medals while the girls outside swarmed and climbed the fences as if they were rebels trying to storm the palace itself, was a surreal moment. The Beatles, the ultimate symbols of this youthful wave of defiance and rebellion, had now been honoured by the very institution they had once seemed to challenge. It was a marriage of counterculture and establishment that felt historic, but in many ways, with the help of the girls, this was exactly what they'd been doing from the start.

THE STUFF THAT SCREAMS ARE MADE OF

The girls first discovered the Beatles at the Cavern Club in Liverpool in 1961 where they'd become a permanent fixture at the lunchtime shows, playing gritty old rock 'n' roll classics and taking requests from the crowd while young working people on their lunch breaks ate the soup and sandwiches served at the snack bar.

There was no thunderbolt here. No one single messianic arrival moment like there had been with Elvis or Sinatra. There wasn't even any screaming at first. OK – they did scream once, but that was because, in the dark, dank corner of the Cavern, someone said they'd seen a rat. That didn't mean what was happening on stage wasn't groundbreaking or that the world wasn't changing before their very eyes. The story of the Beatles is really the story of a revolution hiding in plain sight. One by one, girls and boys would come, see and join up – they were obsessed. By the time the adult world truly noticed or understood the magnitude of what was happening, there was no going back.

The cornerstone of this revolution was new but familiar. On gig days, the girls would whisper and giggle as these four long-haired boys sauntered down those smoky basement steps looking like four little Marlon Brandos with guitars slung over their shoulders. Fresh from a gruelling but formative six-month tenure playing to late-night audiences in the red-light district's Kaiserkeller in Hamburg, they'd brought an edgy, continental vibe back with them. Their scrappy leather jackets and irreverent self-confidence set them apart from the rest of the clean-cut Merseybeat pop acts of the time. Their music was loud, edgy and unpredictable, but their humour, charm and natural charisma made them feel like the neighbourhood boys their early fans might have grown up with.

Their song choices – an eclectic blend of covers, from rock 'n' roll and blues to R&B and girl group hits, mixed in with their own, formative new material – also set them apart. These were four boys who refused to be confined to being one thing, and they were never afraid of speaking directly to and for women in their songs. If there was one thing they'd learned from the prostitutes of Hamburg, it was that women like songs about women who are romantically and sexually in control.

Years later, Paul would look back at these early days with nostalgia: 'My best playing days were at the Cavern,' he said. 'We'd just go on stage with a cheese roll and a Coke and a ciggie and a few requests ... We really got a rapport with the audience that we never got again.'[1] It may never have been repeated, but it was the art of connection they learned here, with their female 'fan-friends', that would set the down-to-earth precedent for how they would relate to audiences for decades to come.

The stage at the Cavern was barely a few centimetres above audience level, putting the Beatles practically nose-to-nose with the crowd. And everyone knew the front rows were reserved for the girls. God help any boy who ventured too far forward; one 'brave lad' who did once was apparently met with 'withering' looks.[2] The girls would shout their song requests, pass notes up to the boys on stage and, when the band finished playing (and despite John's joking decrees of 'get back to work you dossers!'), the band would always stick around to chat.

For the girls, these daytime gigs offered an opportunity for a type of fun and independence that was rare in those days. Many young women would race between Beatles gigs and work or school, sometimes even cutting class or sneaking out during lunch breaks. 'Had anyone watched Mathew Street in the middle of the day they would have seen many lads and lasses haring back to their schools, shops or offices,' says biographer Mark Lewisohn. They were 'incapable of tearing themselves away from the Beatles a moment sooner'.[3] 'I went to school in my uniform with other clothes underneath,' said fifteen-year-old Pat Brady. 'I used to register and then sneak out at morning break, and go back for the end of the day. I got my comeuppance, but I don't regret having done it. It was such an exciting time.'[4]

The intimate nature of the Cavern meant that the fans and the Beatles genuinely got to know each other. The boys would smile

and wave at their regulars, and sixteen-year-old Freda Kelly, a secretary at Princes Foods who would go on to work for them, even
remembered George shouting 'You're late!' down at her from the
stage when she arrived a few minutes after they started.[5] Others
recounted catching rides in the Beatles' van after some of their
evening shows. 'Nothing sexual happened, not even a kiss – when
they dropped us off, they'd just say, "Bye girls!"' recalled Lindy Ness.
'We were fourteen and they were like grown men, a generation
apart, so we never realistically thought we had a chance of shagging
one of them,' but 'riding the van was fun anyway – the Beatles were
always dead funny, and quite hyper after they'd done a gig'.[6] These
relationships were sincere, which created a universe that felt more
like a community than idol worship.

Of course, if you were one of the older girls and wanted to, you
could definitely see about getting a bit closer than car-pool to the
boys after a show (this was one of the reasons they were so excited
when they finally got that van). The idea of hooking up with their
favourite Beatle made perfect sense. The boys were the same age as
them, from similar working-class backgrounds and part of the same
scene. Plus, what made them so attractive, like someone you could
imagine getting together with, was the same thing that made them
so compelling on stage – they were sexy but in a kind, sensitive,
emotionally available kind of way. Many historians have argued
that the Beatles' emotional openness and ability to connect with
their girl fans – from the stage and in real life – was rooted in the
importance women played in their formative years. 'I was always
with the women,' said John, years later. 'I always heard them talk
about men and life, and they always knew what was going on. That
was my feminist education.'[7]

During their time in Hamburg, it was Astrid Kirchherr, the devastatingly cool avant-garde art student, who had taught them about fashion and given them their iconic haircuts. They were, as one fan reflected years later, 'not afraid to be influenced by women'.[8] They weren't afraid of embodying qualities typically seen as 'feminine' either. This shaped their interactions with fans in surprisingly tender ways. When Bobby Brown, emboldened by a drink, was dared by her friend to kiss Paul when he came off stage but ended up with her 'head down the toilet', he showed genuine concern. 'Paul was so lovely,' she recalled. 'He came to see if I was all right, he fetched my coat and bag and looked after me.'[9] In Hamburg, he walked a tearful Swedish fan back to her hotel at 3 a.m. after she confessed she was in love with George. As they said goodbye, he gave her a hug and some brotherly advice.

This community feeling, along with the Beatles' openness and approachability, spilled over into their relationships with fans who had never spoken to them. Something about them seemed to invite girls to connect beyond the Cavern walls. 'There was a very intimate relationship in Liverpool between the Beatles and their fans,' said Tony Barrow, their first press officer. 'Fans could actually ring the Beatles. I mean, you just had to look under "Mc" in the phonebook and ring Paul McCartney and say, "Please will you play 'Some Other Guy' for us at the Cavern on Friday?"'[10] This is exactly what Margaret Hunt did. The first time she phoned, he was asleep, but she was surprised and delighted when he called her back later, and they had a lovely long chat. Another girl told the story of going round to George's house, and his mum letting her have a little snoop in his bedroom while he was out.

By the time the mythic day arrived, when their future manager,

Brian Epstein, walked down the steps into the dark, smoke-filled Cavern to see what all the fuss was about – the Beatles had fully established themselves as local legends. The crowds had grown. The chilled atmosphere of those very earliest shows was now rowdy and intense. 'Here they were,' wrote Bob Wooler in their first ever piece of press coverage. 'Rugged yet romantic, appealing to both sexes. With calculated naivete and an ingenious, throw-away approach to their music. Affecting indifference to audience response and yet always saying "Thank-you" ... Seemingly unambitious, yet fluctuating between the self-assured and the vulnerable. Truly a phenomenon.'[11]

Girls had formed subgroups around their favourite Beatle now. They'd sit in front of them at the Cavern to get the best view. John had started doing this wink from the stage that drove lots of Teddy boys mad, especially when their girlfriends rushed to the front with their mouths open. At the Aintree Institute, chairs were thrown. Even at the mixed night-time shows at the Cavern, there was a bit of a gender divide. 'Boys would bring girls,' remembered Liz Tibbott-Roberts, or rather they would 'pay for them to get in and take them home afterwards, but in between there was no contact at all. Boys would stand around the walls while the girls were in the middle watching the Beatles.'[12]

Some fans were apprehensive about Epstein's influence at first. He dressed the boys in suits, started taking them to London for auditions with record labels, and when he replaced their original heart-throb drummer, Pete Best, with Ringo Starr, there was much drama. Pete had been a favourite with the girls, so they weren't going to take his loss lightly. Ringo's first gig at the Cavern was met with chants of 'Pete for ever! Ringo never!'[13] Girls held vigil outside Pete's family home. When his mum 'opened the front door to pick up her morning milk the next day, she found girls with tear-smudged make-up asleep all over her yard'.[14]

Luckily, Ringo was cute in his own right, and as one Pete fan admitted, he was great for the band musically. 'I used to love Pete and was heartbroken when they sacked him,' she said. 'But it soon passed, and it was as if he'd never been there. They were much better with Ringo, without a doubt. He gave them that solid backbeat – he's a great rock 'n' roll drummer – and he fitted in brilliantly.'[15]

Ringo's arrival was both a blessing and a curse because it deepened the underlying fear that everyone understood innately – that the Beatles were so good, they wouldn't be able to belong just to them for ever. When, on 10 February 1963, Bob Wooler, the resident DJ at the Cavern, walked on stage to announce the good news that the Beatles' second single, 'Please Please Me', had just gotten to No. 1 in the chart, a dejected hush fell over the audience. The moment they dreaded had finally come. The Beatles belonged to everyone now.

Beatlemania officially began on 13 October 1963, when the Beatles arrived in London to record Val Parnell's *Sunday Night at the London Palladium*. Thousands of teenage girls were said to have descended on the theatre, where some managed to get into the band's dressing room while others flooded the street outside, trying to push down the doors. Parnell's show was the British equivalent of *Ed Sullivan*, so that night the show was viewed in 15 million homes around the country.

Beatles biographers and historians like to debate how many girls were actually there that night (theories range from eight to thousands), but in the context of what happened next, facts are pretty much irrelevant. The next day, papers were plastered with photos of girls being held back by police alongside sensationalist headlines like 'Beatlemania: Beatles Flee in Fantastic Palladium Siege'. They described how 'screaming girls launched themselves against the police – sending helmets flying and constables reeling' and how when the show was over, 'police vans sealed off the front of the theatre so that the Beatles could be smuggled out'.[16]

For the adult world, leafing through their newspapers over breakfast, the idea of thousands of schoolgirls behaving so wildly was a curiosity. It seemed to happen overnight, but the truth was that, although Beatlemania had finally been given a name, it had already been going on for months. The true beginning of Beatlemania was back in January when the boys first played 'Please Please Me' live on the teen music TV show *Thank Your Lucky Stars* and then embarked on an intense schedule of tour dates. Wherever they went, they'd been met with screaming girls and adoring boys and pelted with jellybeans (apparently George's favourite). One boy, writing in his diary in 1963, compared the concert he attended to 'a roman orgy'. He was convinced that the Beatles 'were magic'.[17] This was a time when British radio rarely played pop music, and newspapers hardly ever covered it, so the storm that had been brewing had continued to gather under the radar.

The Palladium show was the first time the mainstream press paid attention, and the first time the Beatles were written about outside of specialist music columns. What was different now was the timing. The country was ready. The media, looking for light-hearted distraction from the doom and gloom of the Profumo affair, a political scandal that had been dragging on in the headlines for months, latched onto the scenes of hysterical young girls overcome with what seemed to be a mix of sexual desire and excitement, as if it was somehow emblematic of the era.

England in 1963 was a conservative country standing on the brink of seismic social change or, as historian David Kynaston put it, 'seemingly on the verge of a nervous breakdown'.[18] Sex – this awkward and slightly embarrassing thing that people did but no one liked to talk about – was making itself visible everywhere. The pill was now beginning to be available on the NHS, films like *A Taste of Honey* and *The L-Shaped Room* were putting previously taboo subjects like premarital sex, single motherhood and abortion on the big screen, and three years earlier, the obscenity trial of *Lady Chatterley's Lover* had thrust both sexually explicit language and the question of female sexual autonomy into the news media spotlight, as the prosecution infamously asked: Would you allow your wife or servants to read this book?

The trial was supposed to be about whether the book – a tale of an upper-class lady's epic journey of sexual self-discovery, with the help of her husband's rough-and-ready gamekeeper (a devoted dog dad) – was porn or art but ended up putting its fictional heroine on trial. The charge: sex addiction.

The prosecution's star evidence was the swear word count in the book (fuck/fucking x 30; cunt x 14; balls x 13; shit/arse x 6; cock x 4), but the defence pointed out there were far more instances of words like 'care' and 'tenderness' in the book. As one expert put it: 'Far from setting such liaisons on a pedestal, the whole emphasis of the book was towards the deep and enduring relationship. The depth and enduring quality of the true sex relationship is persistently and carefully worked out.'[19] Not only was this the story of a woman learning how to have great sex (and across class boundaries too) – it was about her reclaiming agency over her body and her life. Lady Chatterley said it herself: 'A woman has to live her life, or live to repent not having lived it.'

The jury agreed. Amid protests from critics and librarians, they ruled that the book, which had been banned since its initial release in 1928, belonged in the hands of readers. Thousands of curious readers and non-readers alike rushed to bookshops, and well-thumbed copies of *Lady Chatterley*, along with Helen Gurley Brown's proto-*Sex and the City* lifestyle guide *Sex and the Single Girl*, would be passed around offices, boarding schools and common rooms for years to come.

As if the prosecution's hysterical scaremongering had been prophetic, it wouldn't be long before reality proved itself more salacious than even that book. The Profumo affair – one of the most notorious political scandals in British history – reminded the nation of the political power that young women could wield through who they were or weren't sleeping with. John Profumo, the Secretary of State for War, was found to be having an affair with Christine Keeler, a nineteen-year-old model who also happened to be involved with a Russian naval attaché (not a good look at the height of the Cold War). When the affair was outed by the press, Profumo denied the relationship to Parliament. Well, he would, wouldn't he?

The truth eventually came out, forcing his resignation. It was a watershed moment – one that offered a compulsively seedy window into the corrupt lives of the British establishment and revealed their hypocrisies around sex, and many saw it as a sign that the country needed new leadership, new honesty, new everything.

Enter the Beatles. When 'Please Please Me' was released in March, it was exactly the joyful, danceable, pop hit British teenagers needed to cheer themselves up in the political uncertainty and economic gloom of 1963. But all that light-hearted charm also made it a musical Trojan horse that aligned perfectly with those sexually charged winds of change. Peel back those sweet harmonies and catchy guitar riffs, and you find a song that has a lot more in common with *Lady Chatterley* than you might think. It's a song about a man who is asking for, and expecting, mutual pleasure and satisfaction in a relationship. More than that in fact: he's the one who's been doing all the pleasing so far. 'There's no getting away from it,' explained a psychologist in a newspaper later that year, 'a revolution is taking place under our noses. It amounts to sexual freedom with a sense of responsibility and honesty ... While other pop stars have reached out to their audiences in artificial terms, the Beatles give honestly as well as receive.'[20]

Whether the lyrics were sexual or really just the pleas of an emotionally unfulfilled man longing for mutual love and connection, it was a radical statement. The idea that sex, emotion and desire were shared experiences; that they could be the same for men and women; that a modern man might be telling his girl that she didn't need him to lead the way – in anything – because she already knew what to do, was a 2.5-minute revolution you could sing and dance along to.

It was so revolutionary, in fact, that even 41-year-old librarian-poet Philip Larkin was feeling it (and mildly sorry he wasn't a few years younger). In his poem 'Annus Mirabilis' – his ode to the cultural revolution that was 1963 – he placed the dawn of sex in Britain somewhere between the end of the Chatterley trial and the arrival of the Beatles. And if you really want to believe 'Please Please Me' isn't about sex, listen for the gritty remnants of the Hamburg red-light district in the way Paul sings 'Come on' in the second half of the song and try not to wet your pants.

For the teenagers of post-war Britain, tired of old-style, manu-factured charm-your-mum-and-grandma pop stars like Cliff Rich-ard, the Beatles radiated an authenticity that felt both inclusive and radical. As four working-class lads from Liverpool joyfully chatting and joking away in their scouse accents in TV interviews, they rep-resented a new type of youthful self-confidence and working-class pride. 'Are you going to get a haircut?' asked a reporter.

'Nope!' said Ringo.

'No thanks,' said Paul.

'I had one yesterday,' said George.

'That's no lie,' said John. 'It's the truth. You should have seen him the day before.'

This was part of a much bigger shift in British society: the boundaries of class and tradition were beginning to break down. As the overwhelmingly swoon-inducing Michael Caine, the cockney son of a fish-market porter, recalled in his autobiography: 'For the first time in British history, the young working class stood up for themselves and said ... "Join us, stay away, like us, hate us – do as you like. We don't care about your opinion anymore."'[21] And as scenes of the screaming, fainting, semi-orgasmic teenage girls of Beatlemania mobbing their idols and clashing with police became a regular feature in the press, it seemed that the Fab Four's au-thenticity and self-assurance were emboldening their girl fans to embrace their own senses of freedom and self-expression in even more dramatic ways.

Outside Birmingham's Alpha Television Studios, where the boys were filming another episode of *Thank Your Lucky Stars*, they were met by 3,500 teenagers who 'swarmed the Beatles' car, bringing traffic to a halt'. In Newcastle, on the day of a Beatles show, 'ambulance crews equipped with gallons of smelling salts toiled to control 7,000 fans lined up at the City Hall, barrelling over the girls who had camped out in the street for nearly two days'. In Liverpool, on the day tickets to two Beatles shows went on sale, 'more than 100 extra police, including some on horseback', were brought in to manage an estimated 12,000 fans, 'mostly teenage girls', who had been camping out for days. Despite a 'predawn stampede down a side street' and over 100 casualties, the chief constable of Liverpool told the papers: 'It all passed off much more quietly than we had dared hope.'[22]

The world had seen screaming girls before. They'd even seen police brought in to manage them. But never on this scale. Beatlemania was relentless and what was even more curious about the whole thing was the relatively minor moral panic it was generating. Just as the Beatles had charmed and connected with the girls at the Cavern and teenagers across Britain, they were now beginning to seduce the press. Their TV and newspaper interviews were natural and adorably irreverent: no formulaic answers or PR scripts, just four lads from Liverpool being themselves. The media were in love. They praised their wit and intelligence as if there was something distinctly British about them – timeless and hopeful – the perfect antidote to the dreariness and austerity of the post-war years.

Their stamp of approval came when the boys were invited to perform for the Queen Mother and Princess Margaret at the Royal Variety Show. During their performance, as John made a request to the audience – 'For the people in the cheaper seats, clap your hands. And the rest of you, if you'd just rattle your jewellery.' – he fell back in a mischievous wince that immediately softened the shocking insolence of what he'd just said. The audience erupted in laughter and applause as the camera cut to the Queen Mother. She gave a wave of acknowledgement, and there was a cheeky little smile on her face. In centuries gone by, that sort of comment would have had John sent straight to the Tower of London, but now here was the Queen Mother herself chuckling along with him.

It was official: while the fans who had braved the rain and fog waited silently outside, thousands of children up and down the country watched at home with their parents and teenage girls lay on their beds, gazing dreamily at posters of these four little rock 'n' roll rebels, now smiling sweetly in their subversively respectable suits, the revolution quietly slipped into the mainstream – endorsed by royalty.

THE OLD WAYS WILL NOT DO

Beatlemania may have started in the UK, but it will forever be associated with the Fab Four's arrival in America. On 7 February 1964, fifteen-year-old Christina Berlin stood wrapped in her best winter coat, looking up at the grey sky above Kennedy Airport. It was one of those classic February days in New York, cold and crisp, but she hardly noticed the tiny ice crystals beginning to form on her scarf. It was 1 p.m. – not long now. According to WMCA radio, which had been tracking their plane since it took off from Heathrow, the Beatles were scheduled to land in America at exactly 1:20 p.m.

All around her, girls were laughing and talking. They'd been here for hours, but the wait – like the cold – seemed like a small price to pay for the chance to actually be here. There was a sense of togetherness in the crowd: a bond that had formed as they huddled in anticipation. 'You could really feel that something important was happening,' she later recalled. 'This was the beginning of something

– a youthquake. We had been bored, and it felt like we were finally taking over the candy store.'[23]

If Christina and her new friends felt like they were part of something bigger, it's because they were. The excitement for the Beatles' arrival had been fuelled by a perfect storm of genuine fan enthusiasm and relentless marketing. Brian Epstein had orchestrated what he was calling 'Operation USA'. Radio stations had been playing their songs nonstop, news features trumpeted 'The Beatles are coming!' and freebies were everywhere. Even the girls waiting at the airport had been plied with Beatles stickers, buttons and memorabilia. But before all that, it had really all started with one teenage girl.

A few months earlier, in December 1963, fifteen-year-old Marsha Albert of Silver Spring, Maryland, had written a letter to her local radio station to ask them to play a song called 'I Want to Hold Your Hand' by a band called the Beatles. She'd seen a short clip on CBS News and then *The Jack Paar Show*, where they'd been featured as a quirky curiosity. Marsha didn't think they were funny. She thought they were brilliant. From that moment on, she made it her mission to get them on the radio. 'I thought they'd be really popular here,' she said.

Intrigued by her letter, DJ Carroll James had managed to track down an imported copy of the single. The moment he heard it, he knew Marsha was right – the song was fantastic. He decided to invite her into the studio for the big moment. And so, at 5 p.m. on 17 December 1963, it was a fifteen-year-old girl who introduced the Beatles to America. 'Ladies and gentlemen,' she said, 'for the very first time on the air in the United States, here are the Beatles singing "I Want to Hold Your Hand".'[24]

American music was in a rut by 1963. The heyday of rock 'n' roll had passed, Elvis was in Hollywood and teen idols like Fabian and

Bobby Vinton were dominating the charts with safe, predictable songs that lacked the rebellious spirit of earlier rock pioneers. 'I Want to Hold Your Hand' was the perfect fusion – it had the romantic earnestness of a teenybopper pop song *and* the raw energy of rock 'n' roll. More than anything, it sounded entirely new. Even Bob Dylan, first hearing it blast over his car radio while driving through California, reportedly exclaimed, 'Fuck! … Man, that was fuckin' great!'[25]

On the eve of their arrival in the States, the daughter of an AP journalist wrote an op-ed to demystify the song's greatness: 'To the average adult,' she wrote, 'it would sound like nothing more than a conglomeration of noises, screams, howls, and other unclassified sounds. To the ecstatic teenager lying in front of her hi-fi, it's sheer heaven.'[26]

Floating above the clouds, on the plane, the Beatles were nervous. 'I Want to Hold Your Hand' had hit No. 1 a few weeks earlier, but you never know. The captain came over the radio to warn them there was going to be a crowd, but they hadn't been expecting it to be anything like this one. There must have been about 3,000 fans and 200 photographers and journalists waiting down below, eyes turned heavenward. The runway and the roof of the air hangar was so packed and swarming with people that, at first, peering out their windows, they thought the mass of people had nothing to do with them. Maybe this was just what America looked like. But as they stepped out of the plane, stopping to wave on the stairway, the familiar sound hit them.

The Beatles' scream is very particular. People have used all kinds of metaphors to try to capture its intensity. One journalist described it as high-pitched and wailing: 'The sound of pigs being slaughtered, only louder.' 'You literally had to hold onto your seat,' explained a fan, 'the noise was so loud that everything vibrated and swayed.'[27] When George Martin tried – and failed – to record a live performance at the Hollywood Bowl, he said the welter of screams sounded like putting a microphone next to the end of a 747 jet.[28] Personally, I like to think of it as a chaotic dawn chorus. What everyone agreed on, however, was that it was a wall of sound that didn't ever stop and followed those four boys wherever they went.

The Beatles had been living with the screams like they had a collective case of tinnitus for quite some time now, but from the moment Christina and all the other girls who had been waiting on the roof of the air hangar welcomed them with their first American scream, the boys realised this was going to be different. 'I FELT New York,' Ringo said, years later. 'It was like an octopus grabbing the plane … I could feel its tentacles coming up. It was so exciting … We'd pulled big crowds before … but America was bigger – just CRAZY … We drove through it … Then we got to the hotel and it was madness!'[29]

The Beatles were staying at the Plaza. Before they even arrived, the management – who hadn't heard of them when they took the booking – had become so alarmed by the thousands of fans massing by the front doors that they'd taken to the radio to offer the band to any other hotel that would take them. No one was interested. Upon arrival, they were bundled into their rooms and told to stay there.

In the street down below, the scene was an epic role reversal of *Romeo and Juliet* – except there were thousands of Juliets, and the four Romeos, hiding in their hotel rooms, had been warned by the police chief to stay away from their windows for fear of causing a riot. The crowd were so hyped that, at one point, a policeman was mobbed because someone said he'd actually touched one of them. Naturally, everyone was there for the Beatles, but the carnival atmosphere in the street made you think that while they were the focus of all the insanity, they were also, in some ways, incidental. As the media circus swirled, girls and boys performed for the cameras – waving, shouting and clowning around. They seemed to be revelling in the attention and the chaos. 'We love the Beatles!!!' shouted a boy while the crowd sung 'yeah yeah yeah' on an infinite loop.

One girl, in a beret and a thick Brooklyn accent, waxed lyrical for the cameras while her friends giggled beside her. 'I love the Beatles and I'll always love them,' she told the reporter. 'Even when I'm 105 and an old grandmother!' Then she turned to the camera, emphatically:

Paul McCartney, if you're listening, Adrienne from Brooklyn loves you with all her heart! I love you, Paul, and please just come to the window so I can see you! I saw you smoking before, and I kissed the limousine you looked out of. I love you, and I want you, Paul! Please look out the window!

Before the Beatles arrived, the press had been describing this as a British invasion, but what this really was, now, was an uprising of children. The average age of a Beatles fan in America was between thirteen and seventeen. Soon it would be even younger. And the Beatles were bringing them out into the streets, emboldening them to something that looked, and sounded, a bit like madness. With stirrings in the press about youth rebellion and the growing power of teenage culture, this could have easily turned into something for the adult world to fear, but the Beatles had a powerful ally. The man who had brought them to America was about to step in and reframe the chaos. Stiff, awkward and square he may have been, but Ed Sullivan was a cultural kingmaker.

According to a fantastical myth that's been retold so many times it has nearly become fact, Sullivan first saw the Beatles at Heathrow Airport in 1963, where, travelling with his wife, by complete chance, he'd experienced Beatlemania first-hand. Intrigued by the throngs of screaming teenage girls, he'd gone to find out what the ruckus was about. 'Who the hell are the Beatles?' he asked, imagining they must be an animal act.[30] When he learned that they were human, he is said to have made the snap decision to book them on the spot. They had released no records in America yet, but judging by the reactions of the girls at the airport, this was something he had to get in on.

Ed Sullivan had always been great at sensing what the American public wanted, but bringing this relatively unknown British act over to the States was still a gamble. He was confident, but even he had no idea just how big this was going to be. Even more than Sinatra's first solo show at the Paramount, or Elvis's first televised bump-and-grind performance, the Beatles' first appearance on *Ed Sullivan* was a cultural earthquake. 'The Beatlecasts are such deeply entrenched landmark moments in the nation's psyche that revisiting them is like watching replays of the Kennedy assassination,' says Sullivan biographer Gerald Nachman.[31] This comparison may seem superficial at first, but many historians believe these two events were actually connected.

The assassination of JFK, just a few months before the Beatles landed at the newly renamed Kennedy Airport, had left the nation heartbroken and desperate for something to bring hope and joy back into their lives. Kennedy's youth, optimism and vision for a new world order had resonated deeply with millions of Americans, especially young people. His assertion in his inaugural address that 'the old ways will not do' was the perfect tagline for the cultural transformation the Beatles had represented in Britain and were now about to bring to America.[32]

Kennedy's appeal was political, but it also spilled over into the world of celebrity. With his Hollywood good looks and cool, casual authenticity, he'd used TV to connect with voters in revolutionary ways. The media were bemused by the fervour of some of his female supporters who were nicknamed 'jumpers', 'touchers' and 'screamers'. As historian Mark White described: 'The frenzied glee with which he was invariably greeted by women on the campaign trail was akin to the adulation usually reserved for Elvis Presley.'[33]

At first, the 'jumpers' had been teenage girls who would 'bounce, jounce, and jump as his cavalcade passed, squealing, "I seen him. I seen him"', but soon middle-aged women and once even a 'row of nuns, all jiggling under their black robes, almost (but not quite) daring to jump' joined in. In Louisville, a student actually shouted, 'We love you! You're better than Elvis,' while another woman was reported to have threatened a journalist: 'You a newspaperman?' she said. 'You better write nice things about him or you watch out' (and she meant it).[34]

This enthusiasm, like Beatlemania, was dismissed as hysteria – a frivolous reaction to Kennedy's devastatingly powerful sex appeal. But as these groups of women gathered and squealed, making their feelings known, it actually pointed to something deeper. Two of the most telling observations came from Theodore White in his Pulitzer Prize-winning account of the 1960 presidential campaign. First, he noted that the number of 'jumpers' grew incrementally as they were featured more and more in the press – almost as if they were inspiring and emboldening each other. Second, he described how, as Kennedy's car passed, 'teenagers would turn to face each other and, in ecstasy, place hands on each other's shoulders and jump up and down together as a partnership'.[35] The significance of this collective euphoria should not be underestimated.

There is no doubt that Kennedy had sex appeal – he was a complete sun-tanned, Wayfarer-wearing, Boston-talking, Hyannis Port hottie (even Marilyn was obsessed). But in a pre-Women's Lib world, all that screaming and jumping also hinted at an emerging energy – a shared excitement and joy among women, a collective sense of optimism for the future and a growing self-confidence in loud, shameless, public displays of emotional and political self-expression.

For the 'jumpers' and for the millions more Kennedy voters who didn't jump or squeal but still felt the energy and youthful vigour he represented, Kennedy embodied the hope of a new era. However much of a mirage that may have been, especially for women (he did relatively little for them during his time in office), his loss shattered that sense of hope and possibility. Even young children felt it – the collective grief that swept the nation was a reflection of how much Kennedy had come to symbolise the future that so many were hoping for.

And so, in quest of a bit of light entertainment, and to find out what this Beatles thing the media had been going on about actually was, on 9 February 1964, 17 million Americans sat down on their sofas to find out. It was the biggest audience in the whole history of *The Ed Sullivan Show* (legend has it that for that one magical hour, even the criminals were watching – calls to the police across America came to a complete stop). Sullivan was on good form that day – clearly excited for what was about to happen or maybe just pumped from the energy of the crowd – 'Ladies and gentlemen, the Beatles! Let's bring them on.'

As the curtain opened and the camera slowly panned in for their first song, the boys looked adorable enough to eat, bouncing along to the beat of 'All My Loving' in their matching suits and mop-top haircuts. Adults were either incensed or amused by their strange appearances and long hair, but millions of teens and pre-teens who were watching remembered being overcome by 'a weird feeling of excitement, like something totally new was happening'. Many felt the irrepressible urge to stand up and join in with the show. 'That was it. I couldn't stop myself,' recalled one girl. 'I started screaming and carrying on, and my mother didn't know what to do … My grandmother thought something was wrong with me.'[36]

'It was just amazing to see them after hearing the record,' explained a high school boy. 'I was knocked out. They were so different from Elvis and Bobby Rydell, and the others. It was their energy – they looked like they were having fun, and you wanted to have fun, too.'[37] At its core was an overwhelming, infectious, almost Lisztian sense of wonder, enthusiasm and joy: 'I was in grade school; not a teenager – so it wasn't about them being hot, it was about the fun; the overriding sense that they were having fun. And the freedom they expressed was palpable.'[38]

Sullivan wasn't just introducing America to four charming British boys that night; he was introducing them to Beatlemania itself. The whole show was an instruction manual for how to be a Beatles fan and a reassurance to parents that this was a safe activity. This was the first time *Ed Sullivan* had ever shown the audience. The screams were right there, front and centre – rising and falling with every close-up of the boys. And the cameras persistently cut back and forth between the Beatles and shots of the girls in the audience joyfully squealing, clapping and dancing in their seats. If you really want to know who the fifth Beatle was, it was those ecstatic teenage girls – the single biggest reason those four boys had arrived at this moment – now screaming along, intent on joining in with the show.

To complete the introduction, while they were singing 'Till There Was You', the camera zoomed in on each of the boys as their names flashed up on screen. PAUL: singing and looking cute as a button. You want to fall in love with him immediately (if you haven't already). He gets screams because he's just so effortlessly romantic and charming – look at those big, fluffy, puppy-dog eyes that make it feel like he's singing just to you. He's trying to pretend he's not completely loving all this attention, and for some reason that makes him even cuter.

RINGO: doing his thing on drums. So cool that he doesn't even notice the camera is on him at first, but when he does, he cracks that massive Ringo smile. He gets screams because he knows you're watching and he's happy you're there and also – just allow me to gush for a moment – because he was almost sexier when he had that secret serious face on: laid back but intense, welcoming but mysterious. He's the boy who will always be there for you: never too much, never too distant. As fun as he is dependable. *Ringo – if you're reading this, come to the window, or better still: DM me!!!*

GEORGE: raising his eyebrows as he really gets into those guitar licks – honestly, as Liszt and Paganini taught us 200 years ago, is there anything more attractive than musical virtuosity!? And then he smiles. Just look at that smile. He gets screams because there's something in the way he plays – so absorbed, so into the music, so good at guitar he makes it all look so effortless. He's loving it. And we are loving him. Look at his guitar face. Well, you just would, wouldn't you?

And finally we come to JOHN. He gets nearly the most screams just for being John (the leader, the wit, the edge – take me down to a strawberry field), but there's an extra little note under his name: 'Sorry girls, he's married.' Interesting. Epstein had always encouraged John to keep his wife Cynthia and their baby out of the public eye, but it was useful now. 'Sorry girls' was a playful reference to his immense popularity with the girls as well as a reminder to potential new fans that crushing on the Beatles was more than OK. Like Sinatra, they were safe fantasy objects.

More than anything, this nod to safe fantasy was a subtle reassurance to parents. These boys might have looked a bit freakish with their bobbing heads and worryingly long hair, but they were safe followers of traditional family values – responsible young men endorsed by Ed Sullivan, who at one point described them as 'tremendous ambassadors of goodwill'.

Just before they went on air, another endorsement had come through. Sullivan was thrilled to announce that a telegram had arrived from The King himself. Now fully settled into respectability in Hollywood, Elvis was writing to wish them 'tremendous success' in America. With this short message, The King had passed the baton of rock 'n' roll royalty to the four little Liverpudlian princes, and Sullivan had sanctified the appointment with his approval.

As the five of them stood together at the end of the show, shaking hands, laughing and talking, it marked the triumph of an artfully executed exercise in intergenerational diplomacy. The Beatles had landed.

Down the eastern seaboard, just as the show ended at 9 p.m., a teacher rang the bell at a girls' boarding school in Washington DC – TV time was over. It was time for Amanda Vaill and her schoolmates, who had just been singing and dancing along with their sisters on screen, to get back to their dorms. 'We certainly didn't think of it then,' she wrote years later, 'but in some ways, she was ringing a funeral knell for one era – our parents' – and ushering in a new one, which, for better or worse, belonged to us.'[39]

LOVE LOVE LOVE

Six months after the Beatles' first appearance on *The Ed Sullivan Show*, the screams outside the Paramount Theatre were deafening – the swoon had come home.

Back in 1944, thousands of bobbysoxers had lined up in this very spot, anxious for a few magical hours in the presence of Frankie Sinatra. There had been frequent traffic jams up and down Broadway in those days, but that was nothing compared to the madness unfolding now. Thousands of wild-haired girls in cardigans and sports jackets – many wearing Beatles buttons with slogans like 'RINGO FOR PRESIDENT' or 'I'M A BEATLES FAN IN CASE OF EMERGENCY CALL PAUL' – had flooded Seventh Avenue, West 43rd and 44th Streets, causing complete gridlock in the whole Times Square area as 240 policemen battled to control them.

Around the corner on West 44th Street there was a commotion. A small group of girls had caught sight of four familiar heads of hair inside a Cadillac trying to slide subtly up onto the sidewalk. Gay Talese, who was there that night, described how a pack of girls 'came rushing and howling toward the car. Forty policemen ringed the singers. The best the girls could do was smear fingerprints over the car and rock it back and forth a bit. By then, however, the Beatles were safely indoors.'[40]

Scenes like this had become everyday life for John, Paul, George and Ringo. The six months between *Ed Sullivan* and this show at the Paramount had been a whirlwind. From Denmark to Tokyo, it was always the same: up and down aeroplane staircases to flashing cameras, running from screaming girls while policemen scooped up the ones who'd jumped the barriers and carried them away, kicking and squealing like Satanic rag dolls. Posing for photo ops. Jumping in and out of decoy cars. Motorcades. Police escorts. Crowds lining the streets as if they were royalty, and, of course, the perpetual hail of jellybeans. As they sat watching TV in their hotel rooms, late into the night – and it didn't even matter how many floors up they put them – the screams.

The craziest part was that it wasn't just teenage girls losing their minds anymore. At a party at the British Embassy in Washington, some drunk old toff had snuck up behind Ringo with a pair of scissors and snipped off a lock of his hair. In Canada, under death threats from a group of radical French-Canadian separatists who wanted to kill him because he was Jewish, Ringo had been forced to play under the protection of an armed guard (he wasn't even Jewish, they had been confused, unfortunately, by his big nose). And at concerts, in multiple countries, respectable, seemingly sane adults had started wheeling sick or disabled children into their dressing rooms, asking the Beatles to bless and cure them, as if they were saints or something.

Maybe they were right. Thousands of freshly minted Beatles fans later described seeing the Beatles for the first time as a miracle or some kind of divine revelation. The press played along. *Newsweek* described them as 'a band of evangelists whose gospel is fun'.[41] In Liszt's day, the ecstasy might have stayed in the concert hall, but by 1965, LP in hand, you could switch it on and off at the crackling touch of a turntable needle.

The Monday after that first *Ed Sullivan Show*, the existing fans proudly arrived at school with their Beatles records balanced on top of their books – a visible badge of belonging – while thousands more rushed to the record stores later that afternoon. Boys were already talking about growing their hair and starting bands, but there was no doubt in anyone's mind: the Beatles belonged to the girls. Watching *Ed Sullivan* at her all-girls boarding school, Amanda Vaill had been struck by the fact that the audience, which would normally have been filled by people her parents' age, was instead made up of young girls like her 'all gasping and clutching their faces in paroxysms of innocent desire'.[42]

There have always been two currents running through the fangirl phenomenon. If you trace it all the way back to its roots, you find the deep, soul-stirring personal identification and romantic fantasy of Byron's readers evolving in parallel with the collective ecstasy first seen during Lisztomania. Each iconic figure of fandom up until Beatlemania had channelled each strand to varying degrees. What made Beatlemania so special was the intensity with which it merged the two. It was a joyful uprising of female fun that gave girls a new sense of connection and belonging. But it also gave them a new way of expressing their own individual dreams and identities because, for the first time in history, there were *four of them*!

One of the most important questions bouncing through classrooms and playgrounds that Monday was: 'Which Beatle is your favourite?' Everything about *Ed Sullivan* – from the songs to the screaming girls to seeing the boys' names flash up on screen

– seemed to be giving heterosexual girls permission to express romantic feelings publicly. As one girl explained: 'We each had a different favourite Beatle. There could be no sharing, because we each were going to meet our favourite, fall in love, and marry them!'[43]

Girls had always used celebrity crushes to express and understand who they were. Pam Rutherford, a childhood friend of Priscilla Beaulieu, once described how, in the early 1950s, the two of them used to lie on her bed for hours talking and playing a game called 'Let's Pretend'. 'Priscilla always pretended that she was gonna marry Elvis,' explained Pam. 'And I was gonna marry Ricky Nelson. We'd pretend what their romance would be like and what mine would be like. We'd play Elvis records and make believe all kinds of glamorous things' (these things were mainly riding in limos and wearing shiny clothes).[44]

Obviously, most girls didn't get to marry their crushes like Priscilla did, but these types of fantasies were common ways for girls to test out and give voice to who they were or wanted to be. What was so special about having your own personal Beatle was that your fantasies could co-exist in the same mythological universe as your friends'. This added an extra layer of fun to the shared joy of loving and fantasising about these boys. It also gave you a new way to signpost who you were within and beyond your friendship group. John was the thinking girl's Beatle. Paul was for sweet, conventional-but-not-boring girls. If you were a bit of a dreamer or had an artistic side, you might pick George. And Ringo was for girls who were just completely obsessed and in love with those big blue eyes and perfectly gigantic nose. He was as adorable as he was hilarious.

Teenage girls, especially in those days, were notoriously concerned with the idea of popularity and fitting in with the group. This new blend of Beatle adoration and identification meant that, for the first time, you could embrace – and be embraced for – your differences. Debbie Geller, for example, had just moved to a new city and a new school and had been struggling to make friends until the Beatles came along. 'Conformity and upward mobility were the most obvious features in the town,' she says.

> It was no place for a left-wing, atheist, divorced family like ours. We were outcasts, treated more with suspicion than curiosity … But then a girlish democracy was created with the arrival of the Beatles. The old nasty prejudices suddenly melted away. Girls who had once teased and mocked me for everything from bad hair to reading too much were suddenly curious to know which Beatle I liked best.

During their performance of 'Till There Was You' on *Ed Sullivan*, as their names flashed up on screen, Debbie, who had always thought she was a Paul kind of girl, discovered that her Beatle was actually George – 'What a revelation! During the postmortem at school the next morning, I announced my discovery with confidence. Although Paul was the undisputed favourite, my choice was accepted with respect. And no one ever made fun of me again.'[45]

Twelve-year-old Noelle Oxenhandler experienced a similar epiphany with John, but hers was even more personally transcendent. She described the feeling triggered during *Ed Sullivan* as akin to being transported through the television screen into another realm. 'In that realm,' she explained, 'John had been waiting for me forever. The predominant emotion for me that night was intense recognition. It was as though, on some altar in primordial space and time, I'd left a request for just this man and now at last he had been given unto me.'[46]

These girls, by their own admission, were too young for boy-friends, many only just on the cusp of having romantic or sexual feelings at all. But the Beatles' fun, playful personalities, along with songs like 'I Want to Hold Your Hand' and 'She Loves You', which celebrated the tentative highs and lows of first love, made them feel approachable and thrilling in equal measure. In many ways, they were the first true boy band: less sexual than Elvis but still sexy enough for you to feel the spark. Soon, a whole industry of magazines and merchandise had sprung up to fuel girls' romantic curiosity and obsessions.

In America, publications like *16*, *Tiger Beat* and *Teen Life* – the first magazines to feature bands like the Beatles and later the Stones – offered access to important behind-the-scenes information like what Paul liked to eat for lunch or John's favourite colour, giant kissable-sized posters and endless opportunities for girls to indulge their feelings and fantasies. Having these magazines, created especially for them – along with Beatles songs that captured the energy and optimism of teenage love and often celebrated young women who were empowered and independent – was both validating and inspiring. If the Beatles liked girls who were bold and confident, then there was only one thing to do.

The Beatles were inundated with marriage proposals and effusive expressions of adoration. 'I love you,' wrote one girl. 'I try so hard to show my love, but what can I do? You are there, and I am here. So I do my best. I have fainted for you six times.'[47] 'My loves,' wrote another, 'I will absolutely suffer and remain in dauntless agony and total despair until the day I may touch you comes.'[48] A particularly optimistic girl told Paul to look out for her at the concert she would be attending. 'You'll recognize me,' she said. 'I'll be in the 1st row in a yellow dress. By the time summer comes my hair will be very long. I will be holding a sign that says "I'M THE ONE".'[49] And yet, when Gloria Steinem approached a tearful girl who claimed to be 'passionately in love with Ringo' at a concert to ask if she would actually go on a date with him, she apparently looked startled and replied, 'I don't think so; I hardly know him.'[50]

This wasn't a contradiction. Crushing on the Beatles, like many a rebel boy before them, was a hardcore blend of fantasy and experimentation. Like Elvis, the emotions they stirred often blurred the line between admiration and identification. They embodied a kind of freedom that was both attractive and aspirational. 'I liked their independence and wanted those things for myself,' explained one girl. 'We were so stifled … If only I could act that way and be strong, sexy, and doing what you want.'[51] 'I didn't want to grow up and be a wife,' reflected another. 'It seemed to me that the Beatles had the kind of freedom I wanted.'[52]

Girls, as much as boys, adopted the Beatles as style icons. They got Beatles haircuts, kitted themselves out in Beatles-inspired clothes and incorporated Liverpudlian slang like 'fab', 'naff' and 'gear' (meaning great) into their vocabularies. Some, however, took the impulse to channel the Beatles' unique brand of irreverence and independence a bit too literally.

In September 1964, America was riveted by the story of thirteen-year-old Elizabeth Freedman who had vanished from her home in Newport, Massachusetts. As far as police could piece together, she'd secretly applied for a passport, withdrawn the whole $405 her grandparents had given her for her savings account and bought a plane ticket. Leaving a note for her mother explaining that she was going to the cinema, she'd boarded a flight to London in the hope of finding and meeting the Beatles. After a fruitless two-week international police search, the papers announced that Brian Epstein was offering Elizabeth a backstage ticket to a Beatles show if she turned herself in.

As she sat happily munching a hotdog in their dressing room and posing for photos with the boys a few days later, the scene could have come straight out of *A Hard Day's Night*.

'The girls back home will never believe me,' she told reporters.

'So this is the little girl we've been reading about,' said Ringo.

'I don't think we've been to Boston,' said George.

'We have,' said Paul. 'That's where we had that tea party.'

'I'm still in a daze,' said Elizabeth. 'I was beginning to think I'd never see them.'[53]

I like to imagine this movie ending with Elizabeth giving a little wink to the camera. Her story may have been the most dramatic, but it wasn't the only one. Throughout the mid-'60s, newspapers across America contained frequent tales of girls who had disappeared from home leaving notes explaining that they'd gone to find the Beatles. Many were supported and encouraged by other Beatles fans they'd met through fan clubs or even by chance. Elizabeth herself had, in fact, been found staying in a boarding house run by a Beatles fan she'd met in a cafe in London. This was a testament to the power of Beatles fandom, which had created a whole network of instant friends as well as a sense of community across countries and borders.

And yet, as these stories remind us, for all the connection and community of fan clubs, the empowerment of shared fantasies, the transcendence of late-night dreaming, the thrill of finding a rare photo, singing and dancing along to records, waiting outside record stores for new releases or chasing down tiny squares of Ringo's bed-sheets or John's boxer shorts that had been cut up and stapled to statements of authenticity signed by hotel laundry workers, noth-ing, *nothing*, NOTHING mattered more than the possibility of seeing the Beatles in person. It was, as historian André Millard put it, 'the only way to consummate the relationship'.[54]

'Having the Beatles come to your town suddenly made your town feel special,' says sociologist and Beatles expert Candy Leonard.[55] Having tickets to a show made you the coolest person in your family or friendship group (younger siblings were often told they were too young to go). Girls saved up their pocket money and nervously sent off for tickets or trekked across town to queue for hours in wind, rain and snow. Those who couldn't afford tickets came up with creative ways to get in, like volunteering to write articles for local newspa-pers. When they finally held those blessed tickets in their hands, they guarded them with their lives. 'It was as if they were the Hope Diamond,' explained a girl called Barbara.[56] They'd buy or even sew themselves new outfits (yellow was popular since it made you stand out, meaning there was a better chance your Beatle might notice you). After that, it was time to prepare for love and chaos.

From the earliest days of Beatlemania, scenes of teenage girls screaming, crying and doing battle with police officers at live events had been presented as inseparable from the experience of Beatles fandom. It was so iconic that girls often discussed their plans for the big day: to scream or not to scream – that was the question. Some, like Sibbie O'Sullivan – who later wrote a memoir called *My Private Lennon: Explorations from a Fan Who Never Screamed* – proudly de-fined themselves as being above screaming. These girls saw it as 'crass and pointless' and argued that the screaming drowned out the music.[57]

For those who did, screaming and crying were essential to fully immersing themselves in the Beatles experience. Beatles shows were one of the few places where this type of behaviour was not only accepted but expected. 'The fans had bought the records and memorised the songs,' says Millard. 'The reason to attend the concert was to be there and affirm their allegiance,' and everyone knew that screaming was part of the show.[58] Sometimes this unladylike behaviour was even encouraged by the Beatles themselves: 'Go ahead and let yourselves go,' said John once. 'It's not our place anyway.'[59]

Leading up to Beatles events, girls often dared each other about what they might be brave enough to do. The unrelenting intensity of their screams and the desperation with which tiny, seemingly fragile girls jumped barriers, charged police officers, shattered windows and, at the Hollywood Bowl, even leapt into the murky water of the moat surrounding the stage were a barometer of the trueness of their love. It said: I am here, my feelings are real and I will be seen and heard.

Even girls who thought they wouldn't scream found themselves carried away and overcome with the intensity of the moment. 'I just screamed; I couldn't help it. It was like I had no control over myself whatsoever,' explained one girl.[60] Others – nervous but resolved to find their voices – anxiously willed themselves on:

I want to scream but I don't know how. My first two attempts fail miserably. On the third attempt, I take in a big breath and emit brief squeals. That's more like it! The next one is perfect: a long, eardrum-piercing shriek. The girls in front grin and nod their approval.[61]

By 1964, loud, visible expressions of fangirl love, desire and devotion were nothing new. The bobbysoxers had swooned for Sinatra. Elvis fans had screamed themselves hoarse and mounted stage invasions too. But Beatlemania was different. It was relentless. Like those never-ending Beatles screams, it was everywhere – in the streets, at airports and hotels, in record stores, in schools and even in homes. From the moment thousands of girls jumped to their feet and began screaming and dancing in their living rooms during that first *Ed Sullivan Show*, it was clear that there was something about Beatlemania that defied containment. As Ehrenreich, Hess and Jacobs put it, if you saw a photo of these crowds out of context, you might think it was a proto-feminist protest of some sort. And in many ways, it was.

Whether they knew it or not, these girls were tired. Tired of having their feelings dismissed. Tired of having to contain their desires. Tired of having to live in a world where boys could have dreams, aspirations and adventures beyond the confines of home while girls had to hold back, be good and make themselves small. Since long before they were born, young women had been told to be good, sit down and shut up, but now – screaming and crying and shouting and dancing with their sisters in screaming – they were, for the first time, experiencing that same sense of togetherness and freedom they'd admired in the Beatles and felt in the irrepressible joy of all their favourite Beatles songs. And for the first time in history, there were too many of them for anyone to tell them to calm down.

Beatlemania – a phenomenon that brought tens of thousands of young women together in a relentless celebration of female love, lust, ecstasy and joy – erupted on the eve of the women's liberation movement. For feminist writer Elizabeth Hess, as for many young women, this first taste of public togetherness and self-expression was a life-changing moment. 'My own consciousness snapped into shape in 1964 at a Beatles concert,' she wrote.

> I still remember melting into a massive crowd of jumping, scream-
> ing girls, all thinking and feeling the same lascivious thoughts. It
> was my generation's turn to let our libidos go public. I was twelve,
> just beginning to understand that sex was power: my first femi-
> nist epiphany. As the '60s tore on, the crowd of girls, now women,
> was still moving together, marching against the war in Vietnam.[62]

ACROSS THE UNIVERSE

As you can imagine, the wildness and intensity of Beatlemania met with many of the same criticisms that this type of fandom always had.

At first, the critics had become obsessed with the Beatles' aes-thetic. 'I took one angry look at those sissy, degenerate Beatles and informed my son if I ever caught him with hair like that I would knock him from one end of the room to the other and give him a good swift kick into the cellar!' fumed one father.[63] 'We put up with that noise from one of our own [Elvis], until the army got him to grow up,' said another. 'Do we have to go through it again with these fugitives from a barber shop?'[64] As a symbol of sexual ambi-guity, youth rebellion and defiance, hair was a serious and ongoing point of contention – a defining battleground for Beatles' boy fans, but the harshest criticism was reserved for the girls.

In Cincinnati, Juvenile Court Judge Benjamin Schwartz stood before an American flag to address TV viewers after experiencing what he called the 'pandemonium' of a Beatles concert attended by '14,000 children, a great majority being girls'. He explained that without proper supervision, these girls had turned into 'unrecognisable beings' – fainting, screaming, pulling their hair out. 'Some girls went up and kissed the very seats [the Beatles had sat on]', he said, in horror, adding that 'one father brought a child who was epileptic, and the child had an epileptic fit'.[65]

This off-hand reference to irresponsible parenting was telling. One of the biggest differences between Beatlemania and previous uprisings of female fan 'hysteria' was that there was much more overlap between parents who appreciated the Beatles too – or at least who understood and engaged with their children's Beatles obsessions. One girl, Joann, remembered her dad, a construction worker, coming home from work one day excited with the news that he'd bumped into the Beatles on a job at the Warwick Hotel. 'You know, they're all kind of homely looking, except that one you like … Paul? He was kind of cute.'[66] Laura's parents were 'very amused' by her devotion.[67] Her mum helped her order personalised stationery in the name of Mrs Paul McCartney, while her dad learned Beatles trivia so she could quiz him on facts like Paul's birthday. For Christmas, they bought her a share in EMI (the Beatles' UK record label) – which sent her dividend checks for 32 cents that she never cashed, forcing them to keep reissuing them in smaller and smaller amounts.

Perhaps these parents remembered their own youthful obsessions with Frank Sinatra. Or perhaps they just thought the Beatles were pretty harmless. 'Now let me ask you a question,' said a concert promoter.

I suppose you were young once. Now maybe you didn't do this, but I'll bet you knew girls who swooned at the very mention of Rudolph Valentino. I've been doing some research. Youngsters not only swooned, but some even committed suicide. So here's the question: 'Which is healthier, to swoon over Valentino or scream at the Beatles? Include Rudy Vallée, Elvis Presley, and Frank Sinatra.'[68]

It seemed that Epstein's decision to dress these four little rebels up in suits and train them to bow in neat unison at the end of their shows had done exactly what it needed to do. Even the mother of cross-continental runaway Elizabeth admitted that the Beatles were nice boys. After meeting them backstage in London, she told the press that she'd become a Beatles fan herself.

Nine-year-old Whoopi Goldberg was another child whose mother understood and engaged deeply. Whoopi had been completely obsessed with the Beatles since she first saw them on TV. Her moment of instant recognition had been one of friendship:

> We watched *Ed Sullivan* every Sunday night: my brother and mom and I. It wasn't even a question, it was just what we did. And man! I'd never seen anyone that looked like that. It was like a revelation. When you're a little kid you don't know it's a revelation, but the whole world lit up and suddenly I felt like I could be friends with them. And I'm Black.

When, in 1965, she heard the Beatles were coming back to New York as part of their summer stadium tour, she asked her mother if they could go. The sad answer was no – they just couldn't afford it, but a few weeks later, her mother came into her room and told her it was time to go. 'Where are we going?' she asked.

Her mother wouldn't say. 'I'll let you know when we get there.'

They took a train and got off at an unfamiliar station. 'Where are we?'

'We're at Shea Stadium,' said her mother.

'Why?'

Whoopi still wells up with tears when she thinks of this moment. 'I don't know how she did it,' she says. 'She got two tickets.'[69]

Shea was a big deal – the biggest actually. It was the first major stadium rock concert in the history of the world, but the Beatles simply had too many fans. Thousands of fans without concert tickets often descended on venues for the pure magic of breathing the same air as the Beatles or maybe catching a glimpse of their car. This was the only way for concert promoters to meet the need and to quell the chaos. It made much more logistical and economic sense to put all these hysterical girls in a stadium than to have them causing chaos in the street.

As 56,000 Beatles fans, many of them children with their parents, descended upon Shea on that sunny August afternoon, you got the sense that something historic was happening. 'It was just great, the anticipation of the entire day … just giggling and carrying on,' said JoAnne McCormack. 'You didn't eat a lot before the concert, 'cause you knew you were gonna be so excited, you didn't want to barf all over people.'[70]

By the time the Beatles' old friend Ed Sullivan, teeth freshly whitened, took to the stage to introduce them, the stadium was a bubbling mass of girls and noise. Along the mesh perimeter of the pitch, clusters of twelve- and thirteen-year-olds in T-shirts or Peter Pan-collared dresses stood gripping the fence, eyes fixed on the stage in expectation. Some were in tears; others were fiercely rattling the wire like little wild animals bellowing to be unleashed.

In the stands, girls in the nose-bleed seats anxiously pointed binoculars. Thousands more were hollering, fainting and crying their hearts out and the Fab Four were still nowhere to be seen (had their helicopter even landed yet?). One girl swooned as a police officer gently tapped her cheeks to revive her and parents looked on, smiling tenderly, because there was something undeniably moving about the sight of all these girls standing and screaming together, beet-red, tear-stained faces twisted in loud, shameless, expectation and longing.

A hundred and fifty years earlier, when thousands of tentative yet flirtatious fan letters landed on the desk of Lord Byron, the authors were anonymous. It wouldn't have been appropriate for a young lady to express passionate emotions in public, let alone put them down on paper and send them to a lord. They did it anyway. Critics genuinely feared that Byron's radical appeal to the minds and emotions of young women might lead to some form of social or political upheaval. Now, halfway across the world, with woman-hood itself on the brink of a revolution, tens of thousands of girls had come together with their parents in a manifestation of desire and devotion so huge that they had to invent the stadium rock con-cert to contain it.

As TV helicopters circled overhead and fourteen TV cameras positioned up and down that stadium immortalised every shout, every shriek and every swoon in glorious Technicolor, the fangirl had come of age.

'Ladies and gentlemen,' said Sullivan. 'Honoured by their country, decorated by their Queen and loved here in America. Here are the Beatles.' And then there it was. The scream to end all screams. The jumbo jet that had first brought the Beatles to America registered a sound of 73 decibels. The screams recorded at Shea that night were

131.35. The sound dwarfed the four boys in tan suits now jogging to the stage. But maybe that was the point. This was the girls' moment.

Shea generated mixed feelings for the Beatles. On one hand, it was a peak. No performer or band had ever played to such a large audience – John said he'd seen 'the top of the mountain' that day.[71] But trying to play a full set through that wall of sound that would have put Phil Spector to shame was… difficult. The footage shows four men exhilarated and overwhelmed, sweating (not in a sexy Elvis *Comeback Special* kind of way), running on pure hysteria and adrenaline. Even their suits, always so cute and charming, now seemed to be strangling them under the stadium lights, and VOX's groundbreaking custom-built new amps were no match for tens of thousands of screaming girls. Somewhere in that tsunami of adoration, John, Paul, George and Ringo had lost themselves. By the time they got to Japan a few months later and, protected by an army of police officers, they could actually hear themselves play for the first time in months, they realised they'd forgotten how to stay in tune.

Many Beatles historians consider Shea and the tours that followed a turning point. It was here that the Beatles began to realise live performance had become nearly impossible amid the frenzy of Beatlemania. They were contractually obliged to continue touring into 1966, but something had changed. The intimacy of live performances was gone, replaced by chaotic stadium shows that left them feeling disconnected and spent. They played their last official concert on 29 August 1966 at Candlestick Park in San Francisco before retreating to the studio. They would only play live together one more time – that final iconic rooftop performance at 3 Savile Row, the HQ of their music empire Apple Corps (not a coincidence: Steve Jobs was a Beatles fan too).

The way the story is most often told is that it was the moment they stopped touring and were 'liberated' from the devotion and demands of their teen girl fans and stopped having to play mindless pop hits like 'She Loves You' and 'I Want To Hold Your Hand' that they were finally free to develop their true musical artistry. But the type of freedom they were given was unheard of. It was a freedom that would only have been bestowed on a band who had proved to their record label that their fans would follow them anywhere.

By 1966, the Beatles and many of their earliest fans were growing up. And as the optimism of the early '60s headed towards the social and political turmoil of 1968, change was inevitable. In the earliest days of Beatlemania, young teenage and pre-teen girls had fallen in love with the sweetness of their sensitive, romantic lyrics. The Beatles sung directly to girls and just like those crooner songs of the 1930s, the magical 'you' in each one of those early love songs was each one of them. Songs like 'If I Fell' took young women seriously. Here was a boy asking a girl if she would be gentle with his heart, admitting he'd been hurt before, seeking reassurance. Boy fans, too, found truths and revelations in these songs: here was proof that it was OK to feel angry and hurt or even afraid and uncertain at times. Kindness, vulnerability and even fear were expressions of authenticity and humanness. It was a hopeful vision of the future.

Now, as both the Beatles and their fans graduated from those early romantic ideals into the more complex realities of their next phase, it was a reflection of how complicated life really was. 'My perception of them was changing,' said one girl. 'I was changing too. Realising the complexity of people, and that the Beatles weren't always happy-go-lucky. It was strange, but you listened.'[72]

What was most meaningful to many fans through this transition, and on into the future as the Beatles became more experimental, was the fact the band was challenging them to think. Beatles fans weren't screaming and dancing anymore. Albums like *Rubber Soul* and *Revolver* were now inviting them to come together to talk, analyse and debate. Fandom was becoming just as much about conversation as adoration. But their special relationship with female listeners was still there. In fact, through this transition, they began to address the feelings, frustrations and aspirations of girls and women even more authentically.

There's a girl. She has no name and she isn't real, but she had been with the Beatles from the start. Paul and John just called her 'her'. She's the girl who got all the pleasing in 'Please Please Me', the one who needed protecting in 'You're Gonna Lose That Girl'. In 'Ticket to Ride', she started tentatively testing the waters of independence, but 1965 was the year she truly began to find herself.

The very first song on *Rubber Soul*, often considered the Beatles' 'transitional' album, opens with a question to her: what does she want to be? 'Drive My Car' is a fun, danceable celebration of her ambitions, because she's the one headed for stardom now – beep beep yeah! In 'Norwegian Wood', she brings some guy home but makes him sleep in the bath. She knows exactly what she's about, and it has nothing to do with pleasing anyone just now.

By the time we get to 'Girl' on that same album, we meet a heroine who is fully formed – a confounding and multifaceted human being: enigmatic, independent and complex. She's tough and resilient in 'For No One', determined and resourceful in 'Lady Madonna'. And when, on Wednesday morning at 5 a.m., she steps out the front door of her mum and dad's house in the push and pull of that gorgeous, haunting string arrangement in 'She's Leaving Home', we feel the weight of the clash between female freedom and expectation in 1967. And so it went on. When it was time for her to make another appearance, Paul and John would just turn to each other and say, 'Shall we bring her back?' and they would know who they were talking about.[73] And if they persistently returned to her in their songwriting, it was because she mattered. Not as some perfect, idealised symbol of romance, but as a reflection of the growing complexity of the world around her. And because she was a part of them.

But in this newly complex and evolving world – a world where the Beatles were now encouraging fans to 'Think for Yourself' – not all of their original fans were interested in following them down their increasingly experimental path. By 1965, as the Beatles began to push the boundaries of pop music and reinvent themselves as 'serious artists', pop music itself was fracturing. Just as Beatlemania reached its peak, it had exploded into a psychedelic kaleidoscope of choices, identities and genres. The revolution of 1964, and the unde-niable spending power of the baby boom teenager that had ignited it, had blown the doors wide open. Record labels, TV shows and magazines were now all clamouring to discover the next big thing.

Younger children – the eight-, nine- and ten-year-olds – who had adored the playful, almost cartoonish image of the early Beatles were now, frankly, quite scared of the warped faces on the cover of *Rubber Soul* and ominous lyrics in darker songs like 'Run for Your Life'. Many shifted their allegiance to lighter pop acts like the Monkees and Herman's Hermits.

The Monkees were the first manufactured boy band. They gave kids four cute boys to love and scream about. Fun, catchy tunes like 'I'm a Believer' lacked the edginess and ambiguity that had begun to permeate the Beatles' music – and thank God for that. Critics sneered at their 'safe' appeal, but what was so wrong with safety if it meant boys who were kind, down to earth and didn't mind laughing at themselves? If loving the Beatles had taught their older sisters anything, it was that tenderness and humour could be just as revolutionary as any hip gyrations. The fact that even manufactured pop stars now wore their hair long and played in bands showed just how much the Beatles had transformed the rules of acceptably desirable masculinity. In a world of Playboy bunnies and beauty queens, where girls were still being taught by advertising and mainstream media that their role was to be decorative and pleasing, what could be more radical than learning to expect and desire kindness and reciprocity – and to be assertive about what you want.

That's not to say that danger was off the table. While the Beatles were off faffing with sitars and tape loops, teenagers looking for something more visceral still had the Rolling Stones. Their concerts were crucibles of chaos. 'It was like they had the Battle of the Crimea going on,' said Keith.

> People gasping, tits hanging out, chicks choking, nurses running around with ambulances ... It was like a living *Hard Day's Night* climbing over rooftops with chief constables who don't know their way, getaways down fire escapes, through laundry chutes, into bakery vans. We ended up being like the Monkees without even realising it.[74]

Newspapers reported an endless stream of riots at their shows and even claimed they'd seen girls being carried out in straightjackets, but the screaming, grabbing, fainting girls who had once struck terror into the hearts of parents and preachers at Elvis shows were now (grudgingly) accepted as a normal part of the rock and pop concert experience. The fact that the Stones were now free to flourish in this atmosphere of beautiful chaos was a testament to how the intensity of Beatlemania had somehow managed to normalise it all.

And these boys didn't just tolerate the pandemonium: they made it their brand. 'Nothing scared me as much as being caught in a crowd of thirteen-year-old girls who have just lost it,' said Keith, years later, 'but if there's one way to die, then that might as well be it, pal.'[75]

The Stones were invited onto panel shows where Mick tried not to roll his eyes while experts quite literally stroked their chins as they dissected and psychoanalysed fangirl love and adoration. 'When these girls pounce upon Mick and seem to want to tear him to pieces, it's not essentially an act of aggression,' explained some professor or other. 'It's an act of devouring him – they want to incorporate his essence' (not a bad theory, actually).[76] Like Elvis, Valentino and Byron before him, Mick Jagger was sexy because he shamelessly refused to conform to anything. He was as beautiful as he was dangerous. And that contradiction still spoke to thousands of girls who couldn't think of anything better than playing with fire – even if it did mean getting a bit burned. Bad boys like the Stones endured because even the surliest sneer contains multitudes.

Two days after Stones guitarist Brian Jones's shocking sudden death in July 1969, Mick stood on stage in Hyde Park in a frilly white Regency tunic and jewelled choker, reading Percy Shelley's 1821 poem *Adonais* to an ocean of fans. When he finished, as the band broke into a blistering cover of Johnny Winter's 'I'm Yours and I'm Hers', thousands of butterflies were released over the crowd. It was the perfect meeting of nineteenth-century Romanticism and 1960s counterculture that reminded the world that beauty and tenderness have a place in rock, that grief and love between men could and should be shared openly and that vulnerability and emotional openness were, in their own way, revolutionary acts. 'I'd really dig it if you would be with us,' he'd said. 'I really don't know how to do this sort of thing, but I'm gonna try.'

The world was changing, and performers and fans now seemed to be evolving together and learning from each other. Whether it was the rebellious spirit of rock, the soul and empowerment of Motown, the political activism of folk or the gritty authenticity of the British blues revival, fans were now aligning themselves with artists who spoke to and for who they were. And where young women had once obsessed over men like Elvis and the Beatles, in part because of the freedom and power they embodied, they now had badass women like Janis Joplin, Aretha Franklin, Joan Baez and Grace Slick beginning to give voice to uniquely female truths, experiences and power. 'It was seeing Janis Joplin that made me resolve, once and for all, not to get my hair straightened,' wrote Ellen Willis, the first pop music critic for the *New Yorker*. 'And there was a direct line from that sort of response to those apocryphal burned bras and all that followed.'[77]

There's a video of Janis on stage in Germany, singing 'Piece of My Heart' in 1969. It's as classic Janis as you can get: shiny blue leggings, sparkly silver top, no make-up, no bra, hair flying everywhere, infinite layers of bangles and beads jingling and jangling with every jump, shimmy and shake – like the true goddess of raw, powerful womanhood that she is. A few years earlier, she'd been a lonely girl in Port Arthur, Texas, desperate for something real. There were no female role models for rebellion back then. After reading that article in *Time* magazine about Jack Kerouac and the Beats, she knew she had to get out. Now, here she is, not just watching it or even living it – she's owning it.

'Piece of My Heart' is a cover. When Erma Franklin took it to

No. 10 on the Billboard R&B chart in 1967, it was a soaring anthem of love and resilience. Her gospel-trained voice transformed all that heartache into something transcendentally beautiful. But now, channelling that raw, untamed lineage of blues women – from Bessie Smith to Ma Rainey – who loved too loud and felt too much, Janis roughs it up. It's something messier here but, in many ways, even more unrestrainable. Superficially, this is a song about loving someone despite getting hurt over and over again. But really, it's a hymn to female autonomy and self-expression – the defiant joy of feeling deeply, shouting loudly and loving hard. And in Janis's version, we can hear the same wild, fearless spirit we heard in the screams of the girls of Beatlemania.

As Janis sings, she starts pulling fans up on stage with her – a boy in a black suit, a girl in a shawl, another boy in plaid. Soon, she doesn't even need to bring them up herself; they're just climbing up on their own. They want to be part of this, and before you know it, the stage is a joyous, undulating sea of people, all singing and dancing together. At one point, when she gets to the line about how a woman can be tough, Janis puts her arm around a shy-looking girl and sings the whole verse to her, as if she's pulled her from the private space of the audience onto the public stage for this exact moment of encouragement.

The Beatles may have chosen to step back from live performances, but they were still there for their fans. 'They put their arms around me with their music,' said one.[78] 'They gave you a sense of what's possible; that you can find what you do well and express yourself doing it,' added another.[79] There are countless stories of Beatles fans who were inspired to pick up pens, guitars, paintbrushes, cameras and laptops. Fan letters became music journalism. Fan clubs became careers. Teen crushes became futures.

But the true beauty of fandom is that its influence really doesn't have to be that grand. For every fan who channelled the energy of Beatlemania into activism or art, there were thousands more who found joy in the pure, unfiltered pleasure of loving something that much. They saved their concert outfits in plastic, tucked ticket stubs into shoeboxes and saved records too worn out to play. Even now, sixty years after that first *Ed Sullivan*, there are millions of women who still feel a little flutter when Paul posts one of his rare personal Instagram pics or when the light is just right and they get a tiny glimpse of Ringo's amazing eyes through those shades. These are the people who can tell you exactly where they were the first time they heard 'I Want to Hold Your Hand', can't help but stop for a second and feel the magic when 'Imagine' comes on in a shop, could debate you all night about the identity of the fifth Beatle (it was the girls, by the way), will cross continents for a Paul or Ringo show or can never not sing along to 'Hey Jude' in the car.

When George died, the youngest fan who came to lay flowers outside Abbey Road was eight. She told the BBC that she'd grown up with Beatles music and her favourite was George. Her mother Laura, of the Mrs Paul McCartney stationery and EMI shares, looked on. 'I was as touched by her devotion as my father had been by mine,' she said.[80]

People who were there during Beatlemania talk about being filled with the feeling that youth is power. But, by January 1969, when the Beatles stepped out onto the rooftop of Apple Corps HQ for that bittersweet final lunchtime show, letting the first chords of 'Get Back' ring out over the grey rooftops of London, the power of that initial burst of collective joy was as alive and unstoppable as the sound waves bouncing between buildings, echoing down alleyways and floating out over the Thames. The love was everywhere now.

Over in Vegas that same year, Sinatra was crooning at his millionth 'pre-retirement' show. The bobbysoxers were in their forties – making a glamorous weekend of it with their husbands in tuxes at the Sands. But when Frank kicked into those high notes in the chorus of 'My Way', it was hard to say who was swooning more.

Across the Strip at the International Hotel, Elvis fans were flying in from around the world, finally meeting friends they'd only known through international fan club letters. Many brought their children to share in the pilgrimage. When the big moment came, mortified teenagers watched through their fingers as their mothers lunged for kisses and grabbed Elvis's sweaty scarves during his 'Love Me Tender' walkabouts.

Back in London, befuddled police officers scratched their heads on the street outside Apple Corp, trying to work out how to shut down a concert happening five floors up as office workers hung out of their windows, teenagers clustered on pavements and suited businessmen squinted and grinned up at the sky. Paul (of course it was Paul) smiled and waved at a group of boys who had climbed up a chimney.

There had always been something revolutionarily democratic about the Beatles, not just in their working-class origins, their blurring of gender boundaries or their ability to erase distinctions between 'high' and 'low' culture – but in the way they invited everyone to experience love as a universal, boundary-breaking force that could bridge divides and inspire connection.

This final rooftop show, with its impromptu audience of office workers, grandmothers and bewildered policemen, was the perfect manifestation of that spirit of unity and wonder. Their music, like their audiences, had always refused to be contained. It spilled out into the streets, turned strangers into conspirators in joy and reminded everyone who heard it that revolution doesn't always come with manifestos and barricades. Sometimes it comes from letting yourself get caught up in the magic of the moment, the transformative power of a song or the realisation that the person standing next to you is a Beatles fan too.

Girls at Shea Stadium (1965)

THANK YOU GIRL

Very late one Saturday night in autumn 1970, Carol, Cathy and Lucy sat on the steps of Abbey Road like they always did, bundled in duffle coats with flasks of tea.

The Beatles had broken up earlier that year, but the Apple Scruffs, as these girls were known, weren't going anywhere. They'd known each other since 1966 when they used to hang around outside the Beatles' houses and recording studios. They officially formed their fan club – complete with membership cards, badges and a hand-drawn monthly magazine – in 1968. There had been seventeen of them originally, but these three were the hardcore. Day in, day out, here they were – standing on the steps outside Apple Corps or Abbey Road, waving hello to studio staff or the Beatles themselves, who were still in and out now and then.

George was in tonight, working on his first solo album. He'd been in nearly every day for the past few months, but something strange was going on today. The girls noticed that the letterbox kept opening and closing as if someone inside was watching them. Every now and then Mal, the Beatles' legendary roadie, would come out like he was checking on them. They briefly wondered what was up but were too busy talking to think about it properly.

It was so late that the sun was just starting to come up when Mal came out again. 'George wants you to come in,' he said. At first, they thought he was joking – they'd never been invited inside before. Mal assured them he wasn't, so they followed him in. George was waiting in the control room of Studio 3 with a smile on his face. 'I've got something I want you to hear,' he said.[1] Then someone hit play. The first thing they heard was a harmonica. After a few bars, it exploded into a beautiful, shimmering Dylan-inspired but unmistakably George love song. When it got to the chorus, they glanced at each other and then over at George in disbelief: the song was about them.

Five years earlier, at the height of Beatlemania, the Beatles had recorded 'Thank You Girl': a joyful, bouncy (and some say strategic) love letter to their girl fans. 'Apple Scruffs', track eleven on the epic three-disc album that would become *All Things Must Pass*, was the evolution of this. It's a celebration of – and meditation on – the enduring but often unspoken bond between artists and fans. 'Now it's finished – and off to the factory. I thought I'd tell you that I haven't a clue whether it's good or bad as I've heard it too much now,' wrote George in a letter to the girls a few weeks later.

During the making of this epic album (the most expensive album EMI ever had to pay for) I have felt positive and negative – pleased and displeased, and all the other opposites expected to be found in this material world. However, the one thing that didn't waver, seems to me, to be 'you three' and Mal, always there as my sole supporters, and even during my worst moments I always felt the encouragement from you was sufficient to make me finish the thing. Thanks a lot, I am really overwhelmed by your apparent undying love, and I don't understand it at all!

Love from George[2]

In this moment of vulnerability, George was acknowledging something that it's easy to forget: there would be no stars without fans. When Byromania and Lisztomania kicked off, or thousands of young women lined up outside the Paramount to see Frankie Sinatra and later the Beatles, they were far from passive consumers. Their fan letters, fan clubs and expressions of adoration and support were actively shaping both their heroes' careers and the future of book, music and movie culture. Their emotional investment was a form of labour that was unacknowledged and unpaid but essential to the mythology and commercial success of their idols. Not to mention their belief in their own work. This was a relationship that had always been reciprocal.

While this book has mainly focused on female fans and their love for male stars, this dynamic was never limited to girls obsessing romantically about men. Sarah Siddons transformed the London stage into a site of collective rapture in the eighteenth century (Lord Byron's mum was a fan). Men and women wept, fainted and mobbed her carriage after performances. Opera singer Jenny Lind drove Berlin to Lindomania a decade before Liszt, and her fans were mainly men (isn't it curious that while Lisztomania became an iconic cultural reference point, Lindomania has faded from historical memory?). And, of course, early screen actresses like Florence Lawrence and Mary Pickford had legions of devoted admirers. These women rose to fame on the back of passionate fan communities that formed around their performances and personas. As Hollywood evolved from its freewheeling early days to the well-oiled commercial dream machine of the 1930s and '40s, studio chiefs took to counting fan letters and monitoring their content to make sure they were clear about what audiences wanted.

And while studios were counting and analysing fan letters for market research, the true impact of actresses and actors on audiences went much deeper than weekly fanmail statistics. For girls, actresses provided new models of modern womanhood – how to be, aspire and imagine a life beyond the ones they were born into. For queer girls, this was especially meaningful. Daydreaming about and expressing love for an actress became a way to explore same-sex desire in an era when feelings like these couldn't be acknowledged or expressed openly. And within the rigid and ridiculous gender expectations of the era – a moment when the world took young women's gushy, overly emotional reactions to things as a universal character trait – the idea that a girl might be in love with her heroine was weirdly accepted. The reality of what 'love' might actually mean in this context often went over potential critics' heads. When an anxious teenage girl wrote into *Motion Picture* magazine in 1916 to ask if it was OK for her to write and tell her favourite actress that she was in love with her, the reply from the 'Answer Man' was a shrug. 'Since you are a girl it is perfectly proper to write to Norma Talmadge to tell her you love her,' he said.[3] It's hard to know whether to laugh or cry.

For male fans of male stars, the situation was often more complicated. Watching Rudolph Valentino be dragged over the coals in the press for his perceived effeminacy and seeing crooners derided as 'sissies' or 'pantywaists' were reminders of the dangers of visible signs of homosexuality in their era. And yet their continued popularity, despite attempts to shame them, validated feelings and identities that had previously remained hidden. Beautiful, sensitive male stars like Valentino and Ramon Novarro and later Montgomery Clift or James Dean invited a radically new kind of male gaze. In doing so, they became cultural touchstones for alternative expressions of masculinity. Whether their fans were gay, questioning or even just fed up of being told what 'real men' were supposed to be like, these stars offered a way to imagine beauty, softness and vulnerability as an increasingly acceptable part of what it meant to be a man.

In the early days of pop culture, like now, fandom was both a deeply personal expression of self and a place where communities of like-minded people could come together to find validation, belonging and shared joy. This was never the domain of just girls, but historically it was female fans who faced the most persistent mockery and moral panic. In early book, theatre and movie culture, women – particularly young women – often made up the largest percentage of readerships and audiences. At moments in history when women were only just beginning to access public life and still had limited agency and autonomy, these were rare places where they could come together in large groups, see themselves and their experiences reflected in meaningful ways and build communities around shared passions. It was a socially acceptable way for them to express who they were and what mattered.

Later, as pop music replaced movies as the primary form of youth entertainment, they continued to be the most visibly enthusiastic participants and highest spenders. As such, they often became flashpoints for much bigger anxieties about mass culture and changing gender roles. It was easier to moralise and ridicule young women's enthusiasm than acknowledge their growing cultural and economic power. This pattern of dismissal stretched all the way back to the birth of mass entertainment – the novel – when women's passionate emotional responses were seen as potentially dangerous, both socially and even politically. As mass entertainment evolved from books to movies and then radio, TV and records, the myth of the mindless, hysterical female fan who was a danger to herself, and others, persisted. The swooning female fan and her obsession with her favourite male star became the perfect symbol of this cultural degradation – that art and culture were being corrupted by the frivolity of female tastes and desires.

When critics scorned Elvis's lustful female fans or derided Movie-Struck Girls for their embarrassingly excessive displays of emotion, they were reinforcing hierarchies that privileged intellectual responses over emotional ones, rational appreciation over passionate engagement. And it emerged at the very moment nineteenth-century divisions – arguably still with us – between high and low culture were gaining momentum. These hierarchies existed to reassert white, male, upper-class authority in the face of growing cultural democratisation. That this female fandom was often bound up with fantasies of love, lust and romance – with pretty, 'feminine' and often foreign or lower-class young men as objects of an actively desiring female gaze – made it even more threatening to the established moral order.

Before the nineteenth century, when 'respectable' women were still a rare sight at the theatre and music hall, it was perfectly normal for men to be brought to tears by a performance or actively engage with the actors on stage. By the late nineteenth century, with the regendering of the theatre in full swing, emotional regulation had taken hold. There was no room for sentimentality in serious cultural discourse, and emotional responses considered 'female' were now scorned. So were the cultural texts that appealed – or at least were marketed – to women: romance novels, women's pictures and sentimental ballads. The scholarly analysis of poetry – or later even 'serious' rock music criticism – was considered valuable intellectual work. An essay in a fan magazine or tear-stained letter from a young woman explaining what Byron or Elvis meant to her was cringeworthy and embarrassing – not worth the perfume-scented notepaper it was written on. And as the rise of celebrity meant that artists themselves became just as fascinating and consumable as their works, 'overly emotional' reactions and attachments to both became even more trivialised and untouchable.

Elvis is a particularly interesting example. For a man who has generated so much attention from critics and scholars – thousands of essays and books – and one whose early career was shaped by young women, I was struck, while researching this book, by the sparse attention from cultural historians on what he might have meant to girls of the 1950s. I guess it was so obvious to them that their interest in Elvis was purely physical that it wasn't worth a closer look. 'What women thought then and now is largely unknown because, quite simply, no one bothered to ask or even thought that our views were worth anything,' wrote sociologist and Elvis fan Sue Wise in 1984.[4] She shared her personal experience of Elvis fandom in an academic journal in the hope of encouraging others to challenge taken-for-granted interpretations of the myths and legends of pop culture. I hope that – in some small way – this book has continued the process of rethinking and reframing that she called for.

We've come a long way since Sue wrote her Elvis essay, thank God – both in terms of our understanding of fandom and cultural respect for the voices and experiences of women and girls. While I was writing this book, Taylor Swift's Eras Tour was smashing records left, right and centre. In the twenty-one months that she was on tour across five continents, playing to more than 10 million fans, she grossed over $2 billion in ticket sales. That made it the highest-grossing tour in the history of the world. With a woman whose music celebrates love, longing and the highs and lows of girlhood as the biggest star in the world – and millions of fans of all ages and genders screaming her lyrics back at her night after night – it seems that we've finally started taking the emotional lives of young women seriously.

This is especially true because it isn't just teenage girls who are obsessed with her. From the *New York Times* gushing about her songcraft to award-winning poets proudly announcing, on social media, that they've been invited to contribute to a book of poems inspired by her *Tortured Poets Department* album, the 'serious' and the 'popular' are in conversation. There's plenty of debate about Swift, of course – her critics argue that her work keeps returning to a narrow idea of straight, white, upper-middle-class girlhood and that this perspective has too often been treated as universal when it's not. But what fans respond to most is her emotional honesty. Her songs document humiliation and rage alongside love, obsession and desire without sanitising any of it. That makes them feel both seen and connected to her. The fact that Swift, more than any other star, has reached an unprecedented level of cultural dominance suggests that feelings and emotions once dismissively labelled 'girl stuff' – or even seen as dangerous in women – are more acceptably relatable than they once were. I bet Caroline Lamb would do a great cover of 'Cruel Summer'.

And then there's the fact that fangirling has officially made it into the dictionary. Everyone has something they fangirl about these days, which is wonderful. But there's a discomfort that lingers – both in the word itself and in the way we use it. We say it with a curious fusion of earnestness and irony, as if passionate enthusiasm is us being reduced to the silly, irrational excitability of a young girl. It's a subtle reminder that we haven't fully escaped the gendered devaluation of enthusing, or feeling 'too much', that is as bound up with what we take seriously as it is with who we take seriously. What would cultural history look like if we acknowledged that emotion is not separate from meaning-making but central to it? If we recognised that the teenage girl screaming and swooning over the early Beatles or more recently the Backstreet Boys or One Direction was engaged in a legitimate – and in fact an important – form of cultural participation? As the stories of the stars in this book, and beyond, remind us, fandom is an activity with the power to shape not only individual experiences and worldviews but collective understandings of art, identity and – this is not an overstatement – culture itself.

I ended this book in the '60s because that was the moment the historical fangirl reached critical mass. There would be countless more cycles of obsession after that – all intense, all influential – but it was Beatlemania that created the template. From Bowie to BTS and Beyoncé, the pattern repeated and is still going strong: fans gathered, girls screamed, stars rose. Every time, there was something particular to its historical moment about the phenomenon and every time – as a result of how audiences responded – art, fashion and culture evolved. Beatlemania exploded at a time when second-wave feminism was just beginning to take shape, when women were starting to demand space in public life beyond the limited roles society had prescribed for them. The silly, screaming swooning girl might not have seen herself as political, but her public displays of love, lust and agency were radical in ways even she might not have recognised in the moment. The moral panics quieted down after that. Female passion gradually became expected, if not respected – less pearl-clutching about corrupted innocence; more cynical marketing aimed at capturing girls' buying power.

In the decades since the '60s, fandom has evolved from a cultural curiosity into a central engine of pop culture. Stars understand how important fans are to their success and work hard to connect with them, and fan studies has emerged as a legitimate academic field. Fandom scholars – many of whom are fans themselves – are now analysing the phenomena critics once mocked. They recognise fandom as a complex, creative and deeply human form of cultural participation and understand the importance of uncovering the meaning beneath the surface.

Interestingly, many fan studies academics call themselves 'aca-fans'. The theory is that being open about their fan identity keeps them honest. It means they're not pretending to be some neutral observer when they're actually emotionally invested. They understand the things they're studying from the inside out, which they believe adds to their work. It's also a response to the derision that fandom has received in the past. They feel it's important to signal to their communities that they're safe to talk to. Honestly, I'm not sure there's much difference between a professor of fan studies who displays her collection of *Twilight* books and posters in her office and a Byron scholar who writes with a bust of his subject on his desk and treasures his complete twelve-volume collection of *Byron's Letters and Journals* – but maybe that's just me.

The final summer I was writing this book, I walked into my living room to find a little girl in a Rolling Stones T-shirt reading a book called *Beatles vs Stones* – a Stones scholar in the making, perhaps. Her dad is a big fan (his favourite is Keith). In the sunshine, I saw the continuity of the thing I'd been writing about: how these attachments to music, movies and books – and the people who make them – create frameworks for identity, meaning and connection across generations. This girl wasn't mindlessly consuming culture; she was actively engaging with it: forming judgements, developing preferences and participating in conversations that began long before she was born.

The emotional labour of fandom – the work of loving, caring and finding meaning in pop culture – continues whether it receives recognition or not. From the Novel-Reading Girls obsessing over delightfully horrid Gothic novels in the eighteenth century to the hundreds of Swifties rushing down to the front of movie theatres to dance to their favourite Taylor Swift songs during the Eras Tour, the history of the fangirl is one that deserves to be told not as a footnote but as an essential force in the history and evolution of pop culture.

And if that little girl can so coolly and nonchalantly wear that Rolling Stones T-shirt, it's because generations of girls and women before her wept over poems, queued for movies, screamed at concerts and joyfully collected Franz Liszt's cigar butts.

ACKNOWLEDGEMENTS

As you probably know by now, I'm a bit of a method writer. That means that while I was researching and then writing this book, I tried to only read, listen and watch in the time period I was working on. As the people who were kind and brave enough to join me on this 200-year odyssey will tell you, every chapter was a new beginning that felt like a sensory and emotional revelation. What I did not expect was how overjoyed and relieved I would be when I got to the '60s and could finally listen to Bob Dylan, wear a miniskirt and leave the house. And so, to wrap things up, I've made you a playlist.

WANDA JACKSON – 'LET'S HAVE A PARTY'

As a first-time author writing about something that is (technically) a niche subject, this book was a leap of faith for the people who made it happen. Thanks to my Liszt-loving agent Jaime Marshall for finding it the perfect home, Lisa Goodrum who acquired it and everyone at Biteback – especially my editors Ella Boardman and Olivia Beattie – for believing in it, whipping it into shape and helping me bring it to life. It really has been a joy.

BILLIE HOLIDAY – 'BLUE MOON'

I love libraries, especially the kind that make it easy for people to access their archives from anywhere. Shoutout to the National Library of Scotland (Byron's fanmail), Hoboken Historical Museum (Frank Sinatra fan club newsletters), the Museo Nazionale del Cinema in Turin (Valentino collection) and to the Apple Scruffs for creating an archive of their experiences and fanzine covers online. These are important historical documents and I'm so glad they've been preserved.

CYNDI LAUPER – 'GIRLS JUST WANT TO HAVE FUN'

People often ask me who I'm a fan of. The answer (after Lord Byron) is that I'm a fan of JSTOR and big fat history books. *Swoon* has been decades in the making. That means it's built on a foundation of research and ideas that shaped and inspired my thinking long before I realised I needed to write it down. These influences are too many to count (see Bibliography), but if I had posters on my wall, they would be of Barbara Ehrenreich, Gloria Jacobs and Elizabeth Hess. 'Girls Just Want to Have Fun', their essay on Beatlemania, was the spark that first got me wanting to think and write seriously about screaming, crying, fainting girls across time.

Years later – with just as much revelatory force – it was Ghislaine McDayter's *Byromania and the Birth of Celebrity Culture* that completely changed how I thought about the relationship between celebrity, enthusiasm and politics and cemented my desire to get properly stuck in. Thanks to Ghislaine and Paul Douglass – the great defender of Caroline – for taking time to answer my Byromania questions.

And to James Deaville for so generously giving his time to talk Liszt, virtuosity and pop culture and giving feedback on Chapter 2. I wrote to a lot of people whose work I was reading while I was working on *Swoon*, but James was by far the most thoughtful, engaged and welcoming. It was wonderful to discover that Franz Liszt's spirit of enthusiasm and generosity is alive and well – and living in Canada. The same goes for Richard Siken, James Kaplan and Elaine Katzenberger. Tiny details can make or break a book (or that's how it feels when you're still polishing two days before your final deadline). This means that small gestures can make a huge difference. Thank you for your last-minute help and advice – the sparkle is you.

JANIS MARTIN – 'GOOD LOVE'

There are so many people who have contributed to the making of this book – both physically and intellectually – that I'm starting to feel like it's 1999 and I'm Gwyneth Paltrow crying in a pink dress. Thanks to Murat, Ezgi and Ali Ozer, Joelle Chang, Royce To, Graham Bates and Lorenzo Spoerry for putting me up (and putting up with me) while I was on research trips. To my favourite folkstar and Beatles fan Dan Raza, my Romanticism consultant and brother in wild and passionate emotions Paul Cuff, Tanc Newbury, Patricia Cordero, Juan Barahona, Sandeep Taylor, Dani Martinez-Gatell, Giorgia Carofiglio and Joe Kimsey for talking ideas, filling gaps, reading bits and pieces and helping me think out loud – way back then and now. And to my personal virtuoso Cristina Cordero for teaching me everything I know about the inner workings of classical music concerts, reading so enthusiastically and most importantly reminding me when it was time to leave the white-hot centre and come out for dinner.

SISTER ROSETTA THARPE – 'UP ABOVE MY HEAD (I HEAR MUSIC IN THE AIR)'

Books need readers, especially when they don't quite exist yet. Ben Dillon, Nora Barnadi and Peter Scott Reid read early drafts and gave feedback that made this a much better book than it would have been without them. I would also not have gotten through the trauma and anxiety of influence involved in having to write about Mr Elvis Presley without their moral and existential support. In that same readerly and creative universe, special and very Byronic thanks to Charlie Hulme for reading, thinking and encouraging from the moment this was the seed of an idea on a couple of sheets of A4 and for being the official music director of this book – destiny works in strange and mysterious ways.

ETHEL MERMAN – 'THERE'S NO BUSINESS LIKE SHOW BUSINESS'

I am blessed to have parents who have been encouraging my inner fangirl and enabling my obsessions since my Robin Hood days aged seven, so it gave me so much joy to find, on a research trip (cough), that the gift shop at Newstead Abbey sells both Robin Hood toys and Lord Byron busts right next to each other. Everything comes full circle. There are no words, so I'm not even going to try. You have encouraged, supported and fangirled this book into existence in every way imaginable, and I am so thankful.

JANIS JOPLIN – 'ME AND BOBBY MCGEE'

Most epic and gushing final thanks to Richard Silk for spending the past two years in the trenches of fangirl love and obsession with me – suffering through all the movies, listening to all the songs, going down all the rabbit holes and reading and editing with Maxwell Perkins-level greatness. It was Ricky, more than anyone, who pushed me to lean into my own voice but also – kindly and frequently – reminded me where the line was. More often than not, he was right. It's so good to know that I have a home away from home, and I'm so happy that the next time I come visit, we can listen to something that isn't the Beatles and talk about something that isn't *The Sheik*.

The night is young so enjoy the party – I'll see you out there soon.

BIBLIOGRAPHY

Adler, Bill, ed., *Love Letters to the Beatles* (New York: Simon & Schuster, 1964).

Bangs, Lester, *Psychotic Reactions and Carburetor Dung* (New York: Vintage Books, 1987).

Barbas, Samantha, *Movie Crazy: Stars, Fans, and the Cult of Celebrity* (New York: Palgrave Macmillan, 2001).

Beisel, Katie Hollenback, "'I Hear Music When I Look at You": Teenage Agency, Mass Media, and Frank Sinatra in World War II America', PhD diss., University of Illinois at Urbana-Champaign, 2018.

Berman, Garry, ed., *We're Going to See the Beatles!: An Oral History of Beatlemania as Told by the Fans Who Were There* (Santa Monica, CA: Santa Monica Press, 2008).

Berry, Helen, *The Castrato and His Wife* (Oxford: Oxford University Press, 2011).

Bertellini, Giorgio, *The Divo and the Duce: Promoting Film Stardom and Political Leadership in 1920s America* (Berkeley: University of California Press, 2019).

Bertrand, Michael T., *Race, Rock, and Elvis* (Champaign: University of Illinois Press, 2000).

Blessington, Lady, *A Journal of the Conversations of Lord Byron* (London: Henry Colburn, 1834).

Bloom, Harold, ed., *George Gordon, Lord Byron* (Philadelphia: Chelsea House, 2004).

Blumer, Herbert, *Movies and Conduct* (New York: Macmillan, 1933).

Bondanella, Peter E., *Hollywood Italian: Dagos, Palookas, Romeos, Wise Guys and Sopranos* (New York: Continuum, 2004).

Bradshaw, David, and Rachel Potter, eds, *Prudes on the Prowl: Fiction and Obscenity in England, 1850 to the Present Day* (Oxford: Oxford University Press, 2013).

Brines, Wini, *Young, White, and Miserable: Growing Up Female in the Fifties* (Chicago: University of Chicago Press, 1992).

Burgess, Anthony, *On Music and Musicians: 1963–1993* (New York: Carroll & Graf, 1997).

Burke, Edmund, *Reflections on the Revolution in France*, edited by Conor Cruise O'Brien (London: Penguin Classics, 1982).

Butsch, Richard, *The Making of American Audiences: From Stage to Television, 1750–1990* (Cambridge: Cambridge University Press, 2000).

Byron, Lord, *Byron's Letters and Journals*, vol. 4, *Wedlock's the Devil*, edited by Leslie Marchand (London: John Murray, 1975).

Byron, Lord, *Letters and Journals*, vol. 10, *A Heart for Every Fate*, edited by Leslie Marchand (London: John Murray, 1975).

Byron, Lord, *Selected Letters and Journals*, edited by Leslie Marchand (London: John Murray, 1982).

Cahn, Susan K., *Sexual Reckonings: Southern Girls in a Troubling Age* (Cambridge, MA: Harvard University Press, 2007).

Caine, Michael, *What's It All About?* (New York: Turtle Bay Books, 1992).

Carroll, David, *The Matinee Idols* (New York: Abbeville Press, 1972).

Cartland, Barbara, *The Sheik: Barbara Cartland's Library of Love Edition* (London: Arrow Books, 1979).

Chandler, Joyce, *James Dean: A Rebel with a Cause: A Fan's Tribute* (Bloomington, IN: AuthorHouse, 1991).

Dalton, David, *James Dean: The Mutant King* (New York: Dell, 1975).

Davis, Hunter, *The Beatles: The Authorised Biography* (London: Heinemann, 1968).

Deaville, James, 'The Making of a Myth: Liszt, The Press, and Virtuosity', in *New Light on Liszt*, edited by Alan Walker (Boston: Northeastern University Press, 1997).

DeLong, Anne, *Mesmerism, Medusa, and the Muse: The Romantic Discourse of Spontaneous Creativity* (Lanham, MD: Lexington Books, 2012).

D'Emilio, John, and Estelle B. Freedman, *Intimate Matters: A History of Sexuality in America* (Chicago: University of Chicago Press, 1997).

Devereaux, Leslie and Roger Hilman, eds, *Fields of Vision: Essays in Film Studies, Visual Anthropology, and Photography* (Berkeley: University of California Press, 1995).

Doss, Erika, *Elvis Culture: Fans, Faith & Image* (Lawrence: University Press of Kansas, 1999).

Douglass, Paul, *Caroline Lamb: A Biography* (Basingstoke: Palgrave Macmillan, 2004).

Dumas, Alexandre, *The Lady of the Camellias* (Philadelphia: Gebbie & Co, 1889).

Eckert, Lindsey, *The Limits of Familiarity: Authorship and Romantic Readers* (New York: Palgrave Macmillan, 2022).

Editors of LIFE, *LIFE Remembering Elvis Presley* (New York: TI Inc. Books, 2020).

Egan, Michael, ed., *Ibsen: The Critical Heritage* (London: Routledge, 1999).

Eisler, Benita, *Byron: Life and Legend* (London: Faber & Faber, 2002).

Elfenbein, Andrew, *Byron and the Victorians* (Cambridge: Cambridge University Press, 1995).

Ellenberger, Allan R., *The Valentino Mystique: The Death and Afterlife of the Silent Film Idol* (Jefferson, NC: McFarland & Company, 2005).

Erenberg, Lewis A., *Steppin' Out: New York Nightlife and the Transformation of American Culture* (Chicago: University of Chicago Press, 1981).

Erenberg, Lewis A., *Swingin' the Dream: Big Band Jazz and the Rebirth of American Culture* (Chicago: University of Chicago Press, 1998).

Erenberg, Lewis A., ed., *The War in American Culture: Society and Consciousness during World War II* (Chicago: University of Chicago Press, 1996).

Fay, Amy, *Music-Study in Germany: The Classic Memoir of the Romantic Era* (Chicago: A. C. McClurg & Co., 1880).

Feldman-Barrett, Christine, *A Women's History of the Beatles* (New York: Bloomsbury Academic, 2021).

Ferris, George Titus, *Great Musical Composers: German, French, and Italian* (New York: D. Appleton and Company, 1887).

Ferris, Ina, *The Achievement of Literary Authority: Gender, History, and the Waverley Novels* (Ithaca, NY: Cornell University Press, 2019).

Finstad, Suzanne, *Child Bride: The Untold Story of Priscilla Beaulieu Presley* (New York: Crown, 1997).

Fitzgerald, F. Scott, *The Crack-Up* (New York: New Directions, 2009).

Fitzgerald, F. Scott, *The Jazz Age: Essays* (New York: New Directions, 2019).

Fitzgerald, F. Scott, *My Lost City: Personal Essays 1920–1940* (Cambridge: Cambridge University Press, 2014).

Franklin, Caroline, *Byron's Heroines* (Oxford: Clarendon Press, 1992).

Franklin, Caroline, *The Female Romantics: Nineteenth-Century Women Novelists and Byronism* (London: Routledge, 2012).

Frith, Simon, and Andrew Goodwin, eds, *On Record: Rock, Pop, and the Written Word* (New York: Routledge, 1990).

Fryer, Paul, ed., *Blockbusters of the Victorian Theater: 1850–1910* (Jefferson, NC: McFarland, 2019).

Gibbs, Christopher H., and Dana Gooley, eds, *Franz Liszt and His World* (Princeton, NJ: Princeton University Press, 2006).

Giordano, Ralph G., *Satan in the Dance Hall: Rev. John Roach Straton, Social Reform, and the Lindy Hop* (New York: NYU Press, 2020).

Goldman, Albert, *Elvis* (New York: McGraw-Hill, 1981).

Gooley, Dana, *The Virtuoso Liszt* (Cambridge: Cambridge University Press, 2004).

Gould, Jonathan, *Can't Buy Me Love: The Beatles, Britain, and America* (New York: Harmony Books, 2007).

Grieveson, Lee, ed., *The Silent Cinema Reader* (London: Routledge, 2004).

Groppa, Carlos G., *The Tango in the United States: A History* (Jefferson, NC: McFarland, 2004).

Guralnick, Peter, *Careless Love: The Unmaking of Elvis Presley* (Boston: Little, Brown, 1999).

Haeussler, Mathias, *Inventing Elvis: An American Icon in a Cold War World* (London: Bloomsbury, 2021).

Hallett, Hilary, *Go West, Young Women! The Rise of Early Hollywood* (Berkeley: University of California Press, 2013).

Hamilton, Kenneth, ed., *The Cambridge Companion to Liszt* (Cambridge: Cambridge University Press, 2005).

Hansen, Miriam, *Babel and Babylon: Spectatorship in American Silent Film* (Cambridge, MA: Harvard University Press, 1991).

Hansen-Miller, David, *Civilized Violence: Subjectivity, Gender, and Popularity in Modern Culture* (London: Routledge, 2011).

Haskell, Mollie, *From Reverence to Rape: The Treatment of Women in the Movies* (Chicago: University of Chicago Press, 2016).

Hay, Daisy, *Young Romantics: The Shelleys, Byron, and Other Tangled Lives* (New York: Farrar, Straus and Giroux, 2010).

Heine, Heinrich, *The Works of Heinrich Heine*, vol. 1 (London: William Heinemann, 1891).

Hellmann, John, *The Kennedy Obsession: The American Myth of JFK* (New York: Columbia University Press, 1997).

Hewitt, Paolo, *Love Me Do: 50 Great Beatles Moments* (London: Quercus, 2012).

Hickman, Tom, *The Sexual Century* (London: Carlton Books, 1999).

Hillard, Dereck, Heikki Lempa and Russell Spinney, eds, *Feelings Materialized: Emotions, Bodies, and Things in Germany, 1500–1950* (New York: Berghahn Books, 2020).

Hilmes, Oliver, *Franz Liszt: Musician, Celebrity, and Visionary*, translated by Stewart Spencer (New Haven, CT: Yale University Press, 2016).

Hunt, Andrew, *Beatlemania in America: Fan Culture from Below* (Liverpool: Liverpool University Press, 2013).

Jacobson, Laurie, *Top of the Mountain: The Beatles at Shea Stadium 1965* (Los Angeles: Dey Street Books, 2016).

Johnson, Joyce, *Minor Characters* (New York: Penguin, 1983).

Kane, Larry, *Ticket to Ride: Inside the Beatles' 1964 Tour that Changed the World* (New York: Running Press, 2003).

Kanfer, Stefan, *Somebody: The Reckless Life of Marlon Brando* (New York: Knopf, 2008).

Kaplan, James, *Frank: The Making of a Legend* (New York: Doubleday, 2010).

Kavanagh, Julie, *The Girl Who Loved Camellias: The Life and Legend of Marie Duplessis* (New York: Knopf, 2013).

Kawabata, Maiko, *Paganini: The 'Demonic' Virtuoso* (Woodbridge, UK: Boydell Press, 2013).

Kelly, Gary, *English Fiction of the Romantic Period, 1789–1830* (London: Longman, 1989).

Kelly, Kitty, *His Way: The Unauthorized Biography of Frank Sinatra* (New York: Bantam Books, 1986).

Knox, Vicesimus, *Essays, Moral and Literary* (London: Edward and Charles Dilly, 1778).

Kordas, Ann, *Female Adolescent Sexuality in the United States, 1850–1965* (Lanham, MD: Lexington Books, 2019).

Kynaston, David, *A Northern Wind: Britain 1962–65* (London: Bloomsbury Publishing, 2022).

Lahr, John, *Show and Tell: New Yorker Profiles* (Woodstock, NY: Overlook Press, 2000).

Lamb, Caroline, *The Whole Disgraceful Truth: Selected Letters of Lady Caroline Lamb*, edited by Paul Douglass (New York: Palgrave Macmillan, 2006).

Larman, Alexander, *Byron's Women* (London: Head of Zeus, 2016).

Leider, Emily, *Dark Lover: The Life and Death of Rudolph Valentino* (New York: Farrar, Straus and Giroux, 2003).

Leonard, Candi, *Beatleness: How the Beatles and Their Fans Remade the World* (New York: Arcade Publishing, 2014).

Leonard, John, *Reading for My Life: Writings, 1958–2008* (New York: Viking, 2009).

Lewis, Lisa A., ed., *The Adoring Audience: Fan Culture and Popular Media* (London: Routledge, 1992).

Lewisohn, Mark, *The Beatles: All These Years – Extended Special Edition, Volume 1: Tune In* (London: Little, Brown, 2013).

Lockhart, John Gibson, *Letter to the Right Hon. Lord Byron* (London: John Murray, 1824).

Looser, Devoney, ed., *The Cambridge Companion to Autobiography* (Cambridge: Cambridge University Press, 2019).

Lovell, Ernest J., *His Very Self and Voice: Collected Conversations of Lord Byron* (New York: Macmillan, 1954).

Macaulay, Thomas Babbington, *Essays Reprinted from the Edinburgh Review* (London: Longman, 1843).

MacCarthy, Fiona, *Byron: Life and Legend* (London: Faber & Faber, 2002).

McCracken, Alison, *Real Men Don't Sing: Crooning in American Culture* (Durham, NC: Duke University Press, 2015).

McDayter, Ghislaine, *Byromania and the Birth of Celebrity Culture* (New York: Palgrave Macmillan, 2009).

McDayter, Ghislaine, *Flirtation and Courtship in Nineteenth-Century British Culture* (London: Routledge, 2017).

McGeary, Thomas, *The Cultural Politics of Opera and the Italian Origins of Romanticism* (Cambridge: Cambridge University Press, 2013).

Manchester, William, *The Glory and the Dream: A Narrative History of America, 1932–1972* (Boston: Little, Brown, 1974).

Marchand, Leslie, *Byron: A Portrait* (London: John Murray, 1971).

Marchand, Leslie, *Byron: Selected Letters and Journals* (London: Pimlico, 1993).

Marcus, Daniel, *Happy Days and Wonder Years: The Fifties and Sixties in American Popular Culture* (New Brunswick, NJ: Rutgers University Press, 2004).

Marcus, Greil, *Mystery Train: Images of America in Rock 'n' Roll Music* (New York: Plume, 1975).

Marks, Edward Bennett, *They All Sang: From Tony Pastor to Rudy Vallée*, as told to Abbott J. Liebling (New York: Viking Press, 1934).

Medwin, Thomas, *Medwin's Conversations of Lord Byron* (London: Henry Colburn, 1824).

Mee, John, *Dangerous Enthusiasm: William Blake and the Culture of Radicalism in the 1790s* (Oxford: Oxford University Press, 1992).

Melman, Billie, *Women and the Popular Imagination in the Twenties: Flappers and Nymphs* (New York: St Martin's Press, 1988).

Mencken, H. L., *The Vintage Mencken* (New York: Vintage Books, 1990).

Millard, André, *Beatlemania: Technology, Business, and Teen Culture in Cold War America* (Baltimore: Johns Hopkins University Press, 2012).

Modleski, Tania, *Loving with a Vengeance: Mass-Produced Fantasies for Women* (New York: Routledge, 2005).

Mole, Tom, *Byron's Romantic Celebrity: Industrial Culture and the Hermeneutic of Intimacy* (Basingstoke: Palgrave Macmillan, 2007).

Moore, Thomas, *The Works of Lord Byron: With His Letters, Journals and His Life* (London: John Murray, 1832).

Nachman, Gerald, *Right Here on Our Stage Tonight! Ed Sullivan's America* (Berkeley: University of California Press, 2009).

Nash, Alanna, *Baby, Let's Play House: Elvis Presley and the Women Who Loved Him* (New York: It Books, 2010).

Nash, Alanna, *Elvis and the Memphis Mafia* (New York: Harper Paperbacks, 2012).

Norman, Philip, *Shout!: The Beatles in Their Generation* (New York: Simon & Schuster, 1981).

Orbanz, Eva, *There Is a New Star in Heaven, Valentino: Biography, Filmography, Essays* (Berlin: Spiess, 1979).

Osborne, Jerry, *Elvis, Elvis: Word for Word* (New York: O'Sullivan Woodside, 1999).

Paston, George, and Peter Quennell, *To Lord Byron* (London: John Lane, 1939).

Peattie, Antony, *The Private Life of Lord Byron* (London: Unbound, 2019).

Perretti, Burton W., *The Leading Man: Hollywood and the Presidential Image* (New Brunswick, NJ: Rutgers University Press, 2012).

Petkov, Steven, and Leonard Mustazza, eds, *The Frank Sinatra Reader* (New York: Oxford University Press, 1995).

Petro, Patrice, ed., *Idols of Modernity: Movie Stars of the 1920s* (New Brunswick, NJ: Rutgers University Press, 2010).

Plath, Sylvia, *The Bell Jar* (New York: Harper & Row, 1971).

Pugliese, Stanislao G., ed., *Frank Sinatra: History, Identity, and Italian American Culture* (New York: Palgrave Macmillan, 2004).

Quinn, Erika, *Franz Liszt: A Story of Central European Subjectivity* (Boston: Brill, 2014).

Radway, Janice, *Reading the Romance: Women, Patriarchy, and Popular Literature* (Chapel Hill: University of North Carolina Press, 1984).

Ritter, Richard, *Imagining Women Readers, 1789–1920* (New York: Palgrave Macmillan, 2021).

Robins, Elizabeth, *Ibsen and the Actress* (London, Hogarth Press, 1928).

Rodman, Gilbert D., *Elvis After Elvis: The Posthumous Career of a Living Legend* (New York: Routledge, 1996).

Rogers, Samuel, *Recollections of the Table-Talk of Samuel Rogers* (London: Edward Moxon, 1856).

Rowbotham, Sheila, *Woman's Consciousness, Man's World* (London: Penguin Books, 1973).

Rowlands, Penelope, ed., *The Beatles Are Here!* (Chapel Hill, NC: Algonquin Books, 2014).

Rutherford, Andrew, ed., *Byron: The Critical Heritage* (London: Routledge, 2010).

Saffle, Michael, *Germany 1840–1845: A Study in Sources, Documents, and the History of Reception* (Hildesheim: Georg Olms Verlag, 2011).

Saffle, Michael, ed., *Liszt and His World: Proceedings of the International Liszt Conference held at Virginia Polytechnic Institute and State University, 20–23 May 1993* (New York: Pendragon Press, 1998).

Saffle, Michael, ed., *New Light on Liszt* (Stuyvesant, NY: Pendragon Press, 1997).

Sampson, Jim, *Virtuosity and the Musical Work: The Transcendental Studies of Liszt* (Cambridge: Cambridge University Press, 2003).

Sawyers, June Skinner, ed., *Read the Beatles: Classic and New Writings on the Beatles, Their Legacy, and Why They Still Matter* (New York: Penguin Books, 2006).

Schweitzer, Marlis, *When Broadway Was the Runway: Theater, Fashion, and American Culture* (Philadelphia: University of Pennsylvania Press, 2009).

Shaw, Arnold, *Sinatra: Twentieth-Century Romantic* (New York: Holt, Rinehart and Winston, 1968).

Soderholm, James, *Fantasy, Forgery, and the Byron Legend* (Lexington: University Press of Kentucky, 1996).

Stabler, Jane, *Byron, Poetics and History* (Cambridge: Cambridge University Press, 2002).

Stark, Steven D., *Meet the Beatles: A Cultural History of the Band that Shook Youth, Gender, and the World* (New York: HarperEntertainment, 2005).

Studlar, Gaylyn, *This Mad Masquerade: Stardom and Masculinity in the Jazz Age* (New York: Columbia University Press, 1996).

Summers, Anthony, *Sinatra: The Life* (New York: Alfred A. Knopf, 2006).

Taraborrelli, J. Randy., *Sinatra: Behind the Legend* (New York: Birch Lane Press, 2015).

Teo, Hsu-Ming, *Desert Passions: Orientalism and Romance Novels* (Austin: University of Texas Press, 2012).

Tuite, Clara, *Lord Byron and Scandalous Celebrity* (Cambridge: Cambridge University Press, 2015).

Ullman, S. George, *The Real Valentino* (London: C. A. Pearson, 1927).

Vare, Ethlie Ann, *Legend: Frank Sinatra and the American Dream* (New York: Boulevard Books, 1995).

Walker, Alan, *Franz Liszt: The Virtuoso Years, 1811–1847* (Ithaca, NY: Cornell University Press, 1987).

Walker, Keith, *Byron's Readers: A Study of Attitudes Towards Byron, 1812–1832* (Bern: Peter Lang, 2008).

Watt, Ian, *The Rise of the Novel* (London: Chatto & Windus, 1957).

Weber, William, *Music and the Middle Class: The Social Structure of Concert Life in London, Paris, and Vienna* (New York: Holmes & Meier, 1975).

Weis, René, *The Real Traviata: The Song of Marie Duplessis* (Oxford: Oxford University Press, 2015).

Welsch, Tricia, *Gloria Swanson: Ready for Her Close-Up* (Jackson: University Press of Mississippi, 2013).

Wheeler, Kay and W. A. Harbinson, *Growing Up with the Memphis Flash* (Amsterdam: Tutti Frutti Productions, 1994).

White, Mark, *Kennedy: A Cultural History of an American Icon* (London: Bloomsbury Academic, 2013).

Williams, Adrian, *Portrait of Liszt: By Himself and His Contemporaries* (Oxford: Clarendon Press, 1990).

Williamson, Joel, *Elvis Presley: A Southern Life* (New York: Oxford University Press, 2014).

Willis, Ellen, *The Essential Ellen Willis*, edited by Nona Willis Aronowitz (Minneapolis: University of Minnesota Press, 2014).

Wilson, Frances, ed., *Byromania: Portraits of the Artist in Nineteenth- and Twentieth-Century Culture* (London: Macmillan, 1999).

Wolfson, Susan J., *Romantic Interactions: Social Being and the Turns of Literary Action* (Baltimore: Johns Hopkins University Press, 2010).

Womack, Kenneth, and Kit O'Toole, eds, *Fandom and the Beatles: The Act You've Known for All These Years* (New York: Oxford University Press, 2021).

Wootton, Sarah, *Byronic Heroes in Nineteenth-Century Women's Writing* (Basingstoke: Palgrave Macmillan, 2016).

Wouters, Cas, *Sex and Manners: Female Emancipation in the West 1890–2000* (London: SAGE Publications, 2004).

Wright, Angela, *Gothic Fiction* (Basingstoke: Palgrave Macmillan, 2007).

Zionkowski, Linda, *Women and Music in the Age of Austen* (Albany: State University of New York Press, 2021).

PAPERS/ESSAYS

Barstow, Susan Torrey, '"Hedda Is All of Us": Late-Victorian Women at the Matinee', *Victorian Studies*, 43, no. 3 (Spring 2001).

Chow, Karen, 'Popular Sexual Knowledge and Women's Agency in 1920s England', *Feminist Review*, 63, no. 1 (Autumn 1999).

Deaville, James, 'Writing Liszt: Lina Ramann, Marie Lipsius, and Early Musicology', *Journal of Musicological Research*, 23, no. 1 (2004).

McCracken, Alison, '"God's Gift to Us Girls": Crooning, Gender, and the Re-Creation of American Popular Song, 1928–1933', *American Music*, 17, no. 4 (Winter 1999).

Origo, Iris, 'The Innocent Miss Francis and the Truly Noble Lord Byron', *Keats-Shelley Journal*, 1 (January 1952).

Stamp, Shelley, 'It's a Long Way to Film Land: Screen Hopefuls and Extras in Early Hollywood', *Camera Obscura*, 14, no. 3 (1999).

Vorachek, Laura, '"The Instrument of the Century": The Piano as an Icon of Female Sexuality in the Nineteenth Century', *George Eliot–George Henry Lewes Studies*, 38–39 (September 2000).

Woollacott, Angela, '"Khaki Fever" and Its Control: Gender, Class, Age and Sexual Morality on the British Homefront in the First World War', *Journal of Contemporary History*, 29, no. 2 (April 1994).

ARCHIVES

Apple Scruffs, www.applescruffs.co.uk.

Byron fan letters, National Library of Scotland, Edinburgh, UK.

Sinatra fan club newsletters, Hoboken Historical Museum, Hoboken, NJ.

NOTES

PREFACE

1   Gaylyn Studlar, 'Barrymore, the Body, and Bliss', in *Fields of Vision: Essays in Film Studies, Visual Anthropology, and Photography*, edited by Leslie Devereaux and Roger Hillman (Berkeley: University of California Press, 1995), p. 166.

2   'The American Girl's Damning Influence on the Drama', in *Current Literature*, 43 (December 1907).

PROLOGUE: THE HEROINE

1   Caroline Lamb, *The Whole Disgraceful Truth: Selected Letters of Lady Caroline Lamb*, edited by Paul Douglass (New York: Palgrave Macmillan, 2006), p. 77.

2   Leslie Marchand, *Byron: A Portrait* (London: John Murray, 1971), p. 124.

3   Paul Douglass, *Caroline Lamb: A Biography* (Basingstoke: Palgrave Macmillan, 2004), p. 110.

4   Samuel Rogers, *Recollections of the Table-Talk of Samuel Rogers* (London: Edward Moxon, 1856), p. 231.

5   Douglass, p. 120.

6   Frances Wilson, 'An Exaggerated Woman: The Melodramas of Lady Caroline Lamb', in *Byromania: Portraits of the Artist in Nineteenth- and Twentieth-Century Culture*, edited by Frances Wilson (London: Macmillan, 1999), p. 196.

7   Alexander Larman, *Byron's Women* (London: Head of Zeus, 2016), p. 124.

8   Ghislaine McDayter, *Byromania and the Birth of Celebrity Culture* (New York: Palgrave Macmillan, 2009), p. 47.

9   *London Magazine*, 9 (1824), p. 425.

10 Lord Byron, *Byron: Selected Letters and Journals*, edited by Leslie Marchand (London: John Murray, 1982), p. 233.

11 John Wilson, *Edinburgh Review* of *Childe Harold Canto IV*, in *Lord Byron: The Critical Heritage*, edited by Andrew Rutherford (London: Routledge & Kegan Paul, 1970), p. 152.

12 Charles Dickens, *All the Year Round*, 29 (1892), p. 201.

1. IMAGINATION, LONDON, 1812: BAD ROMANCE

1   Ghislaine McDayter, *Flirtation and Courtship in Nineteenth-Century British Culture* (London: Routledge, 2017), p. 81.

2   Byron, letter to John Murray, in Thomas Moore, *The Works of Lord Byron: With His Letters, Journals and His Life* (London: John Murray, 1832), p. 47.

3   Fiona MacCarthy, *Byron: Life and Legend* (London: Faber & Faber, 2002), p. 238.

4   Ibid., p. 34.

5   Betina Eisler, *Byron: Child of Passion, Fool of Fame* (New York: Knopf, 1999), p. 102.

6   Moore, p. 137.

7   Duchess of Devonshire, quoted in *Lord Byron: The Critical Heritage*, p. 26.
8   Lady Falkland, quoted in *To Lord Byron*, edited by George Paston and Peter Quennell (London: John Lane, 1939), p. 19.
9   Fanmail sent to Lord Byron, National Library of Scotland.
10 Clara Tuite, *Lord Byron and Scandalous Celebrity* (Cambridge: Cambridge University Press, 2015), p. 146.
11 Thomas Babington Macaulay, review of *Moore's Life of Byron*, in *Essays Reprinted from the Edinburgh Review* (London: Longman, Green, Longman, and Roberts, 1860), p. 170.
12 Matthew Arnold, in *Lord Byron: The Critical Heritage*, p. 459.
13 Andrew Elfenbein, *Byron and the Victorians* (Cambridge: Cambridge University Press, 1995), p. 14.
14 Sarah Wootton, *Byronic Heroes in Nineteenth-Century Women's Writing* (Basingstoke: Palgrave Macmillan, 2016), p. 2.
15 Fanmail to Lord Byron, National Library of Scotland.
16 Annabella Milbanke, quoted in Ernest J. Lovell, *His Very Self and Voice: Collected Conversations of Lord Byron* (New York: Macmillan, 1954), p. 52.
17 Lord Byron, *Byron's Letters and Journals*, vol. 4, edited by Leslie Marchand (London: John Murray, 1975), pp. 182–5.
18 Tania Modleski, *Loving with a Vengeance: Mass-Produced Fantasies for Women* (New York: Routledge, 2005), p. 37.
19 Fanmail to Lord Byron, National Library of Scotland.
20 Ibid.
21 Isabella Harvey, in *To Lord Byron*, p. 261.
22 Byron, *Selected Letters and Journals*, edited by Leslie Marchand (London: John Murray, 1982), p. 190.
23 Byron, quoted in Thomas Medwin, *Medwin's Conversations of Lord Byron* (London: Henry Colburn, 1824), p. 206.
24 Sir Walter Scott, quoted in Wilson.
25 Lord Byron, *Manfred* in *The Major Works*, edited by Jerome J. McGann (Oxford: Oxford University Press).
26 Tom Mole, *Byron's Romantic Celebrity: Industrial Culture and the Hermeneutic of Intimacy* (Basingstoke: Palgrave Macmillan, 2007), p. 72.
27 John Gibson Lockhart, *Letter to the Right Hon. Lord Byron* (London: John Murray, 1824), p. 29.
28 John Wilson in *Lord Byron: The Critical Heritage*, p. 148; Crabb Robinson, in *George Gordon, Lord Byron*, edited by Harold Bloom (Philadelphia: Chelsea House, 2004).
29 Lindsey Eckert, *The Limits of Familiarity: Authorship and Romantic Readers* (New York: Palgrave Macmillan, 2022), p. 73.
30 Caroline Franklin, *Byron's Heroines* (Oxford: Clarendon Press, 1992), p. 56.
31 Keith Walker, *Byron's Readers: A Study of Attitudes towards Byron, 1812–1832* (Bern: Peter Lang, 2008).
32 McDayter, *Byromania*, p. 56.
33 Gary Kelly, *English Fiction of the Romantic Period, 1789–1830* (London: Longman, 1989), p. 9.
34 Ina Ferris, *The Achievement of Literary Authority: Gender, History, and the Waverly Novels* (Ithaca, NY: Cornell University Press, 2019), p. 40.
35 Jane Austen, *Northanger Abbey* (London: Penguin Books, 1995), p. 82.
36 Vicesimus Knox, 'On Novel Reading', in *Essays, Moral and Literary*, 2nd ed. (London: Charles Dilly, 1779).
37 Ian Watt, *The Rise of the Novel* (London: Chatto & Windus, 1957), p. 152.
38 *Gentleman's Magazine*, 67, pt 2 (1797), p. 912.
39 Angela Wright, *Gothic Fiction* (Basingstoke: Palgrave Macmillan, 2007), p. 20.
40 Edmund Burke, *Reflections on the Revolution in France*, edited by Conor Cruise O'Brien (London: Penguin Classics, 1982).
41 John Mee, *Dangerous Enthusiasm: William Blake and the Culture of Radicalism in the 1790s* (Oxford: Oxford University Press, 1992).

42 McDayter, *Byromania*, p. 136.

43 Miranda Burgess, quoted in Richard Ritter, *Imagining Women Readers, 1789–1920* (New York: Palgrave Macmillan, 2021), p. 5.

44 Byron, *Selected Letters and Journals*, p. 58.

45 Byron, quoted in Jane Stabler, *Byron, Poetics and History* (Cambridge: Cambridge University Press, 2002), p. 82.

46 Byron, quoted in James Soderholm, *Fantasy, Forgery, and the Byron Legend* (Lexington: University Press of Kentucky, 1996), p. 28.

47 Byron, *Letters and Journals*, vol. 10, *A Heart for Every Fate*, edited by Leslie Marchand (London: John Murray, 1972).

48 Lady Blessington, *A Journal of the Conversations of Lord Byron* (London: Henry Colburn, 1834), p. 86.

49 Isabella Harvey, in *To Lord Byron*, pp. 260–66.

50 Byron, *Letters and Journals*, vol. 10, p. 180.

51 Eliza Francis, in Lovell, *His Very Self and Voice*.

52 Harriette Wilson, quoted in Jillian Heydt-Stevenson, 'Sexualities', in *The Cambridge Companion to Autobiography*, edited by Devoney Looser (Cambridge: Cambridge University Press, 2019).

53 Harriette Wilson, quoted in Susan J. Wolfson, *Romantic Interactions: Social Being and the Turns of Literary Action* (Baltimore: Johns Hopkins University Press, 2010), p. 27.

54 Caroline Franklin, *The Female Romantics: Nineteenth-Century Women Novelists and Byronism* (London: Routledge, 2012), p. 1.

2. ECSTASY, BERLIN, 1842: IN LOVE WITH A FEELING

1 Mary Shelley, quoted in Anne DeLong, *Mesmerism, Medusa, and the Muse: The Romantic Discourse of Spontaneous Creativity* (Lanham, MD: Lexington Books, 2012), p. 68.

2 Ibid.

3 Liszt, quoted in Jim Samson, *Virtuosity and the Musical Work: The Transcendental Studies of Liszt* (Cambridge: Cambridge University Press, 2003), p. 80.

4 Alan Walker, *Franz Liszt: The Virtuoso Years, 1811–1847* (Ithaca, NY: Cornell University Press, 1987), p. 136.

5 Ibid., p. 150.

6 Ibid., p. 130.

7 Oliver Hilmes, *Franz Liszt: Musician, Celebrity, and Visionary*, translated by Stewart Spencer (New Haven, CT: Yale University Press, 2016), p. 8.

8 Walker, p. 63.

9 Ibid., p. 162.

10 Hans Chrisian Anderson in *Portrait of Liszt: By Himself and His Contemporaries*, edited by Adrian Williams (Oxford: Clarendon Press, 1990), p. 146.

11 Ibid.

12 Amy Fay, *Music-Study in Germany: The Classic Memoir of the Romantic Era* (Chicago: A. C. McClurg & Co., 1880), p. 269.

13 Robert Schumann, quoted in Dana Gooley, *The Virtuoso Liszt* (Cambridge: Cambridge University Press, 2004), p. 47.

14 Clara Wieck (later Schumann), quoted in Hilmes, p. 81.

15 Maiko Kawabata, *Paganini: The 'Demonic' Virtuoso* (Woodbridge, UK: Boydell Press, 2013), p. 74.

16 George Titus Ferris, *Great Musical Composers: German, French, and Italian* (New York: D. Appleton and Company, 1887), p. 77.

17 Jeffrey A. Nigro, 'Georgian Fangirls: Women and Castrati in Eighteenth-Century London', in *Women and Music in the Age of Austen*, edited by Linda Zionkowski and Miriam Hart (Albany: State University of New York Press, 2021).

18 Helen Berry, *The Castrato and His Wife* (Oxford: Oxford University Press, 2011), p. 83.

19 Thomas McGeary, *The Cultural Politics of Opera and the Italian Origins of Romanticism* (Cambridge: Cambridge University Press, 2013), p. 120.

20 Heinrich Heine, 'Musical Season in Paris, 29 July 1844', reprinted in *Franz Liszt and His World*, edited by Christopher H. Gibbs and Dana Gooley (Princeton, NJ: Princeton University Press, 2006), p. 460.

21 Heinrich Heine, *Florentine Nights*, in *The Works of Heinrich Heine*, vol. 1 (London: William Heinemann, 1891), p. 72.

22 Fanny Lewald, quoted in *Portrait of Liszt: By Himself and His Contemporaries*, p. 185.

23 Adalbert Cohnfeld, quoted in Hilmes.

24 Walker, p. 371.

25 Ludwig Rellstab, quoted in Walker, p. 374.

26 Ibid.

27 Gooley, *The Virtuoso Liszt*, p. 121.

28 Ibid., p. 9.

29 Heine, in *Franz Liszt and His World*, p. 460.

30 Walker, p. 287.

31 Gooley, *The Virtuoso Liszt*, p. 107.

32 Heine, in *Franz Liszt and His World*, p. 468.

33 Ibid.

34 Gooley, *The Virtuoso Liszt*, p. 211.

35 Heine, in *Franz Liszt and His World*, p. 468.

36 Hannu Salmi, 'Emotional Contagions: Franz Liszt and the Materiality of Celebrity Culture in the 1830s and 1840s', in *Feelings Materialized: Emotions, Bodies, and Things in Germany, 1500–1950*, edited by Dereck Hillard, Heikki Lempa and Russell Spinney (New York: Berghahn Books, 2020), p. 50.

37 Ibid.

38 Christopher H. Gibbs, '"Just Two Words. Enormous Success": Liszt's 1838 Vienna Concerts', in *Franz Liszt and His World*, p. 205.

39 Gibbs, in *Franz Liszt and His World*, p. 205.

40 James Deaville, 'The Making of a Myth: Liszt, the Press, and Virtuosity', in *New Light on Liszt*, edited by Michael Saffle (Stuyvesant, NY: Pendragon Press, 1997), p. 186.

41 Sheila Rowbotham, *Woman's Consciousness, Man's World* (London: Penguin Books, 1973), p. 14.

42 Erika Quinn, *Franz Liszt: A Story of Central European Subjectivity* (Boston: Brill, 2014), p. 48.

43 Franz Liszt, 'On the Situation of Artists and Their Condition in Society', quoted in Katharine Ellis, 'Liszt: The Romantic Artist', in *The Cambridge Companion to Liszt*, edited by Kenneth Hamilton (Cambridge: Cambridge University Press, 2005), p. 12.

44 Malwida von Meysenbug, in *Portrait of Liszt: By Himself and His Contemporaries*, p. 191.

45 Gooley, *The Virtuoso Liszt*, p. 69.

46 Ibid.

47 Vladimir Stasov, in *Portrait of Liszt: By Himself and His Contemporaries*, p. 188.

48 Yuri Arnold, in *Portrait of Liszt: By Himself and His Contemporaries*.

49 Maria Edgeworth, quoted in Laura Vorachek, '"The Instrument of the Century": The Piano as Icon of Female Sexuality in the Nineteenth Century', in *George Eliot–George Henry Lewes Studies*, 62 (2012), p. 32.

50 Anthony Burgess, 'The Devil Prefers Mozart', in *On Music and Musicians: 1963–1993* (New York: Carroll & Graf, 1997), p. 16.

51 Eva Hanska, quoted in Walker, p. 377.

52 Amy Fay, *Music-Study in Germany*, p. 227.

53 Clara Wieck, in *Portrait of Liszt: By Himself and His Contemporaries*, p. 102.

54 Marie Duplessis, quoted by Jules Janin in his introduction to Alexandre Dumas Jr, *The Lady of the Camellias* (Philadelphia: Gebbie & Co, 1889), p. viii.

55 Franz Liszt, quoted in René Weis, *The Real Traviata: The Song of Marie Duplessis* (Oxford: Oxford University Press, 2015), p. 232.

56 Marie Duplessis, quoted in Julie Kavanagh, *The Girl Who Loved Camellias: The Life and Legend of Marie Duplessis* (New York: Knopf, 2013), p. 146.

57 Malwida von Meysenbug, in *Portrait of Liszt: By Himself and His Contemporaries*, p. 191.

58 Hilmes, p. 88.

59 Ibid.

60 Liszt, in Michael Saffle, *Liszt in Germany 1840–1845: A Study in Sources, Documents, and the History of Reception* (Hildesheim: Georg Olms Verlag, 2011), p. 131.

61 *Politique* newspaper review in *Portrait of Liszt: By Himself and His Contemporaries*, p. 222.

62 William Webber, *Music and the Middle Class: The Social Structure of Concert Life in London, Paris, and Vienna* (New York: Holmes & Meier, 1975), p. 42.

63 Robert Schumann, quoted in Quinn, p. 33.

64 Hector Berlioz, ibid.

65 Walker, p. 289.

66 Liszt, quoted in Gooley, p. 8.

67 Richard Butsch, *The Making of American Audiences: From Stage to Television, 1750–1990* (Cambridge: Cambridge University Press, 2000), p. 50.

68 Ibid., p. 74.

69 Heather Jeanne Violanti, 'From the Matinee to the Long Run', in *Blockbusters of the Victorian Theater: 1850–1910*, edited by Paul Fryer (Jefferson, NC: McFarland, 2019), p. 172.

70 Marlis Schweitzer, *When Broadway Was the Runway: Theater, Fashion, and American Culture* (Philadelphia: University of Pennsylvania Press, 2009), p. 41.

71 Gaylyn Studlar, *This Mad Masquerade: Stardom and Masculinity in the Jazz Age* (New York: Columbia University Press, 1996), p. 95.

72 Butsch, p. 69.

73 Studlar, p. 106.

74 David Carroll, *The Matinee Idols* (New York: Abbeville Press, 1972), p. 38.

75 Studlar, p. 106.

76 Ibid., p. 109.

77 Carroll, p. 17.

78 *Munsey's Magazine*, October 1897, pp. 37–8.

79 Studlar, p. 122.

80 Ibid., p. 134.

81 Schweitzer, p. 12.

82 Ibid., p. 14.

83 Ibid., p. 42.

84 Susan Torrey Barstow, '"Hedda is All of Us": Late Victorian Women at the Matinee', *Victorian Studies*, vol. 43, no. 3 (Spring 2001), p. 389.

85 Ibid.

86 An unsigned notice, Licensed Victuallers' Mirror, 17 March 1981, in *Ibsen: The Critical Heritage*, edited by Michael Egan (London: Routledge, 1999), p. 202.

87 Elizabeth Robbins, *Ibsen and the Actress* (London: Hogarth Press, 1928), p. 50.

88 Barstow, p. 397.

89 Ibid.

90 Ibid.

91 Heine, in *Franz Liszt and His World*, p. 461.

92 Deaville, James. 'Writing Liszt: Lina Ramann, Marie Lipsius, and Early Musicology', *Journal of Musicological Research*, 23, no. 1 (2004), pp. 74–5.

3. DESIRE, HOLLYWOOD, 1926: THE LURE OF THE FLESH

1 *Daily Mail*, 29 August 1926, p. 11.

2   *Miami Herald*, 3 October 1926, p. 43.
3   Peggy left two notes for Rosa and newspapers excerpted different parts, often changing some words. For readability, my version combines *Sunday Sun*, 29 August; *Manchester Evening News*, 27 August; and the *Daily Telegraph*, 28 August 1926.
4   Emily Leider, *Dark Lover: The Life and Death of Rudolph Valentino* (New York: Farrar, Straus and Giroux, 2003), p. 387.
5   Samantha Barbas, *Movie Crazy: Stars, Fans, and the Cult of Celebrity* (New York: Palgrave Macmillan, 2001), p. 171.
6   Tom Hickman, *The Sexual Century* (London: Carlton Books, 1999), p. 53.
7   Carlos G. Groppa, *The Tango in the United States: A History* (Jefferson, NC: McFarland, 2004), p. 31.
8   Ralph G. Giordano, *Satan in the Dance Hall: Rev. John Roach Straton, Social Reform, and the Lindy Hop* (New York: NYU Press, 2020), p. 26.
9   Lewis A. Erenberg, *Steppin' Out: New York Nightlife and the Transformation of American Culture* (Chicago: University of Chicago Press, 1981), p. 83.
10 Studlar, p. 163.
11 John D'Emilio and Estelle B. Freedman, *Intimate Matters: A History of Sexuality in America* (Chicago: University of Chicago Press, 1997), p. 231.
12 Studlar, p. 182.
13 Erenberg, *Steppin' Out*, p. 82.
14 Margaret Turnbull, quoted in Hilary Hallett, *Go West, Young Women! The Rise of Early Hollywood* (Berkeley: University of California Press, 2013).
15 Studlar, p. 174.
16 Constance Talmadge, quoted in Leider, p. 123.
17 Miriam Hansen, *Babel and Babylon: Spectatorship in American Silent Film* (Cambridge, MA: Harvard University Press, 1991), p. 256.
18 *Photoplay*, June 1922.
19 Gaylyn Studlar, '"The Perfect Lover": Valentino and Ethnic Masculinity in the 1920s', in *The Silent Cinema Reader*, edited by Lee Grieveson and Peter Krämer (London: Routledge, 2004), p. 296.
20 Giorgio Bertellini, *The Divo and the Duce: Promoting Film Stardom and Political Leadership in 1920s America* (Berkeley: University of California Press, 2019), p. 113.
21 Hsu-Ming Teo, *Desert Passions: Orientalism and Romance Novels* (Austin: University of Texas Press, 2012), p. 88.
22 Angela Woollacott, '"Khaki Fever" and Its Control: Gender, Class, Age and Sexual Morality on the British Home Front in the First World War', *Journal of Contemporary History*, 29, no. 2 (1994), p. 331.
23 Gaylyn Studlar, 'Barrymore, the Body, and Bliss', in *Fields of Vision: Essays in Film Studies, Visual Anthropology, and Photography*, edited by Leslie Devereaux and Roger Hillman (Berkeley: University of California Press, 1995), p. 275.
24 Karen Chow, 'Popular Sexual Knowledge and Women's Agency in 1920s England', *Feminist Review*, 63 (1999), p. 73.
25 Billie Melman, *Women and the Popular Imagination in the Twenties: Flappers and Nymphs* (New York: St Martin's Press, 1988), p. 45.
26 Janice Radway, *Reading the Romance: Women, Patriarchy, and Popular Literature* (Chapel Hill: University of North Carolina Press, 1984).
27 Quoted in David Hansen-Miller, *Civilized Violence: Subjectivity, Gender, and Popularity in Modern Culture* (London: Routledge, 2011), p. 72.
28 Quoted in Hallett, p. 138.
29 Barbara Cartland, introduction to *The Sheik*, *Barbara Cartland's Library of Love Edition* (London: Arrow Books, 1979), p. 2.
30 Tricia Welsch, *Gloria Swanson: Ready for Her Close-Up* (Jackson: University Press of Mississippi, 2013), p. 96.
31 Leider, p. 167.

32 *Pittsburgh Post-Gazette*, 5 June 1924, p. 1.

33 F. Scott Fitzgerald, 'Echoes of the Jazz Age', in *The Jazz Age: Essays* (New York: New Directions, 2019), p. 5.

34 *Photoplay*, July 1922, p. 119.

35 Gabriel Vaughn, 'Why Are Women Hero-Worshippers?', *San Francisco Examiner*, 17 January 1926, p. 22.

36 Herbert Blumer, *Movies and Conduct* (New York: Macmillan, 1933), p. 70.

37 Ibid., pp. 70–74.

38 Adela Rogers St John, 'What Kind of Man Attracts Women Most', *Photoplay*, April 1924, pp. 40–41.

39 Fitzgerald, F. Scott.,'Echoes of the Jazz Age', in *My Lost City: Personal Essays 1920–1940*, p. 135.

40 Hallett, p. 138.

41 Elinor Glyn quoted in Burton W. Peretti, *The Leading Man: Hollywood and the Presidential Image* (New Brunswick, NJ: Rutgers University Press, 2012), p. 64.

42 Hallett, p. 130.

43 *Photoplay*, December 1922, p. 8.

44 *Photoplay*, March 1922, p. 41.

45 Leider, p. 171.

46 *Photoplay*, January 1922–July 1923.

47 Dorgan, Dick, 'A Song of Hate', *Photoplay*, July 1922, p. 26.

48 Studlar, *This Mad Masquerade*, p. 28.

49 *Motion Picture Classic*, May 1926, p. 69.

50 *The Nation*, 1927, pp. 125, 190.

51 Leider, p. 172.

52 Amy Lawrence, 'Rudolph Valentino: Italian American', in *Idols of Modernity: Movie Stars of the 1920s*, edited by Patrice Petro (New Brunswick, NJ: Rutgers University Press, 2010), p. 99.

53 Leider, p. 304.

54 Ibid., p. 312.

55 Bertellini, p. 140.

56 Until very recently, it was thought that the power puffs article was genuine. The true extent of Shapiro's involvement was uncovered by Giorgio Bertellini. Read his full account in *The Divo and the Duce*, pp. 149–56.

57 Leider, p. 375.

58 Bertellini, p. 153.

59 Allan R. Ellenberger, *The Valentino Mystique: The Death and Afterlife of the Silent Film Idol* (Jefferson, NC: McFarland & Company, 2005), p. 42.

60 Eva Orbanz, *There Is a New Star in Heaven, Valentino: Biography, Filmography, Essays* (Berlin: Spiess, 1979), p. 86.

61 Ibid.

62 S. George Ullman, *The Real Valentino* (London: C. A. Pearson, 1927), p. 122.

63 Leider, p. 389.

64 Ibid., pp. 388–9.

65 H. L. Mencken, 'Valentino', in *The Vintage Mencken: The Finest and Fiercest Essays of the Great Literary Iconoclast*, edited by Alistair Cooke (New York: Vintage Books, 1990), pp. 170–74.

66 Mollie Haskell, *From Reverence to Rape: The Treatment of Women in the Movies* (Chicago: University of Chicago Press, 2016), p. 187.

67 *Sunday Sun*, 29 August 1926, p. 6.

68 *Sunday Mirror*, 10 October 1926, p. 7.

69 *Sunday Sun*, 29 August 1926, p. 6.

70 *San Francisco Enquirer*, 24 October 1926, p. 119.

71 *Sunday Mirror*, 10 October 1926, p. 7.

72 Shelley Stamp, *Movie-Struck Girls: Women and Motion Picture Culture after the Nickelodeon* (Princeton, NJ: Princeton University Press, 2000), p. 39.

73 Studlar, *Fields of Vision*, p. 160.
74 *Photoplay*, December 1914, p. 109.
75 Mary Pickford, 'Talks by Mary Pickford: The Magic Wand', *New Journal*, 12 September 1917.
76 *Photoplay*, December 1915, pp. 48–9.
77 Shelley Stamp, 'It's a Long Way to Film Land: Screen Hopefuls and Extras in Early Hollywood', *Camera Obscura*, 16, no. 3 (2001), p. 335.
78 Quoted in Hallett, p. 151.
79 Ibid., p. 93.
80 Ibid., p. 148.
81 Stamp, 'It's a Long Way to Film Land', p. 333.
82 *Literary Digest*, February 1921.
83 Ibid.
84 Stamp, 'It's a Long Way to Film Land', p. 347.
85 Hallett, p. 149.
86 Quoted in Barbas, p. 76.
87 Ellenberger, p. 69.
88 Bertellini, p. 154.
89 *Daily Mirror*, 28 August 1926.

4. ROMANCE, NEW YORK CITY, 1944: IT'S ALWAYS YOU

1   James Kaplan, *Frank: The Making of a Legend* (New York: Doubleday, 2010), p. 5.
2   J. Randy Taraborrelli, *Sinatra: Behind the Legend* (New York: Birch Lane Press, 2015), p. 40.
3   Anthony Summers, *Sinatra: The Life* (New York: Alfred A. Knopf, 2006), p. 91.
4   Summers, p. 102.
5   Lewis A. Erenberg, *Swinging the Dream: Big Band Jazz and the Rebirth of American Culture* (Chicago: University of Chicago Press, 1998), p. 59.
6   Artie Shaw, ibid.
7   Kaplan, p. 176.
8   Ibid.
9   Frank Sinatra interview in Alex Gibney, *Sinatra: All or Nothing at All* (HBO Documentary Films, 2015).
10 Kaplan, p. 149.
11 Ibid., p. 150.
12 Ethlie Ann Vare, ed., *Legend: Frank Sinatra and the American Dream* (New York: Boulevard Books, 1995), p. 18.
13 *Sinatra-ly Yours* newsletter from the Semper Sinatra Fan Club, Winter 1944.
14 Kitty Kelley, *His Way: The Unauthorized Biography of Frank Sinatra* (New York: Bantam Books, 1986), p. 76.
15 Summers, p. 104.
16 Kelley, p. 68.
17 Arnold Shaw, *Sinatra: Twentieth-Century Romantic* (New York: Holt, Rinehart and Winston, 1968), p. 42.
18 Steven Petkov and Leonard Mustazza, eds, *The Frank Sinatra Reader* (New York: Oxford University Press, 1995), p. 21.
19 Kaplan, p. 162.
20 Kahn, *The Frank Sinatra Reader*, p. 37.
21 Janice L. Booker, 'Why the Bobby Soxers?', in *Frank Sinatra: History, Identity, and Italian American Culture*, edited by Stanislao G. Pugliese (New York: Palgrave Macmillan, 2004), pp. 73–82.
22 Kahn in *The Frank Sinatra Reader*, p. 35.
23 Ibid.

24 Summers, p. 108.
25 William Manchester, *The Glory and the Dream: A Narrative History of America, 1932–1972* (Boston: Little, Brown, 1974), p. 377.
26 Martha Weinman Lear, 'The Bobby Sox Have Wilted, but the Memory Remains Fresh', in *The Frank Sinatra Reader*, p. 48.
27 Bliven in *The Frank Sinatra Reader*, p. 33.
28 Ibid., p. 36.
29 Cas Wouters, *Sex and Manners: Female Emancipation in the West 1890–2000* (London: SAGE Publications, 2004), p. 98.
30 Ibid., p. 101.
31 Ann Kordas, *Female Adolescent Sexuality in the United States, 1850–1965* (Lanham, MD: Lexington Books, 2019), p. 309.
32 Wouters, p. 98.
33 Kordas, p. 309.
34 Summers, p. 81.
35 Weinman Lear, p. 48.
36 Kaplan, p. 176.
37 'Embraceable You', George and Ira Gershwin, 1930.
38 Kaplan, p. 176.
39 Weinman Lear, p. 48.
40 Kaplan, p. 176.
41 Kahn in *The Frank Sinatra Reader*, p. 42.
42 Ibid.
43 Ibid.
44 *Sinatra-ly Yours* newsletter from the Semper Sinatra Fan Club, Winter 1944.
45 All newsletter quotes from documents in the Sinatra fan club collection at the Hoboken Historical Museum.
46 *The Voice*, Vol. 1, No. 3, September 1944, from by the Slaves of Sinatra fan club.
47 *Sinatra-ly Yours* newsletter from the Semper Sinatra fan club, Summer 1945.
48 *New York Daily News*, 16 October 1944.
49 Erenberg, *Swingin' the Dream*, p. 197.
50 Manchester, p. 377.
51 Ava Garner quoted in Kaplan, p. 49.
52 Sinatra quoted in John Lahr, *Show and Tell: New Yorker Profiles* (Woodstock, NY: Overlook Press, 2000).
53 E. B. White, quoted in Summers, p. 51.
54 Edward B. Marks, *They All Sang: From Tony Pastor to Rudy Vallee*, as told to Abbott J. Liebling (New York: Viking Press, 1934), p. 68.
55 Martha Gellhorn quoted in Allison McCracken, *Real Men Don't Sing: Crooning in American Culture* (Durham, NC: Duke University Press, 2015).
56 Allison McCracken, '"God's Gift to Us Girls": Crooning, Gender, and the Re-Creation of American Popular Song, 1928–1933', *American Music*, 17, no. 4 (Winter 1999), pp. 365–95.
57 Ibid.
58 Ibid.
59 McCracken, *Real Men Don't Sing*, p. 202.
60 Ibid., p. 206.
61 Ibid., p. 234.
62 Cardinal William O'Connell in *The Musical Leader 1932 – Volume 62*.
63 McCracken, *Real Men Don't Sing*, p. 239.
64 Ibid.
65 Kaplan, p. 186.

66 Erenberg, *Swinging the Dream*, p. 193.
67 Elaine Tyler May, 'Rosie the Riveter Gets Married', in *The War in American Culture: Society and Consciousness during World War II*, edited by Lewis A. Erenberg and Susan E. Hirsch (Chicago: University of Chicago Press, 1996), p. 128.
68 Ibid., p. 134.
69 Ibid., p. 133.
70 Ibid., p. 134.
71 Kordas, p. 268.
72 Booker, p. 73.
73 Blivern, *The Frank Sinatra Reader*, p. 36.
74 Kahn, *The Frank Sinatra Reader*, p. 35.
75 Stephen Holden, 'Guide to Middle Age', in *The Frank Sinatra Reader*, p. 189.
76 Summers, p. 264.
77 Nancy Sinatra obituary, *New York Times*, 15 July 2018.
78 Katie Beisel Hollenbach, '"I Hear Music When I Look at You": Teenage Agency, Mass Media, and Frank Sinatra in World War II America', PhD dissertation (University of Illinois at Urbana-Champaign, 2018).
79 Ibid.
80 F. Scott. Fitzgerald, *The Crack-Up*, edited by Edmund Wilson (New York: New Directions, 2009).
81 Booker, p. 76.
82 Ibid.
83 Weiman Lear in *The Frank Sinatra Reader*, p. 47.
84 Kelly, p. 97.

5. SEX, MEMPHIS, 1954: SACRED AND PROFANE

1 Kay told this story many times. The details and dialogue in this section is an amalgamation of accounts from her autobiography, Kay Wheeler and W. A. Harbinson, *Growing Up with the Memphis Flash* (Amsterdam: Tutti Frutti Productions, 1994), Alanna Nash, *Baby, Let's Play House: Elvis Presley and the Women Who Loved Him* (New York: It Books, 2010) and a 2017 interview she did with Peter Alden and Krista Joy on TCB Radio (YouTube).
2 Lester Bangs, *Psychotic Reactions and Carburetor Dung* (New York: Vintage Books, 1987), p. 216.
3 Erika Doss, *Elvis Culture: Fans, Faith & Image* (Lawrence: University Press of Kansas, 1999), p. 141.
4 Joel Williamson, *Elvis Presley: A Southern Life* (New York: Oxford University Press, 2014), p. 44.
5 Ibid., p. 45.
6 *Los Angeles Mirror News*, 31 October 1957.
7 Mathias Haeussler, *Inventing Elvis: An American Icon in a Cold War World* (London: Bloomsbury, 2021), p. 35; *Sioux City Journal*, 23 May 1956.
8 *San Francisco Chronicle*, 4 June 1956.
9 Williamson, p. 46.
10 *Vancouver Sun*, 31 August 1957.
11 *Miami Daily News*, 4 August 1956.
12 Haeussler, p. 36.
13 Kordas, p. 283.
14 Ibid., p. 281.
15 Williamson, pp. 31–2.
16 Sylvia Plath, *The Bell Jar* (New York: Harper Perennial, 2005), p. 85.
17 Joyce Johnson, *Minor Characters* (New York: Penguin, 1983), p. 30.
18 Priscilla Presley, interview in *The Searcher*, directed by Thom Zimny (HBO, 2018).
19 Michael T. Bertrand, *Race, Rock, and Elvis* (Champaign: University of Illinois Press, 2000), p. 140.
20 Haeussler, p. 35.

21 Greil Marcus, *Mystery Train: Images of America in Rock 'n' Roll Music* (New York: Plume, 1975), p. 147.

22 Williamson, p. 60.

23 Susan K. Cahn, *Sexual Reckonings: Southern Girls in a Troubling Age* (Cambridge, MA: Harvard University Press, 2007), p. 254.

24 Frank Sinatra, quoted in Stefan Kanfer, *Somebody: The Reckless Life of Marlon Brando* (New York: Knopf, 2008), p. 138.

25 Haeussler, p. 36.

26 Maureen Orth, quoted in Daniel Marcus, *Happy Days and Wonder Years: The Fifties and Sixties in American Popular Culture* (New Brunswick, NJ: Rutgers University Press, 2004).

27 P. F. Sloan, interview in *The Searcher*.

28 David Dalton, *James Dean: The Mutant King* (New York: Dell, 1975), p. 317.

29 Robert Altman, *The James Dean Story* (Warner Bros, 1957).

30 Joyce Chandler, *James Dean: A Rebel with a Cause: A Fan's Tribute* (AuthorsHouse, 1991), p. 2.

31 Barbara G. Harrison, 'Oh How We Worshipped the Gods of the Fifties', in *Legend: Frank Sinatra and the American Dream*, p. 128.

32 Sheila Rowbotham, *Woman's Consciousness, Man's World* (London: Penguin Books, 1973), pp. 15–16.

33 Annie Dillard, quoted in Wini Breines, *Young, White, and Miserable: Growing Up Female in the Fifties* (Chicago: University of Chicago Press, 1992), p. 139.

34 Janis Joplin, quoted in ibid.

35 Joyce Johnson, *Minor Characters: A Beat Memoir* (New York: Penguin, 1983), pp. 29–30.

36 Cher, quoted in Alanna Nash, *Baby, Let's Play House*, pp. 277–8.

37 Doss, p. 133.

38 Ibid., p. 125.

39 Ibid., p. 133.

40 *Life*, 25 March 1957, p. 55.

41 Breines, p. 15.

42 Cahn, p. 263.

43 Studlar, *This Mad Masquerade*, p. 113.

44 Ibid., p. 116.

45 Ibid., p. 113.

46 Ibid., p. 114.

47 Anthony Peattie, *The Private Life of Lord Byron* (London: Unbound, 2019), Chapter 22.

48 Byron, quoted in Marchand, *Byron: A Portrait*, p. 250.

49 Byron, quoted in MacCarthy, p. 297.

50 Claire Clairmont, quoted in Daisy Hay, *Young Romantics: The Shelleys, Byron, and Other Tangled Lives* (New York: Farrar, Straus and Giroux, 2010), p. 292.

51 Eliza Francis, *His Very Self and Voice*, p. 91.

52 Iris Origo, *The Innocent Miss Francis and the Truly Noble Lord Byron*, Keats-Shelley Journal, 1 (1952), p. 9.

53 Eliza Francis, *His Very Self and Voice*, pp. 90–91.

54 Kay Wheeler interview in *Elvis' Women*, directed by Barbara Shearer (USA: Passport Video, 2005).

55 Kay Wheeler, quoted in Nash, *Baby, Let's Play House*, p. 165.

56 Gilbert D. Rodman, *Elvis After Elvis: The Posthumous Career of a Living Legend* (New York: Routledge, 1996), p. 59.

57 Horace Logan quoted in Nash, p. 108.

58 Nash, p. 10.

59 Diane Keaton quoted in Nash, p. 180.

60 Bobbi Owens TV interview, WTVR TV News, 2016 (YouTube).

61 Bangs, p. 216.

62 Elvis, quoted in Jerry Osborne, *Elvis: Word for Word* (New York: O'Sullivan Woodside, 1999), p. 65.

63 Nash, p. 264.

64 Ibid.

65 Gloria Mowel, quoted in Albert Goldman, *Elvis* (New York: McGraw-Hill, 1981), p. 315.

66 Jackie Rowland, interview in *Elvis' Women*, directed by Barbara Shearer (USA: Passport Video, 2005).

67 Elisabeth Stefaniak, interview in ibid.

68 Nash, p. 323.

69 Elvis, quoted in Alanna Nash, *Elvis and the Memphis Mafia* (New York: Harper Paperbacks, 2012).

70 For discussion of Elvis, Priscilla and technical virginity, see Suzanne Finstad, *Child Bride: The Untold Story of Priscilla Beaulieu Presley* (New York: Crown, 1997); Nash, *Baby, Let's Play House*, Chapter 20.

71 *60 Minutes*, TV interview, 2023 (YouTube).

72 Nash, p. 240.

73 Nash, pp. 232–3.

74 Marucs, p. 266.

75 *Elvis Monthly*, 76, 1966.

76 Haeussler, p. 115.

77 Doss, p. 137.

78 *Elvis Monthly*, 12, 1963; *Elvis Monthly*, 11, 1964.

79 *Elvis Monthly*, 12, 1963.

80 Sue Wise is now an emeritus professor of sociology Lancaster University. Her reflections were part of an academic essay called 'Sexing Elvis' in Simon Frith and Andrew Goodwin, eds, *On Record: Rock, Pop, and the Written Word* (New York: Routledge, 1990).

81 Ibid., p. 395.

82 Doss, p. 13.

83 Ibid., p. 108.

84 Ibid.

85 *LIFE: Remembering Elvis Presley* (New York: Time Inc., 1999), p. 191.

86 Williamson, p. 49.

87 Barbara Ehrenreich, Elizabeth Hess and Gloria Jacobs, 'Beatlemania: Girl's Just Want to Have Fun', in *The Adoring Audience: Fan Culture and Popular Media*, edited by Lisa A. Lewis (London: Routledge, 1992), p. 85.

88 Haeussler, p. 138.

89 Peter Guralnick, *Careless Love: The Unmaking of Elvis Presley* (Boston: Little, Brown, 1999), p. 317.

90 Ehrenreich, Hess and Jacobs, p. 86.

91 Franz Liszt quoted in Gerhard J. Winkler, 'Liszt's Weimar Mythology', in *Liszt and His World: Proceedings of the International Liszt Conference held at Virginia Polytechnic Institute and State University, 20–23 May 1993*, edited by Michael Saffle (New York: Pendragon Press, 1998), p. 69.

6. REVOLUTION, LIVERPOOL, 1963: FROM ME TO YOU

1   Mark Lewisohn, *The Beatles: All These Years – Extended Special Edition, Volume 1: Tune In* (London: Little, Brown, 2013), p. 83.

2   Christine Feldman-Barrett, *A Women's History of the Beatles* (New York: Bloomsbury Academic, 2021), p. 14.

3   Lewisohn, p. 148.

4   Ibid.

5   Ibid.

6   Ibid., p. 224.

7   John Lennon, quoted in Feldman-Barrett, p. 23.

8   Feldman-Barrett, p. 87.

9   Lewisohn, p. 225.

10 Ibid.

11 Hunter Davis, *The Beatles: The Authorised Biography* (London: Heinemann, 1968), p. 183.

12 Lewisohn, p. 300.

13 Ibid., p. 355.

14 Philip Norman, *Shout!: The Beatles in Their Generation* (New York: Simon & Schuster, 1981), p. 202.

15 Elsa Breden, quoted in Lewisohn, p. 355.

16 David Kynaston, *A Northern Wind: Britain 1962–65* (London: Bloomsbury Publishing, 2022), p. 273.

17 Ibid., p. 180.

18 Ibid., p. 231.

19 Rod Mengham, 'Bollocks to Respectability: British Fiction After *The Trial of Chatterley's Lover* (1960–1970)', in *Prudes on the Prowl: Fiction and Obscenity in England, 1850 to the Present Day*, edited by David Bradshaw and Rachel Potter (Oxford: Oxford University Press, 2013), p. 181.

20 Kynaston, p. 240

21 Michael Caine, *What's It All About?* (New York: Turtle Bay Books, 1992), p. 187.

22 Kenneth Womack and Kit O'Toole, eds, *Fandom and the Beatles: The Act You've Known for All These Years* (New York: Oxford University Press, 2021).

23 Christina Berlin, quoted in Steven D. Stark, *Meet the Beatles: A Cultural History of the Band that Shook Youth, Gender, and the World* (New York: HarperEntertainment, 2005), p. 15.

24 Paolo Hewitt, *Love Me Do: 50 Great Beatles Moments* (London: Quercus, 2012).

25 Bob Dylan, quoted in John Leonard, *Reading for My Life: Writings, 1958–2008* (New York: Viking, 2009), p. 299.

26 Gay Stilley, quoted in Andrew Hunt, *Beatlemania in America: Fan Culture from Below* (Liverpool: Liverpool University Press, 2013), p. 48.

27 Stark, p. 15.

28 *The Beatles Anthology*, directed by Geoff Wonfor and Bob Smeaton (London: Apple Corps Ltd., 1995), DVD.

29 Ringo Starr, interview with Elliot Mintz, *Inner-View*, 29 August 1977.

30 Gerald Nachman, *Right Here on Our Stage Tonight! Ed Sullivan's America* (Berkeley: University of California Press, 2009), p. 356.

31 Ibid., p. 354.

32 John F. Kennedy quoted in Mark White, *Kennedy: A Cultural History of an American Icon* (London: Bloomsbury Academic, 2013), p. 28.

33 White, p. 24.

34 John Hellmann, *The Kennedy Obsession: The American Myth of JFK* (New York: Columbia University Press, 1997), p. 126.

35 Ibid.

36 Hunt, p. 13.

37 Candy Leonard, *Beatleness: How the Beatles and Their Fans Remade the World* (New York: Arcade Publishing, 2014).

38 Ibid.

39 Amanda Vaill, 'We Saw Them Standing There', in *The Beatles Are Here!*, edited by Penelope Rowlands (Chapel Hill, NC: Algonquin Books, 2014), p. 24.

40 Gay Talese, 'Beatles and Fans Meet Social Set', in *The Beatles Are Here!*, p. 28.

41 Candy Leonard, 'Beatles Fandom: A De Facto Religion', in *Fandom and the Beatles*, p. 24.

42 Vaill in *The Beatles Are Here!*, p. 24.

43 Leonard, *Beatleness*, p. 58.

44 Pam Rutherford, quoted in Finstad, p. 28.

45 Debbie Geller, 'America's Beatlemania Hangover', in *The Beatles Are Here!*, p. 78.

46 Noelle Oxenhandler, 'Swimming to John', in *The Beatles Are Here!*, p. 58.

47 André Millard, *Beatlemania: Technology, Business, and Teen Culture in Cold War America* (Baltimore: Johns Hopkins University Press, 2012), p. 159.

48 Bill Adler, ed., *Love Letters to the Beatles* (New York: Simon & Schuster, 1964).

49 Millard, p. 163.

50 Gloria Steinem, 'Beatle with a Future', *Cosmopolitan*, December 1963, in *Read the Beatles: Classic and New Writings on the Beatles, Their Legacy, and Why They Still Matter*, edited by June Skinner Sawyers (New York: Penguin Books, 2006), p. 63.

51 Millard, p. 161.

52 Ibid.

53 Elizabeth Freedman, quoted in 'Runaway Beatle "Bug" Sees Idols Has Fun', *Sacramento Bee*, 2 November 1964, p. 6.

54 Millard, p. 157.

55 Leonard, *Beatleness*, p. 82.

56 Barbara Allen in *We're Going to See the Beatles!: An Oral History of Beatlemania as Told by the Fans Who Were There*, edited by Garry Berman (Santa Monica, CA: Santa Monica Press, 2008), p. 109.

57 Feldman-Barrett, p. 45

58 Millard, p. 157

59 John Lennon, quoted in Jonathan Gould, *Can't Buy Me Love: The Beatles, Britain, and America* (New York: Harmony Books, 2007), p. 267.

60 Millard, p. 158.

61 Larry Kane, *Ticket to Ride: Inside the Beatles' 1964 Tour that Changed the World* (New York: Running Press, 2003), p. 120.

62 Elizabeth Hess, 'The Women', *Village Voice*, 8 November 1994.

63 Millard, p. 101.

64 Ibid., p. 102.

65 Judge Benjamin Schwartz, TV broadcast, 28 August 1964 (YouTube).

66 Joann Marie Puglise Flood, in *The Beatles Are Here!*, p. 140.

67 Laura Tarrish, in *The Beatles Are Here!*, p. 175.

68 Hunt, p. 62.

69 Whoopi Goldberg, interview in *The Beatles: Eight Days a Week – The Touring Years*, directed by Ron Howard (2016).

70 JoAnne McCormack, in *We're Going to See The Beatles!*, p. 167.

71 John Lennon, quoted in Laurie Jacobson, *Top of the Mountain: The Beatles at Shea Stadium 1965* (Los Angeles: Dey Street Books, 2016), p. 5.

72 Leonard, *Beatleness*, p. 108.

73 Kenneth Womack, interview in 'Baby You Can Drive My Car', *Harvard Gazette*, 10 December 2019.

74 Keith Richards, interview in *Rolling Stone*, January 2015.

75 Keith Richards, interview in *60 Minutes Australia*, 2013.

76 *Crossfire Hurricane*, directed by Brett Morgen (2012).

77 Ellen Willis, 'Janis Joplin', in *The Essential Ellen Willis*, edited by Nona Willis Aronowitz (Minneapolis: University of Minnesota Press, 2014), p. 6.

78 Leonard, *Beatleness*, p. 255.

79 Ibid., p. 261.

80 Laura Tarrish, in *The Beatles Are Here!*, p. 176.

AFTERWORD: THANK YOU GIRL

1 Apple Scruffs, 'Our Song', www.applescruffs.co.uk (accessed 1 April 2025).

2 Ibid.

3 Diana W. Anselmo, *A Queer Way of Feeling: Girl Fans and Personal Archives of Early Hollywood* (Oakland: University of California Press, 2023), p. 46.

4 Wise, p. 397.

INDEX

'68 Comeback Special 235–7

activism 289
actors 76, 78, 100, 129, 298
actresses 131, 133, 136, 159, 183, 297
adventure 9, 17, 94, 98, 131, 133–4,
    136–7, 201, 210, 218, 277
Albert, Marsha 257–8
animal magnetism 57, 91, 102, 111
Apple Scruffs 295
Arbuckle, Fatty 136
art 55, 56, 62, 67–69, 72, 75, 81, 84,
    114–15, 122, 172, 251, 299–303
artistry 59, 61, 74, 121–2, 130, 187
authenticity 5, 100, 131, 148–9,
    245–6, 254, 262, 284, 289
Awakening Conscience, The 67–8

backlash 81, 117–22, 135–7, 146,
    169–71, 166–171, 174–6, 177,
    179–80, 197–199, 203, 278–9
bad boys 13–14, 99, 194, 222,
    226, 268
bad readers 18, 22, 26–7
Baez, Joan 209
Barrymore, John 79–81, 84, 120
Beat generation 209–10
Beatles, The 148, 235, 241–51,
    253–93
    Beatlemania in America
        256–67
    Cavern Club 245–8
    early Beatlemania (UK) 249,
        50, 254
    final rooftop performance
        291–3
    first *Ed Sullivan* appearances
        263–7
    Royal Variety performance
        255–6
    songs 284–6
beatniks 208–210
Beaulieu, Priscilla 202–3, 226, 270
Beecher Stowe, Harriet 36
van Beethoven, Ludwig 45–6, 74

Blumer, Herbert 111–13
bobbysoxers 150–68, 180–88, 267,
    277, 292
Bonaparte, Napoleon 54–5
Brando, Marlon 206–8, 213, 222–3,
    230, 244
Brontë, Anne 37
Brontë, Charlotte xxii, 37
Brontë, Emily 29, 37
Byron, Lord xv–xxiii, 1–22, 27–39,
    42–3, 46, 56, 58, 63, 69, 98, 103,
    107, 128, 148, 185, 216–18, 267,
    269, 282, 288, 300, 304
    Byromania, 1812 7–10
    Byronic Hero 10, 36–9, 187
    Byronic Heroine 36
    early celebrity culture 17–18,
        148
    exile 16, 33
    in-person relationships with
        fans 34, 216–18
    marriage to Annabella/
        separation 12, 36
    Milton/Satan influence 10

Caine, Michael 254
Castrati 49–50, 71, 171
Cavern Club 243–9
Chaplin, Charlie 99, 127
Cher 211–12
Childe Harold's Pilgrimage xvi,
    xvii, xxiii, 1–2, 5–9, 15
children 10–11, 28, 30, 35–8, 260,
    286–7
cinemas 89, 105, 131–2
Clairmont, Claire 216
class 2, 18, 23, 27, 45, 155, 203, 237,
    251–2, 254, 292, 300, 302
community 78, 84, 154, 163–4, 247,
    274, 298
concert souvenirs 49, 51, 70–73
concerts 243–5, 275–78
conduct books 2; *see also* etiquette
    books
Corsair, The 9–11, 16

crooners 145, 171–176
Crosby, Bing 145, 149, 168, 176
crying xi, xvi, 47, 55, 60–62, 65, 80,
    83, 91–2, 138, 182, 222–3, 225,
    281, 300
cultural hierarchies xi, 71–5,
    299, 304

dance 94–8, 100, 202–4
dating 104, 199, 208
Dean, James 206–8, 298
department stores 70–71
desert romance 103–4, 108
desire, female 2–3, 21–2, 196–7,
    214, 269, 299
Dorogokupetz, Alexander 169–70
Duplessis, Marie 65–7
Dylan, Bob 5, 148, 235, 242, 258,
    296

ecstasy 21, 43, 50, 55, 68, 84, 182,
    232, 263, 269, 277
Ed Sullivan Show, The 148, 202,
    206, 211, 221, 249, 261, 263–6
emotional connection 61, 148–9,
    187
emotional labour 304
emotions 64, 226
enthusiasm 13, 28, 49–50, 68–9, 72,
    83, 257, 262, 264, 299, 302
etiquette books 159–60; *see also*
    conduct books
Evans, George 151, 154–5, 164–7

fainting 137, 165, 170, 222, 235, 279,
    282, 287
Fairbanks, Douglas 99, 100,
    110, 123
Falkland, Lady 7
fan club newsletters 167–9
fan clubs 166–17, 192, 229
fan magazines 101–2, 116–18,
    132–3, 231–2
fan poetry 168
fan studies 304

fangirling x, 57, 302
fanmail xvi, xvii, xxiii, 1–2, 7–8,
    14–16, 31–5, 101, 110–11, 225,
    234, 282, 297
fantasy 105–8, 111–13, 179–82, 214,
    222, 227, 234, 272–3
Farinelli 49–50
fashion 9, 213, 247
Fay, Amy 48, 65
FBI 234
feelings, romantic xix, 12, 154,
    161–2, 173
feelings xi, xvii, xxiii, 6, 8, 13–15,
    21–2, 32–3, 35, 38, 61, 64, 150,
    154, 158, 166, 168, 171, 186–8,
    233–4
female filmmakers 98, 114
female gaze 19, 50, 299
feminisation of culture 30, 119,
    300
feminism 232, 234–5, 277–8, 282,
    289, 303
film audiences, female 98, 108,
    111–12, 131–3
First World War 100, 103, 104
Fitzgerald, Scott F. 109, 114, 185
Four Horsemen of the Apocalypse,
    The 99–101
Francis, Eliza 34, 217–18
Franklin, Erma 289–9
Freedman, Elizabeth 273–4, 280
freedom 5, 67–8, 84–5, 285
French Revolution 27, 45

Gable, Clark 160–62
Garland, Judy 161–2
gate girls 214–15, 223
genius 5, 47, 58, 62–3, 71
Glenarvon xxi, 29, 30, 35
Glyn, Elinor 114–15, 120
Goldberg, Whoopi 280
Gothic literature 18, 22, 24–9
Great Depression 155, 158, 171,
    173, 175
growing up 161, 184, 207, 284–9

hair xv, xvi, 9, 17–18, 43–4, 47,
    51–2, 54, 59, 62, 89, 97, 110, 118,
    150, 168, 173, 193, 211, 212–13,
    237, 264, 266, 268–9, 271, 278,
    287, 289
Hard Day's Night (film) 287
Harvey, Isabella ('Zorina') 1–5,
    15, 17, 31–4
Hedda Gabler 82, 84
Heine, Henrich 50, 54–8, 74
heroines xv, xxi, xxiii, 25, 36,
    112, 115, 133, 173, 218, 251, 285,
    288, 298
Hollywood 9, 95, 98–102, 115,
    119–21, 127, 133, 174, 230–33,
    297
homosexuality 5, 298
hysteria 28, 42, 50–51, 53, 57, 59, 63,
    83, 91–3, 125, 129, 138, 165, 176,
    205, 224, 235, 251, 281 299

'I Want to Hold Your Hand'
    257–8, 272, 291, 297
Ibsen, Henrik 81–3
imagination 6, 12, 16, 30–33, 129,
    214, 233–4, 270
infatuation 49, 130, 159, 165
intimacy 162, 166, 172, 174, 187,
    221, 283

Jagger, Mick 287, 288–9
Johnson, Joyce 201, 209–10
Joplin, Janis 289–90
joy 39, 51, 59, 82, 89, 167, 173, 206,
    214, 234, 237, 253–4, 261, 263–5,
    269–70, 277, 290–92, 296,
    299, 305

Keisker, Marion 231
Kennedy, John F. 261–3
Kerouac, Jack 5, 208, 289
khaki fever 104–5
kindness 14, 167, 284, 287
Kinsey Report 195–6, 200
Kiss, The (photograph) 220–21
kissing xviii, 220–23, 238–9, 247

Lady Chatterley's Lover 251–3
Lamb, Caroline xvi, 2, 19, 29–31,
    217, 302
Landon, Letitia 35
Latin Lover 114–16, 118, 120, 126
letters xvi, 3, 7–8, 11, 13–18, 31–5,
    73, 78, 90, 101, 110, 117, 130, 132,
    145, 153–5, 167, 181, 192, 207,
    225, 234, 282, 290, 292, 297
libraries 23–6, 101
Lipsius, Marie (La Mara) 86–7
Liszt, Franz 43–75, 84–7, 238,
    264–5, 269, 305
    female patronage 71–3, 85–7
    Lisztomania 50–58, 297
    performance style 46–8, 54–5
    piano recital innovation 48,
        58–66
    women as fans/supporters
        50–53, 58–9, 65–7
    women mentors/
        collaborators 85–7
love 5, 10–12, 173–4, 187, 292
lust xxi–xxii, 19, 21, 28, 159, 202,
    277, 299, 300, 303
lyrics 149–50, 180, 213–14, 253, 284,
    286, 302

madness xxii, 8, 50, 53, 259, 260,
    267, 287
male beauty 19, 43–4, 47, 62, 64,
    96–7, 110, 202, 298
male body 18, 110, 202
male fans 50, 112–13, 186–7, 206–7,
    230, 284
Manfred 9, 17, 37–8
marriage 134, 181–4
Martin, Janis 213–14
masculinity 96, 106, 118, 123–4,
    170–71, 175, 186, 212, 223, 287, 298

masquerade 2, 35
Mathis, June 98–100
Matinee Girls 78–84, 215–16
Matinee Idols 79–80, 215, 220
medals and honours 54, 242–3
media 53, 55, 92, 121, 198, 250–51,
    255, 260, 262–3, 228–9, 287,
    302
melodrama xviii, 8, 15, 29, 31, 81,
    127, 130
Mencken, H. L. 127
Methodism 56
von Meysenbug, Malwida 60, 67
Milbanke, Annabella (Lady
    Byron) 7–8, 12–13, 16, 31, 36, 38
Monkees, The 286
Movie-Struck Girl 131–9, 300

Novel-Reading Girl 24, 38, 131,
    305
novels 25, 28, 210, 299

Owens, Bobbi 220–21, 223

Paganini, Niccolò 41–3, 46, 49
Pamela 13–14
Paramount Theatre 53–4, 144,
    147–52, 156, 163–4, 169–70, 184,
    261, 267–8
parents 164, 183–5, 192, 199, 202,
    207, 210, 215, 232, 256, 264,
    266–7, 269, 278–82, 287
participation xvi, 68, 131, 138,
    303–4
passion 8, 11, 26, 30, 36, 39, 49, 50,
    61, 66, 97, 107, 111
performance 41–4, 46–8, 51, 54,
    58–61, 64–5, 70, 80, 82–3, 138,
    146–7, 197
Photoplay 101, 102, 107, 110, 113–19,
    122, 133–6
physical responses to art 23–5,
    59–62, 68
piano 44, 46–8, 50–51, 54–5, 60,
    63–8, 166
Pickford, Mary 110, 131–3, 297
'Piece of My Heart' 289
pink powder puff article 123–4
pirates 9, 304
Plath, Sylvia 210
'Please Please Me' 249, 253–4
pleasure 5, 20, 38, 95–8, 171, 195,
    214
poetry xvi, xviii, 9–10, 14–15, 18,
    20–21, 39, 56, 99, 120, 125, 168,
    209–10, 300
police 79, 92, 109, 135, 198, 205,
    214, 242, 250, 254–5, 259, 263,
    267–8, 273–6, 282–3, 292
popular culture xi, xxii, 53, 69,
    73, 95, 127, 148, 162, 170, 179,
    213–15, 299–305
portraits and posters xvi, 17, 20,
    33–5, 42, 49, 68, 156, 179–80,
    256, 272, 304
pregnancy 3, 50, 135

Presley, Elvis 44, 63, 184, 193–206,
   210–15, 219–39, 257, 262, 264,
   266, 270, 272–3, 277, 278, 280,
   287–9, 292, 300–301
   clothing/style 212–13
   Elvis films 230–32
   first *Ed Sullivan Show*
      appearances, 1956 202
   first performances, Overton
      Shell, 1954 194–202
   Las Vegas 1970s 237–9, 292
   military reset 228–9
   racial dynamics/Black
      influence 203–5
   relationships with underage
      girls 223–8
   sexual relationships with fans
      219–20
Profumo affair 252–3

queer fandom 232–3, 298

race 93–4, 102–3, 107–8, 126, 203–5
radio 171–5, 192, 299
Rainey, Ma 290
rake reform 6–7, 13–14, 20, 25
Ramann, Lina 85–6
reading 2, 22–8
rebellion 9, 29, 204–14, 230, 242–3,
   260, 278, 289
reciprocity 189, 197, 237–8, 289,
   296–7
records 286
respectability 81, 95–6, 119, 176,
   183, 256, 268, 300
revolution 187, 196, 223, 235, 242,
   244, 253, 256, 282, 286, 288,
   292–3
Richards, Keith 48, 287–8
riots 76, 79, 91–2, 126, 130, 137–8,
   156–7, 287
rock 'n' roll 204–5, 229, 257
Rolling Stones 287–8, 303
romance xxi, 10, 22, 24–6, 29,
   38–9, 64, 81, 97, 102–3, 106, 128,
   130, 144, 149, 157–62, 173–4,
   180–81, 187, 270, 284, 286
romantic feelings 270, 272
Romanticism 288, 17, 35, 46–7, 56,
   62–3, 69
Rowbotham, Sheila 60
runaways 273–4

salon culture 71–3
salon patronage 179–81
Sand, George 50, 73, 85
Satan 10, 193, 229
Scott, Peggy 89–90, 129–30, 139
screaming 202, 205, 236, 242,
   258–9, 276, 282–3, 287
Second World War 142–4, 176–82,
   176–82
segregation/desegregation era
   203–5
self-expression 64–5, 153–4, 214,
   248, 269–70, 276, 290

sensation 19
sex, celebrity–fan 215–28
sex 50, 68, 104–5, 112–15, 177–8, 195,
   199, 201–2, 214, 215–28, 244,
   246, 251–4, 244, 246, 251–4
Shapiro, Victor Mansfield 123–4
Shea Stadium 281–3
Sheik Fever 171–2
Sheik, The 102–3, 171
Shelley, Mary 41
Shelley, Percy Bysshe 216–17, 288
shopping 26, 70, 76, 131
Sinatra, Frank 142–72, 176–89,
   192, 195, 205, 229–30, 235, 277,
   279, 292
   crooning style/microphone
      use 172
   first solo shows, Paramount,
      1942–43 147–52
   Frankie vs Frank (teen idol
      to artist) 185–7
   hatred from servicemen/
      veterans 170–71, 176–7
   Las Vegas performances
      185, 292
   Sinatramania 150–57
Sinatra, Nancy (née Barbato) 143,
   153, 166, 181–4
Slick, Grace 289
Smith, Bessie 290
social change 71–2, 75–6, 104–5,
   113, 177–8, 181, 251,
   299
soul-saving xii, 12–14, 42, 100, 205;
   see also rake reform
Stefaniak, Elisabeth 225
Stopes, Marie 105
Stowe, Harriet Beecher 36–7
Streetcar Named Desire, A 222
suicide 26, 82, 90, 280
Sullivan, Ed 202, 260–61, 263–7,
   269–70, 271, 280,
   282
*Sunday Night at the London
   Palladium* 249
Swift, Taylor 301–2, 305
swooning 50, 163–6

tango dancing 91, 94–7, 100–102,
   120
tango pirate 95–8, 101–2, 107,
   120
taste 16, 299–30
teen girl magazines 262
teen idol 157, 222, 229, 257
teenage girls 178–9
teenagers 157–61, 206–7
theatre 76–84
troubadours 171
Turkish Tales, The 9, 18
TV 202, 206, 210–11, 213, 228, 234,
   236, 250, 254–5, 262, 263–7,
   278, 280, 282, 286, 299

Valentino, Rudolph 90–102,
   107–31, 137–9, 150, 152, 156, 171,

   173, 175, 202, 208, 212, 235, 279,
      288, 298
   death 126–7
   foreign/racial tensions 101–2,
      118–19
   Four Horsemen success
      100–101
   funeral 92–3, 137–8, 156
   pink powder puff controversy
      123–5
   Sheik role/character 102,
      107–8, 116–17, 171
Vallée, Rudy 129, 171–6, 279
virginity 200–201, 219, 226
virtuoso/virtuosity 42–3, 45–6,
   63–4
voice 35, 49, 143–4, 146–9, 155, 158,
   162–5, 171, 173–6, 184–6, 192,
   195, 197, 204, 210–11, 214, 222,
   270, 276, 289, 290, 301
vulnerability 143, 173, 187, 212, 237,
   284, 288, 297, 299

Wheeler, Kay 191–2, 193, 218–19,
   227, 231
Whitefield, George 56
Wieck, Clara (later Clara
   Schumann) 48–9, 54, 65, 85
wildness 8, 12, 38, 91, 209, 237, 278
Willis, Ellen 289
Wilson, Harriette 16, 34–5
woman-made men 119–20,
   159, 175
writers, female 23, 31, 35–9, 98, 210
Wuthering Heights 29, 37–9, 17